the BORDER

the BORDER

Canada, the U.S. and Dispatches from the 49th Parallel

JAMES LAXER

DOUBLEDAY CANADA

COPYRIGHT © JAMES LAXER 2003

Doubleday Canada and colophon are trademarks.

National Library of Canada Cataloguing in Publication

Laxer, James, 1941–
    The border : Canada, the U.S. and dispatches from the 49th parallel / James Laxer.

ISBN 0–385–65981–4

1. Canada—Boundaries—United States. 2. United States—Boundaries— Canada. 3. Canada—Relations—United States. 4. United States—Relations—Canada. I. Title.

FC76.L39 2003   971   C2003–900903–3   F1017.L39 2003

JACKET IMAGE: Zoran Milich/Masterfile
JACKET AND TEXT DESIGN: Daniel Cullen
Printed and bound in the USA

Published in Canada by Doubleday Canada,
a division of Random House of Canada Limited

Visit Random House of Canada Limited's website: www.randomhouse.ca

BVG 10 9 8 7 6 5 4 3 2 1

To Nathaniel

Contents

Canada's Alaskan boundary.

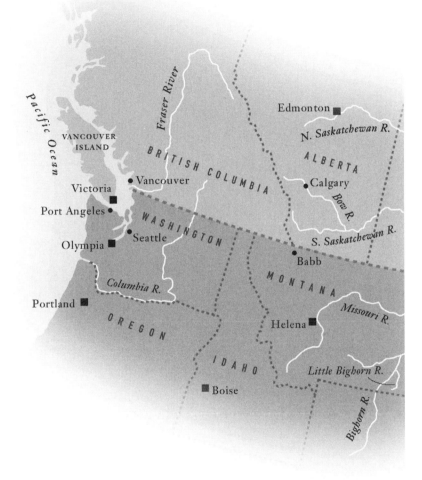

The forty-ninth parallel became the boundary to the Pacific coast in 1846.

The Prairie boundary runs through a dry land where rivers flood.

The Great Lakes, a natural frontier.

The Maine–New Brunswick border, a nineteenth-century powder keg.

Preface

I set out to write *The Border* in an age that has now passed—the less fearful time prior to the terrorist attacks on New York and Washington, DC, on September 11, 2001. I first conceived the book in the sunset days of the longest bull market in history, when the "new" tech-based economy still seemed to hold the promise that we would all become rich. For those who didn't like the way the spoils and the power were being divvied up, there were demonstrations against globalization, the World Trade Organization, the proposed Free Trade Area of the Americas, the IMF and the World Bank to attend in places like Seattle, Washington, DC, Quebec City or Genoa.

Travelling across the continent to places where social issues play themselves out simply to watch people is a favourite activity of mine. My goal was to journey along the Canada–U.S. border to observe communities on both sides, to consider the history of the border and to reflect on the Canadian-American relationship. Even in those halcyon times, it was clear that Canada was headed for a reckoning in its relationship with the United States. Free trade had taken Canada too far into an economic union with the

U.S. for those who had won the free trade fight not to want to take the next steps toward full economic integration and possible political union.

One day early on in the project I drove down to Niagara-on-the-Lake, the picturesque old town located across the Niagara River from New York State, to think about the book. I sprawled on the grass in a big park that slopes to the shore of Lake Ontario. The cold waves were rolling ashore. As I sat in the bright, late May sun at midday, across the water I saw the skyline of Toronto—the CN Tower a little off to the left and the big banks all in a clump. There was Canada's biggest city, visible from U.S. territory. Off to my right, less than a kilometre away on the far side of the Niagara River, was Fort Niagara, the fort at Youngstown, New York. Niagara-on-the-Lake is only a few kilometres from Queenston Heights, where Sir Isaac Brock and his British and Canadian troops defeated American attackers in 1813.

The frontier, in question that day in 1813, has stood for over two centuries since the American Revolution. What does the border signify, I wanted to know. Is it merely a dividing line drawn by contending forces long ago that no longer matters? Or is it the boundary of a nation, with its own values and outlook, that can endure next door to a superpower?

Over a period of eighteen months, I travelled along the border, from Campobello, New Brunswick, in the east to Vancouver Island in the west. And I took a cruise ship north from Vancouver to the Alaska Panhandle for a look at the most mysterious of Canada's frontiers with the United States, the one that held the key to the riches of the Klondike. I went by car, train, bus, ferry, cruise ship and air to the seven provinces that have land borders with the U.S. and to twelve of the thirteen states that border on Canada—leaving only Idaho for another day.

Inevitably, my approach to the book changed after September 11. In the end I was afforded a unique perspective on the border before and after a date when the world changed. For North America, September 11 brought on a twin crisis, that of the role of the United States in the world, and that of Canada's relationship with the United States. *The Border* addresses that twin crisis.

Introduction

We are near the Alberta–Saskatchewan border en route to Saskatoon when I retire to my railway-car roomette and climb into the narrow bed. I push up the window shade and turn out the light. As I lie on my side and look out, the sky fills the picture from the top of my window to very near the bottom, where the shadows of trees erupt from the flat surface of the prairie. The sky is so luminous that the stubble of the prairie appears like the edge of a grainy film.

Feeling fine but saddled with a mild ear infection, and therefore unable to fly home from Edmonton to Toronto, I'm taking the train, something I haven't done for many years.

The stars in the window are an indecipherable jumble to me. I regret that I haven't studied the constellations so I can read the great hieroglyphic in the sky.

I drift off to sleep and awaken a while later. I look out the window again and this time see a hieroglyph I can read. The seven stars of the Big Dipper fill the frame. And looking up from the last star of the cup of the Dipper, I find the North Star. Now I can read the sky. We are heading due east.

Much later still, I wake up again and look out. The Dipper is on its side now—its handle down toward the prairie and the cup high above, its last star pointing back to the North Star, which lies in the left of the frame. We have turned to the south.

At the corner of the frame, a glow is beginning to light the sky. The hard prairie is elemental, like the surface of an unknown planet, as the light that is stealing across it casts its darkness into stark relief. The Dipper and the pole star are fading as the light spills outward from the corner of the frame. The harsh surface of the planet is about to explode in light.

The stars in my window, some I can read and others I cannot, are a metaphor for my country. For all that humans have done here for thousands of years, Canada remains vast and inscrutable. Its largest cities and its arable land lie on the edge of one of the world's great land masses, a half continent that is as alien to human concerns as any terrain on the planet. There are now more than 30 million of us living mostly in the southern extremity of this immense land. The land itself remains the first and last fact of Canadian existence.

As a great continental nation, the second largest in area in the world, Canada is in the unique position of having only one border. Along the whole southern perimeter of our country is the line that marks us off from the United States. To the north, where most of us have never been and will never go, our country continues all the way to the North Pole. It's true that in the polar north we meet up with Russia and Scandinavia, and that we have a marine frontier with Greenland, but that doesn't change the fact that for Canadians *the border* means one thing only. In our region of the world, the Americans are our only neighbours, and that makes the border between us and them uniquely important, as a fetter for some, and for many others as a guarantee of nationhood, for which we stand on guard.

In places the border feels arbitrary. When I drive along the Saint John River on the Trans-Canada Highway just south of

Edmundston, New Brunswick, I look across the narrow water and see the State of Maine only a few hundred metres away. There is the United States separated from Canada by a river that is not very majestic in its upper reaches. Over there in Maine it is one hour earlier, Eastern Time, while it is Atlantic Time in New Brunswick. On both sides of the river, much of the population is of Acadian origin. In Maine, English is the official language, and most of the people of French background have become English speakers. On the New Brunswick side, both French and English are official languages, and the French culture is vibrant and alive. Here, the border runs north and south, with the Americans on the west side and the Canadians on the east. It's hard to believe that this stretch of the vast Canada–U.S. border was the scene of violence and turmoil in the mid-nineteenth century that very nearly triggered a war between Britain and the United States.

Elsewhere in its long reach across the continent, the border seems natural, located as it is in a majestic setting. From just west of Montreal to within five hundred kilometres of Winnipeg, the border between Ontario and the United States follows the line of the continent's greatest waterway. Separating Ontario from New York State, the border runs down the centre of the St. Lawrence River to Lake Ontario, and from there through the Great Lakes all the way to a point on the shore of Lake Superior between Thunder Bay, Ontario, and Duluth, Minnesota. The line runs around the islands in the immense waterway. In cases where the border would naturally bisect an island, the sensible arrangement is that the country that would have the greater share of the island gets the whole of it.

Far past the Great Lakes, the border runs along its most arbitrary line, the forty-ninth parallel, across the Prairies and over the mountain ranges all the way to the Pacific coast. From the air, the border is clearly visible, a dark, narrow shadow as straight as an arrow, looking for all the world like a sharply focused ray of dark light. The line is at the centre of a tiny clearing between fields and forests, across cliffs and mountain ridges. Far to the north, just opposite Prince Rupert, British Columbia, the border sets out again on a northward course around the Alaska Panhandle and then north to the Arctic Ocean, dividing Alaska from B.C. and the Yukon.

Warfare, diplomacy, chance, chicanery, ignorance, pigheadedness and compromise forged the Canada–U.S. border. Centuries of turmoil went into making the line that exists today. The border was born of struggles that began with the first European settlements in North America, in the early seventeenth century. The border reflects the ebb and flow of global struggles for primacy on the part of the European imperial powers as well as arrangements between the rising United States and fledgling Canada. The states of the American republic, the provinces and territories of Canada, and the border between the two countries are all successors to the divisions of the continent that existed among Aboriginal peoples into a much more distant past.

The struggle between the British and French empires in North America set the stage for the evolution of boundaries that would later have a major impact on the drawing of the boundary between the United States and British North America. By 1763, with the signing of the Treaty of Paris, all of New France with the exception of the islands of St. Pierre and Miquelon had become British territory. Little would those drawing the boundaries between Quebec and Nova Scotia (which then included the territory of present-day New Brunswick), and between these two colonies and those to the south, have imagined that they were helping etch the future border between two transcontinental nations.

In an important sense, they were also drawing the boundary between North America and Europe, or at least between that portion of North America that was soon to cut its ties with Europe and the portion that was to retain its transatlantic connection.

Much of the historical meaning of the Canada–U.S. border and of the differences between the societies on either side of it turns precisely on this point: the border divided America from Europe. Today, the border marks off two nations from one another. Historically, it was the line along which the tectonic plates of two empires rubbed up against each other, one a receding empire, the other the world's rising superpower.

Long dismissed as a topic worthy of serious discussion with the clichéd label "world's longest undefended border," the Canada–U.S. border is now a stress point. The terrorist attacks on New York and Washington, DC, on September 11, 2001, announced to the world that North America was no longer a quiet neighbourhood. The attacks immediately made Canada's relationship with the United States the most important question to face our country. A storm had been gathering in the Canadian-American relationship for years prior to September 11, but on that date the tempest struck. Canadians would no longer be able to put off a wrenching debate about the future of their nation and of its most important external tie.

Would September 11 push Canadians closer to their southern neighbours, unleashing a chain of events that could lead not only to a tighter military and security union but also to a more embracing economic union, perhaps even to a political union? Or would September 11 drive a wedge between Canada and the United States that would force Canadians to look to the strengthening of their own country? As always, when the Canadian-American relationship has been shaken to the core, the first shock came from south of the border. Only after it has been fully absorbed will it be possible to determine the long-term nature of the Canadian response.

Over the past fifteen years, there has been so much talk about globalization and the "borderless world" that it is easy to overlook the ways in which borders remain essential to the operations of the sovereign state. Borders are much more than lines to mark off one jurisdiction from the next. They are crucial control points that regulate the passage of people. They are, above all, the most visible symbols of sovereignty. Throughout history, tribes, empires and nations have measured their effectiveness as sovereign entities through their ability to maintain their territorial integrity against their neighbours. Between potentially hostile states, borders are heavily fortified, with watchtowers and guards patrolling the frontier itself and, farther back, military units ready to move into action in the event of a hostile incursion. Borders distinguish between the domestic and the foreign. Without them, citizenship is inconceivable.

Frontier posts are important administrative units in the operations of the sovereign state. Typically, a number of government departments exercise authority at border control points. In addition to officials who collect duties on imported goods, there are officials whose job is to check on who is crossing, to ensure that illegal migrants, criminals and terrorists are kept out. At border posts, officials monitor whether citizens exceed the duty-free allowances they are permitted. They enforce restrictions on the import of banned drugs, weapons, explosives, pornography, toxic waste, and certain categories of animals, plants and food.

In the age of the nation-state, which began in the era of the French Revolution, borders have marked off the boundaries between nations. While there have been plenty of exceptions to this, as in the case of multi-ethnic states, borders have gained enormous legitimacy as markers between nations, each with its own customs and way of life. At the core of the idea of the nation-state is the notion that because nations have distinctive customs and therefore form an extended community, they ought to be self-governing. This idea emerged in tandem with the rise of capitalism and democracy. If nations ought to enjoy self-determination, the allied concept is that it is the people of the nation who ought to govern it and not an aristocracy or oligarchy. Canada and the United States emerged during the high tide of the era of the nation-state.

The twentieth century was to overturn the easy notion that there was a necessary connection tying nationalism to liberalism and democracy. In a Europe crowded with nation-states, a new variety of nationalism, linking blood to theories of racial and ethnic distinctiveness and superiority, was to leave a dark stain on history. The experience of the 1920s, 1930s and World War II revealed what came of a strain of nationalism that legitimated the absolute exclusion of those castigated as racial foes. While the right of national self-determination remained a basic principle of the United Nations Charter after the war, the Cold War, which generated a call for solidarity in the face of the common Soviet foe, had the effect of further undermining the legitimacy of nationalism in Western thought.

As the role of the state in society has increased, the stake people hold as a consequence of their citizenship has also increased. Being a Canadian or a permanent resident of Canada means you are entitled to medicare. It means, as well, that your children can expect to gain admission to publicly financed universities for tuition fees that are far lower than those in the neighbouring United States. Upon retirement, you are entitled to receive Old Age Security and to payments from the Canada Pension Plan, depending on the contributions you and your employer have made to the Plan. In the past, citizenship centred more on what could be called "freedom from" than these examples of "freedom to." The traditional tasks of the state have been to maintain the peace internally, to protect personal safety and property, as well as to prepare for the defence of the nation against foreign invaders. The shift in the role of the state has had a great deal to do with a shift in the perceptions people have concerning what they obtain from their citizenship and what would be lost without it.

Canadians have always been overwhelmed by the sheer size of their country, and just as overwhelmed by the vast population and energy of their southern neighbour. Perpetually an uneasy country, knitted together from the English- and French-speaking pieces of British North America, Canada in recent decades has seen its largest cities transformed by immigration from Asia, the Middle East and the Caribbean. As a consequence of its complexity, its regionalism and the shadow cast over it by the power of the United States, Canada is a naturally conservative country—conservative not in the contemporary sense of enthusiasm for radical free market experiments but in the deeply ingrained conviction that wrenching change threatens the country's fragile unity.

Given the prevailing assumptions of our times, it has been natural for people to think that borders are withering away, and that Canada and the United States are becoming ever more alike and are bound to continue becoming more alike. In one very important respect, this is not true, a point worth making at the outset. In recent decades, there has been very little migration across the Canada–U.S. border in either direction. Fewer than 3 percent of immigrants to Canada in the past twenty years have come from the United States. And while Canada was once a major source of immigrants for the U.S., that is not so today. Only 300,000 Canadians now live in the United States, about 1 percent of the Canadian population. By contrast, in the 1880s, when the Canadian population was fewer than five million people, about one million Canadians headed for the United States, some in search of land to farm and others, especially French Canadians, looking for factory jobs in New England.

In other words, about 20 percent of the Canadian population chose to abandon Canada for the United States. Those wanting to make a case that there is an alarming drain of Canadian brains to the United States would have been far better off making their argument in 1885 than today. At times, Americans have moved north into Canada. Notably, and with great effect, this occurred at the end of the American Revolution, when tens of thousands of United Empire Loyalists headed north to British North America. Later, there was the heroic migration of American slaves to Canada in the quest for freedom during the days of the Underground Railroad. When the American frontier was filled by the early 1890s, thousands were drawn to Canada's "last best West," where they settled on the land, especially in southern Alberta. In the 1960s and 1970s, a unique brand of American immigrants who were to leave their mark on Canada came north as Vietnam War resisters.

In addition to the fact that few Canadians and Americans are now moving across the border to settle on the other side, the sources of immigration of the two countries are quite dissimilar. Fifty-eight percent of immigrants to Canada in the past two decades have been from Asia. By far the largest sources of immigrants to the United States have been Mexico and other Latin American countries. Current U.S. population projections forecast that by the middle of this century, Hispanics, now more numerous than African Americans, will constitute 25 percent of the U.S. population. Canada, also rapidly becoming a multicutural society, is drawing its new population from different cultures than the U.S. Indeed, not only are the two populations not becoming more alike, they are actually becoming increasingly divergent.

Today the shock waves emanating from the United States are wreaking havoc in Canada. Through the ages, Canadians have been taken aback by the Jekyll and Hyde personality of their great neighbour—sunny, effusive, liberal and grandiose for long stretches, followed by startling bursts of isolationism, self-absorption, bellicosity and compulsive patriotism. The election (*accession* is perhaps a better word) of George W. Bush to the presidency in 2000 signalled a shift from the madcap money-making 1990s to the darker passions of religious fundamentalism at home and muscular unilateralism abroad. But it was the

September 11 attacks that transformed a darkening sky into a full-blown tempest.

The United States now plays a role that is unprecedented for any country in the history of the modern world. Even at the peak of its power in the mid-nineteenth century, the sway of the British Empire did not approximate the power of the United States in today's global system. The hegemonic position of the United States is quite unlike anything the world has seen at least since the days of the Roman Empire. Nearly half of all the military spending in the world is now done by the United States. No military in modern times has ever achieved this level of dominance. In the nineteenth century, British hegemony was sustained through the might of the Royal Navy. To keep its lead, it was British policy to ensure that its navy was equivalent to the strength of the next two navies combined. When British hegemony came to an end with the outbreak of the World War I, the world entered an era of continuous struggle for supremacy among the great powers that lasted from 1914 until the collapse of the Soviet Union in 1991.

The first phase of the struggle was the era of the two world wars. During the two titanic wars that were fought between 1914 and 1945, all but two of the great contenders for global power were knocked out of the ring. After World War II came the Cold War. While the United States and the Soviet Union were by no means equal, they both qualified as superpowers in a world divided between a Soviet sphere and a much larger American one. The sudden, and unanticipated, disintegration of the Soviet Empire and of the Soviet Union itself between 1989 and 1991 ushered in the age of the single superpower.

The twentieth century was an epoch of gigantic struggles for global supremacy. The century that has just opened has begun uniquely—with one superpower at the centre of the world power structure. What makes this immensely significant is that the norms for dealing with international relations that exist in the world today are based on the implicit assumption that no single power utterly dominates the system.

In theory, all states in the international system have equal rights. They have a basic right to self-determination, to govern themselves on their own territory. This right to self-government is by no means absolute. The United Nations Charter espouses a set of broad principles that limit the rights of nations to absolute self-government. Of great importance, nations are not allowed to practise systematic racial discrimination on their territories. In principle, other nations can intervene in such cases to limit what a nation is allowed to do within its own boundaries. Broadly speaking, though, the right of self-government is still the essential principle on which the system theoretically rests.

In practice, of course, there have been all kinds of limits on the hallowed principle of self-determination. During the Cold War, the Soviet Union called the shots in Eastern Europe. In 1956 and 1968, when Hungary and Czechoslovakia respectively departed from a course that was acceptable to Moscow, the Soviet Union dispatched tanks to these countries to turn out the offending regimes. Similarly, the United States used force, overtly or covertly, during the Cold War to overturn regimes of which it did not approve in Iran, Guatemala, Panama, Nicaragua, Chile, the Dominican Republic and Grenada.

Despite these interventions, the principle of self-determination remained in place as the cornerstone of international relations. What made the principle more than a mere formality was the reality of struggles for power among the world's great states. Since the rise of capitalism and the demise of feudalism in early modern times, there has been a more or less constant balance among great powers. This balance has shifted dramatically, of course—so much so that the nineteenth century was rightly called the age of the Pax Britannica. Today, however, the balance has been replaced by the sway of the United States. Can the norms of international relations conceived in an age in which there was a balance of power survive in an age when there is no longer such a balance? To put it another way, what happens when a single nation acquires unprecedented power? What is to stop its rulers from changing international norms and running roughshod over the rights of other nations?

The Bush administration has transformed the U.S. view of what a superpower is permitted to do. The United States is streets ahead of every other power in the world in military technology and military capability. As a consequence, the U.S. government has shown that it is no longer much interested in international accords to limit the arms race. The Bush administration shuns the idea of signing the treaty to ban the testing of nuclear weapons. Like its predecessor, the Clinton administration, it will not sign on to the treaty conceived in Canada to ban land mines. And the Bush administration has taken the radical step of tearing up an existing treaty—the Anti-Ballistic Missile Treaty signed with the Soviet Union in 1972. Washington calculates that though the Russians and the Chinese may not like what the U.S. is doing, there is nothing they can do about it. The Bush administration believes that if the United States is successful in developing and deploying a system that can reliably shoot down approaching enemy missiles, it will protect the U.S. from attack. But it will do much more than that. A workable missile shield would liberate the United States to do what no power has been willing to do since the early Cold War years: use nuclear weapons in certain extreme circumstances.

The so-called missile defence shield (MDS) is a bold attempt to shift the global system even further in the direction of U.S. military power as the grand arbiter of human affairs. The Pentagon is anticipating this new age by developing custom-designed nuclear weapons that can be used on the field of battle in certain cases. Even the threat of such use, with no credible counterthreat of a nuclear attack on the United States, would change in a dramatic way what the United States could do against foes.

The United States' military doctrine and its concept of international relations are shifting as a consequence of its unprecedented military supremacy. The Bush administration has proclaimed the right to mount pre-emptive strikes against foes that are said to pose a threat to the United States and its allies. The argument goes like this: if the United States has reason to believe that other countries are developing weapons of mass destruction that could be used against the U.S., it is proper for the U.S. to regard pre-emptive strikes against such powers as legitimate. In the aftermath of September 11, when George W. Bush labelled three countries—Iraq, Iran and North Korea—the "Axis of Evil," he was taking the first step toward claiming the right to make pre-emptive strikes against these nations.

The Bush doctrine amounts to no less than the idea that the strongest power can do what it likes, that the strongest need not be constrained by norms such as the right of nations to self-government. The U.S. is behaving as though it is a universal state with unlimited rights to intervene where it likes. Call it a universal state or call it an imperial state—it amounts to the same thing.

Americans have no intention of ever forgetting September 11. But remembering goes far beyond the television specials and the staged events that pay tribute to those who died. September 11, laden as it is with heavy meaning—"Patriot Day," as President George W. Bush has named it—has become the basis for a new American approach to international relations. September 11 is now inseparably linked to the idea that the United States has the right to undertake pre-emptive military action against states that pose a threat to American national security—or that, *in the opinion of the administration*, pose such a threat.

Saddam Hussein's Iraq became the test case for the new doctrine, one that has enormous implications for the world. Even though there was no evidence linking the Iraqi government to the attacks of September 11, and there was no evidence that Iraq was planning a September 11–type attack in the future, the U.S. invasion of Iraq had everything to do with the uses to which the memory of September 11 is being put.

It was perhaps inevitable that this era would turn on the question of how much power the Americans would wield in the world. However, September 11 brought that question to a head more brutally than might otherwise have been the case. And that has forced a fundamental choice on Canadians, much as they may not want to face it. They will have to decide to travel down one of two divergent roads.

The first is the road of "deep integration." The deep-integrationists want Canada to go beyond its free trade agreement with the U.S. and Mexico to embrace the goal of a much fuller economic and security union with the United States. One element of their program is the removal of customs and immigration controls at the Canada–U.S. border. They are aware that the removal of border controls would require a deal with the United States to harmonize immigration, visa, refugee and security policies. They insist that since, in the aftermath of September 11, the U.S. is constructing a security fortress, Canada must do whatever is necessary to be *inside* the perimeter of that fortress—regardless of the effect on Canada's nationhood.

The alternative road is to maintain our border, to choose to sustain a sovereign Canada, separate from the United States, able to make key decisions about our economy, social order, and foreign and defence policies in Canada. The case for the Canadian option is that we have our own values and outlook on the world, and that there is no sign whatsoever that Canadian and American attitudes are converging. Indeed, a strong case can be made that since September 11 the two societies are diverging even more in their priorities and outlook. The Canadian option rests on the proposition that the quality of life of the average Canadian is superior to that enjoyed south of the border and that while deep integration could bring huge rewards for a few, it would condemn most Canadians to a deteriorating quality of life. Moreover, it would rob Canadians of the democratic right to govern our own society.

The question at the heart of this book is what becomes of Canada, and of the Canadian border with the United States, in a transformed world. Under pressure from Canadian elites who have long sought a tighter union with the United States, will Canada move to embrace the U.S. more closely? And as a consequence, will a line be crossed where Canada is no longer a sovereign state in any meaningful sense and must seek to establish a new place for itself—essentially inside the American union? Or, as the United States acts out the logic of its new role in the world, will Canadians step back, as we have at crucial points in our history, to reassert our own nationhood, to unite to reconstitute our country as best we can next door to the colossus? In short, will Canada defend its border?

Chapter 1 | The Meaning of the Border

It was the one great river which led from the eastern shore into the heart of the continent. It possessed a geographical monopoly; and it shouted its uniqueness to adventurers. The river meant mobility and distance; it invited journeyings; it promised immense expanses, unfolding, flowing away into remote and changing horizons. The whole west, with all its riches was the dominion of the river . . . The river was to be the basis of a great transportation system by which the manufactures of the old world could be exchanged for the staple products of the new. This was the faith of successive generations of northerners. The dream of the commercial empire of the St. Lawrence runs like an obsession through the whole of Canadian history; and men followed each other through life, planning and toiling to achieve it. The river was not only a great actuality: it was the central truth of a religion. Men lived by it, at once consoled and inspired by its promises, its whispered suggestions, and its shouted commands; and it was a force in history, not merely because of its accomplishments, but because of its shining, ever-receding possibilities.

— DONALD CREIGHTON, *The Empire of the St. Lawrence*

A great debate has raged over many decades about Canada's border with the United States, between those who think it an artificial boundary and those who want to keep it securely in place as marking off a society worth preserving next door to what is now the world's only superpower. Historians and economists, as well as politicians and poets, have shaped our conception of the border.

In the late nineteenth century, Canadian historians typically belonged to what can be called the "blood is thicker than water" school of Canadian history. To these thinkers, steeped in the worthiness of the British connection, Canada was a country that had emerged in defiance of geography. When they looked at maps of North America, they saw the continent cordoned off into regions that marched along north-south lines. There was the West Coast, flanked by the Rocky Mountains, which in turn butted up against the Great Plains. East of the Great Plains were the Appalachian Mountains and beyond them the Eastern Seaboard. From this point of view, it seemed that North America had been designed along north-south lines. For patriotic historians, the moral of the story was that Canada had been forged by those loyal to the British crown despite the counter-pull of geography. The great event in Canadian history, then, had been the northern migration of the United Empire Loyalists at the end of the American Revolution. These worthy believers in the British cause had left their comfortable homes in the south to make new ones in the northern wilderness.

Thinkers with a very different outlook used the same view of North American geography to reach a contrary conclusion. According to late-nineteenth-century writers like the English-born Canadian historian Goldwin Smith, who favoured the union of Canada with the United States, Canada was nothing more than a series of northern extensions of continental regions loosely tethered together through Confederation. And these Canadian regions, Smith believed, had more in common with neighbouring

U.S. regions than they did with each other. The idea of Canada as a freak in defiance of the natural lines of the continent has survived to the present day, particularly among economists who fervently espouse economic union between Canada and the United States. Especially for economists who believe in the perfection or near perfection of the market system, Canada's historic reliance on government intervention to sustain an east-west economy has been seen as a denial of sacred principles.

The view of Canada as a country composed of regions whose logic ran north-south was reinforced by an influential interpretation of U.S. history that first appeared in the 1890s. The American historian Frederick Jackson Turner developed the thesis that what differentiated America from Europe was the continual presence of the frontier from the early seventeenth century to the last decade of the nineteenth century. It was not accidental that he came up with his seminal idea when he did. It was in the 1890s that the U.S. Department of the Interior announced that there was no longer an open frontier in the continental United States. At the moment of the passing of the frontier, Turner seized on it as having been the central influence in American life. His argument will be easily recognized since what came to be called "the frontier thesis" has had such a huge impact on American culture. Turner contended that the frontier, that zone on the edge where Americans could migrate to leave behind settled ways and hierarchies, constantly re-created a society populated by free people who had not yet made a compact to form a government. To Turner, the experience of individuals in a virtual state of nature on the frontier was an intensely democratizing force in American life. He contended that the experience on the frontier, where it mattered what you did, not who you were, had a determining impact on the rest of America. From the frontier, individualism and a penchant for democracy helped break down hierarchies and established ways in the East, in the long-settled regions of the country. The frontier thesis is the paradigm that underlies that staple of Hollywood films, the western. The cowboy, the hardy worker-frontiersman, became the quintessential character in the America of the margin.

Boiled down to its essence, Turner's thesis held that the open frontier had allowed Americans who were tired of settled social norms to take off on their own to start life over. Not surprisingly, some historians in Canada were influenced by the thesis and used it as a tool for analyzing the development of early Upper Canada and other regions of the country in the nineteenth century. When Canadian historians picked up the frontier thesis, their work suggested that Canadian development involved variations on the same themes that were evident south of the border. By its very logic, the frontier thesis emphasized those things common to the American and Canadian experience. Canada, seen this way, was a northern extension of the United States.

Beginning in the 1920s, the Canadian political economist Harold Innis developed a sharply different outlook on Canada, its geography and its history. Innis and the historian Donald Creighton became the foremost exponents of the view that far from being a creation in defiance of geography, Canada was shaped by its natural setting and the commercial-communications systems that grew out of it. Innis and Creighton were not impressed by the theory that the regions of North America ran along north-south axes. What they looked at as the key to development were the continent's waterways. Understood this way, the logic of a Canada that was separate from the United States jumped out at them. For Innis and Creighton, the first fact of Canadian existence was the Great Lakes–St. Lawrence waterway, which thrust right into the heart of the continent. It was a natural route for the extraction of the treasures of North America by Europeans.

Harold Innis observed that west of the Great Lakes, the Great Plains were divided at close to the forty-ninth parallel—the boundary between Canada and the United States—between north-flowing and south-flowing rivers. North of the forty-ninth parallel, the major rivers flow north into Hudson Bay and the Arctic Ocean. South of the parallel, most of the major rivers flow south into the Missouri and Mississippi rivers and their tributaries. Innis made the point that in the era when the United States and the British North American provinces that later formed Canada were developing, major waterways were the lifelines of commerce and communications. North of the forty-ninth parallel, these waterways pulled commerce along the east-west lines that had grown up with the fur trade, whose ultimate market lay in Europe. Innis and Creighton concluded that Canada emerged from its natural setting, and that its waterways and the resources of the Canadian Shield gave it the potential for an existence distinct from that of the United States.

In their approach to the political economy of North America, Innis and Creighton turned the assumptions of Frederick Jackson Turner upside down. Turner had stressed how the frontier transformed American society. Innis and Creighton, however, insisted that metropolitan centres shaped the life and values of satellite settlements and of the hinterland. In their interpretation, it was the centre that shaped the margin, not vice versa. This understanding of Canadian history placed Montreal, with its English-speaking commercial capitalists, at the focus of nineteenth-century Canadian life. From there, along the pathways of commerce and communications, influence was directed outward to satellite centres and from there to the resource-producing hinterland. By the end of the nineteenth century, with the Canadian Pacific Railway completed, Montreal's main satellite in the West was Winnipeg. Winnipeg remained the largest city in western Canada until the completion of the Panama Canal, on the eve of World War I, promoted the takeoff of Vancouver. With the opening of the canal, shipments from the port of Vancouver gained access to markets in eastern North America at competitive shipping rates.

For Innis and Creighton, the American cowboy myth was not convincing. It was the powerful in London, New York, Montreal and Winnipeg who called the tune in the hinterland, not the other way around. In any case, the very geography of Canada conspired against the development of a cowboy myth on the northern side of the border. In the United States, it was possible for those seeking new land and a new life in the West to set out on their own or with a few others to head for the new territory. We can all recall those movies with wagon trains taking settlers west. But the Canadian Shield, the barrier between Central Canada and the Prairies, meant there could be no wagon trains to the Canadian West. Large-scale migrations from Central Canada to the West had to wait for the completion of the CPR. When settlers migrated to the Prairies, they did not arrive in a covered wagon in a lawless territory. They took the CPR, detraining in a region where the North West Mounted Police were on duty, and where the eastern banks had set up shop. Government, railway and banks were already on the scene. There was no return to a "state of nature" on the Canadian side of the line.

The American experience and, even more, the relating of that experience promoted the notion of a stark conflict between the individual and society. In *High Noon*, Gary Cooper, deserted by the townspeople, walks down the main street to face the four desperadoes. When he has dispatched them, he throws down his sheriff's badge in disgust and leaves town with his bride. Escaping from society and its norms and avoiding the grasp of government remain powerful, almost instinctual, responses in American culture. The American theory of society and government as a coming together of individuals in a state of nature to form a limited compact has its roots in the writings of John Locke and is enshrined in the Declaration of Independence and the U.S.

Constitution. Frederick Jackson Turner's insistence on the frontier as the feature that most distinguished America from Europe reshaped the legacy of Locke and the founding documents. The emphasis on the frontier elevated the role of a very particular kind of common man in American myth and culture. It was not the labourer, the factory worker or even the farmer who was the exemplar of this culture. Rather it was the free spirit, the cowboy, the rancher, the troubadour, the outlaw, the solitary avenger. The anti-societal loner became the hero.

In contrast, the Canadian experience promoted important variations within a common North American culture. Developing a country with a colder climate and a more forbidding terrain pressured British North Americans and then Canadians to temper individualism and to promote a strong belief in the utility of social cohesion. Consider the settlement of the Canadian West from this perspective. The point has already been made that for large numbers of settlers to move from Central Canada to the Canadian West, the railway had to be in place. And the building of the CPR required not only a change of government policies in Canada but the reconstruction of the Canadian state itself.

In the 1860s, the Canadian state was completely overhauled. The Confederation of 1867 was undertaken to cope with a number of threats to the viability of the British North American provinces. Those threats included the undoing of the balance of power on the continent as a consequence of the American Civil War. Early in the Civil War, the British government was sufficiently sympathetic to the Southern cause that it sold two warships to the Confederacy, an act that enflamed the relationship between Britain and the United States. A consequence of Anglo-American tension was the abrogation of the reciprocity trade deal with British North America by the U.S. government. By the end of the Civil War, not only had the federalists regained control over the South, but the Union army had become the supreme military force in North America. The British government had to recognize that its forces in British North America could not conceivably hold out against an invasion by the United States. Under the circumstances, the British inclination was to support the drive for union among the British North American provinces and to give up its military bases on British North American soil, apart from its naval base in Halifax.

British North Americans were impelled to union for other reasons too, which do not concern us in detail. Among them was the need to overcome the deadlock between English and French in the post–1841 Province of Canada through a move to federalism and the division of Quebec and Ontario into two separate provinces. And by the time of Confederation, there was a shortage of arable land in the Province of Canada. That fact, along with the loss of reciprocity with the U.S., increased the desire of British North Americans to expand westward into the lands held in the Prairies by the Hudson's Bay Company. It would surely be a race against time. If the newly formed Dominion of Canada was unable to extend its sway to British territory in the West, it would not be long before the United States would do so. And for Canada to move west, there would have to be a transcontinental railway.

Confederation gave the federal government the political and financial clout to oversee the construction of the Pacific railway. But political scandal and disagreement about how to get the job done delayed the completion of the railway until the 1880s. Returned to power in 1878, Sir John A. Macdonald's Conservatives came up with a set of national development policies that finally led to the completion of the CPR in 1885. To build the railway, the government had to make extraordinary deals with the CPR. The railway was granted a twenty-year monopoly of the traffic of the West. In addition, the federal government granted the CPR $20 million and twenty million acres (eight million hectares) of land. The land was some of the most valuable in the

Prairies, since it was taken along the rail line right-of-way. Especially valuable were the portions that ended up in the hearts of the cities that rose along with the line, such as Regina and Calgary. Just to make the pie especially delectable for the CPR, the government declared those lands exempt from property tax.

The second prong of Macdonald's east-west nation-building effort was the introduction of a protectionist tariff policy. In 1879, John A. Macdonald did what he had promised during his successful election campaign the preceding year. He unveiled a revision of the tariff schedule whose purpose was to promote manufacturing in Canada. The average tariff on manufactured goods was nearly doubled, to over 30 percent. The manufacturing tariff was to have a long and controversial history. Its first consequence was to encourage Canadians and foreigners to set up manufacturing establishments in Canada, a fact of particular importance for Ontario and Quebec. A further consequence, and one that fostered long-term resentment, was that westerners were pressured to purchase their finished products from Central Canada. For prairie farmers, who had to sell their grain in world markets, it seemed immensely unfair that they were impelled to purchase their farm machinery and other manufactured goods from protected central Canadian manufacturers rather than from the U.S. A longer-term consequence was the branch-plant economy in Canada, which emerged when U.S. firms jumped over the tariff and set up subsidiaries in Canada.

The Canadian experience, in which government policies were absolutely crucial to the development of a transcontinental economy, embedded Canadians in a web of corporate and state relationships. They could not look back in fond remembrance to a golden age when rugged individuals did their thing unencumbered by large institutions. For Canadians, there never was a Garden of Eden, real or imagined. Prairie farmers, wage earners, eastern railway owners and manufacturers were all driven by their circumstances to pressure the state to act on their behalf, and just as often against the interests of others. As they did so, there was much less inclination than in the United States to raise the cry that the state should get off their backs and leave them alone.

No region of Canada has ever surpassed Saskatchewan for the level of citizen involvement in community or provincial affairs, farm politics or formal politics. In 1944, when the social democratic Co-operative Commonwealth Federation (CCF) won office in Saskatchewan, the party had thirty thousand members. Out of a population of one million, that represented about 7 percent of the active adult population, an extraordinarily high level of participation compared with other parties in other regions or countries. It was no exaggeration to say that the CCF could achieve office if party members won over their relatives and close friends. By the time the CCF came to power, the people of Saskatchewan had had a long experience of wide popular involvement in public and farm community affairs. The Saskatchewan Wheat Pool, established by farmers to market grain collectively, had been a quasi-public institution in which thousands of farmers gained experience in how to engage in politics. Co-operation, not rugged individualism, was the ethic that took hold in Saskatchewan.

In the Saskatchewan case, the effects of terrain and climate were reinforced by a national culture that contained elements distinct from that of the United States to produce and sustain a political movement that would not have fitted anywhere south of the border. Crucial to that political culture was the Canadian tie to Britain that continued as a vital force for more than 150 years after the American Revolution.

The Canada–U.S. border is intimately connected to the great struggle that tore the English-speaking world apart in the late eighteenth century, when the Thirteen Colonies fought for their independence from Britain. The revolution that led to the founding of the United States played a critical role in reinforcing a very particular set of values among Americans. To this day, Americans are profoundly influenced by the social ideas embodied in the Declaration of Independence and the Constitution of 1787. In the United States, these founding documents are the living texts in an American civic religion. The notions of the market economy and of individuals coming together to form a limited government—a compact between the governors and the governed—are the very essence of Americanism. The newly created United States locked itself into its very particular version of a bourgeois revolution at about the moment when the Industrial Revolution was beginning to transform Britain.

To the north, where British rule remained intact, a different experiment was getting under way in the aftermath of the American Revolution. If the United States was born of revolution, Canada was the product of counter-revolution, and that includes both French Canada and English Canada, although in different ways. France ceded New France to Britain in 1763, following the Conquest of 1759. When the French Revolution erupted in 1789, French Canada remained subject to British rule, and as a consequence the society of the St. Lawrence missed out on the political and social effects of the great upheaval. While the revolution vastly lessened the role of the Church in French society, the Church, if anything, grew even more important in French Canada. When the Conquest devastated New France, the only important indigenous institution to remain intact was the Church. It became the intellectual and even political centre of French-Canadian society. It is not surprising that Church leaders in French Canada came to see the fact that their society was spared the apostasy of the French Revolution as a kind of salvation. For them, perverse as this may seem, the British Conquest came to be understood as God's way of sparing them what befell their brethren in France. During the nineteenth century and well into the twentieth, French-Canadian thinkers exhibited an ambivalent attitude toward their old mother country. On the one hand, they saw it as an essential source of cultural nourishment for their small society, which was surrounded by the preponderance of English-speaking North America. On the other hand, they feared the potential infection of their Catholic society with republican, liberal, socialist and anti-clerical nostrums. It was only with the Quiet Revolution of the 1960s that Quebec shed its old Catholic outlook and adopted a much more favourable attitude to France.

In English Canada, the counter-revolution was directly linked to the American Revolution. The patriots fought and defeated the British and the Tories. Some of the Tories came north to British North America as Loyalists. The first English-speaking settlers in what was to become Canada had settled in Nova Scotia decades before the American Revolution, and there were some English settlers in Quebec by the time of the revolution. But substantial settlement in Upper Canada and New Brunswick began with the United Empire Loyalists. It certainly overstates it to picture the Loyalists as a band of migrants who had a well thought out vision of society and of the British connection that marked them off from the supporters of the revolution. That said, it is clear that the Loyalists brought an outlook to English Canada that differed from the American outlook in important ways. As American historian Louis Hartz once remarked in a felicitous phrase, English Canada has a "Tory touch." The Loyalists, while sharing many of the social attitudes of their fellow colonists, were most distinguished from them on one single point: their attitude to the British connection. The patriots in the Thirteen Colonies had fought a lengthy war for their independence. The Loyalists gave up their homes, often forced to do so by the victors, because they had supported the losing British side. When they crossed the newly established frontier into British North America, the Loyalists were embittered refugees who were sure about one thing—their detestation of the new regime south of the border.

Three decades after the Loyalists made their trek north, they and their descendants were given a new reason to detest the United States when American armies invaded their territory. Particularly in Ontario, where American troops burned down farmhouses and villages, seized food and livestock, and paid farmers with worthless paper money, the legacy of the War of 1812 was long and bitter. A century after the war, tens of thousands of Ontario schoolchildren were taken to Queenston Heights, near Niagara Falls, to celebrate Sir Isaac Brock's victory over the American invaders.

In 1883, there was a huge centenary celebration of the coming of the Loyalists to Canada. A distinct Tory Anglo-Canadian sensibility had grown up by this time, and it formed a clear contrast to the outlook on the other side of the border. It has often been observed that the conscious rejection of the United States is and has been stronger in English Canada than in French Canada. Quebec nationalists have often attributed this to the fact that English Canadians, who speak the same language as Americans, are therefore much more vulnerable to American domination than are francophones. While this explanation is not entirely without merit, what it misses is the cogent fact that English Canada and the United States were created out of the two sides in a very bitter civil war. Civil wars leave behind them people with long memories, particularly among those on the losing side. Witness the enduring identity of the U.S. South, nearly a century and a half after the defeat of the "lost cause." English Canada, of course, was more successful than the South. It succeeded in making itself the majority component of a large country that managed to stay clear of the American republic, in a formal sense at least.

Just what was the difference in outlook that was being nurtured in English Canada? The first difference was a tendency to reject the American political model in favour of the English. In the nineteenth century, indeed during the first half of the twentieth century, the American political system was eyed with deep suspicion in

English Canada. I can remember, as a child attending a public school in Toronto in 1950, being taught by my teacher the conventional Canadian wisdom about politics. In my eyes the teacher was ancient; I figured she had probably known Queen Victoria personally. She taught our class that we were privileged to live in the greatest empire in the history of the world, by which she meant, of course, the British Empire. In Kiplingesque language, she informed us that the British had shouldered the heavy burden of civilizing a very large part of the world. As Canada grew in population and importance, we could expect to take up a larger part of the burden of sustaining the empire. Our teacher had a much less positive view of the United States, which she insisted on calling "the Thirteen Colonies," in a derisive tone. The problem with the neighbour to the south, she told us, was that a republic was more or less fated to become a tyranny, as had happened to Rome. Canadians, on the other hand, lived in a constitutional monarchy, by far the best guarantee of our liberty, because of the separation between the monarch, the head of state, and the prime minister, the head of government. In the U.S., the president is the head of state, the head of government and the commander-in-chief of the armed forces—a very dangerous cocktail.

The folk wisdom I was receiving from my teacher was the Canadian image of the United States that was the Canadian Tory outlook. This outlook was in part a legacy of the historic relationship with the United States, dating back to the American Revolution, and in part the product of Canada's continuing connection with Britain. On display in this perspective is what we can call "colonial nationalism." The colonial nationalism of English Canada was cultural as well as political. The heirs to the Loyalist tradition saw the United States as a violent, corrupt country, where aggressive business practices were the norm. It was a place where innocents had to be constantly on their guard. In the minds of northerners, the violence of the United States was reflected both in individual behaviour and in great historical events.

In the minds of Canadians, there was a definite link between the revolutionary origins of the United States, the terrible Civil War of the mid-nineteenth century and the lawlessness of the American frontier. The *Canadian Methodist Magazine* in 1880, in a self-congratulatory tone, wrote: "We are free from many of the social cancers which are empoisoning the national life of our neighbours. We have no polygamous Mormondom; no Ku-Klux terrorism; no Oneida communism; no Illinois divorce system; no cruel Indian massacres."[1]

There was an ingrained conviction in the conservative Canadian consciousness that the United States was an inherently unstable society, that its experiment in excessive democracy was fraught with peril. In the 1880s, when Loyalist sentiment was at a peak in Canada, it was not difficult for Canadians to perceive the United States as deeply flawed. The Civil War, with its terrible casualties—there were as many Unionist and Confederate deaths at Gettysburg in a three-day battle in 1863 as there were Canadians killed in World War II—was fresh in the minds of Canadians. And the Civil War was followed in the 1870s and 1880s by an epoch in American politics that was chiefly noteworthy for its venality.

The political strategy for Canadian survival on the North American continent in the decades following the American Civil War was mostly worked out by one remarkable man—John A. Macdonald.

Macdonald was the political embodiment of colonial nationalism. Over the course of his long career, he established the party that dominated Canadian politics in the latter half of the nineteenth century, presided over the achievement of Confederation and elaborated the National Policy, the economic doctrine that created a transcontinental Canadian economy and drew a clear line between

Canada and the United States. He was at times corrupt, and utterly contemptuous of the rights of Native people and the Metis.

Hugely important in the divergence of the two nations have been experiences unique to each. Crucial things have happened to the United States that have not happened in Canada. And the same is true of Canadian experiences that have little or no echo south of the border. Canada has missed out on three formative realities that have shaped much of the culture and outlook of the United States: revolution, slavery and global power.

The United States has been called the "first new nation," as a consequence of its revolution and its severing of ties with Europe. Like other nations that have had revolutions, the United States went through a history of power struggles as the institutions and values of the new country won their legitimacy. This period did not end until the climactic struggle of the Civil War left hundreds of thousands of Americans dead. The Canadian experience, in both English and French Canada, could not have been more different. Canada never severed its ties to Europe. Canadian institutions developed within the bosom of the link to Britain. At times, there was rebellion, violence and difficult adjustment to changing realities. But there was never as stark a need for the development of a new national character with new institutions that commanded legitimacy. The consequence, of course, has been a nation of multiple identities and two main languages. National identity has been weaker, in part because it never needed to be as strong.

The second seminal event in the United States that was almost entirely absent in Canada was slavery. Slavery and race have been central themes in American life, and like revolution, they were central ingredients in the great paroxysm of the Civil War. And slavery and race have been intimately connected to the rise of the gun culture of the United States. Slavery is an institution that can only be sustained through the threat and the use of force. Keeping a sizable proportion of the American population in bondage required the arming of the masters. The gun culture of America was reinforced by the Civil War and by the relatively anarchic conditions that prevailed during the Indian wars and the settling of much of the West. Without slavery and with a much more centralized impetus behind the settling of the Canadian West, the gun culture put down roots in few parts of Canada.

The third great formative fact about the United States has been its march to global power. The acquisition of great power alters a society, reshapes its institutions and changes the outlook of its people. Despite huge cultural differences and differences of historical era, it is not inaccurate to suggest that nations that wield power over others have what can be called a Great Power outlook, which affects both leaders and the population as a whole. During its imperial days, Rome saw itself as the centre of the world, a universal state on whose flanks were located lesser peoples who could be dismissed as barbarians. The proudest boast of Romans was "Civis Romanus Sum"—I am a Roman citizen. The epithet "Roman" announced that the citizen was a member of the most powerful human civilization of all time, that the Roman was to be respected and feared, that if foreigners mistreated him, the wrath of the Roman state and army would be wielded against them. Imperial China had a similar outlook, styling itself the Middle Kingdom. By definition, this relegated other states to the periphery. At the height of its world power in the eighteenth century and up until the defeat of Napoleon at Waterloo, France regarded itself as the most civilized and important of countries. Benjamin Franklin, citizen of a peripheral new nation, once said: "Each man has two countries, his own and France." One reason the French Revolution was such an epochal event was that it took place in the country that everyone in the West at the time agreed was the most important. The British and the Americans, long convinced that their nations occupy the first rank in the world, are infuriated by the haughty air of the French, which seems even today to convey to them the idea that what is French is superior.

After Waterloo, during the century of the Pax Britannica, the British were the world's special people. Other Europeans watched in a mixture of awe and amusement as the British visited their countries. *Milords anglais,* they were called in France. Wherever the British travelled, things had to be done their way by those who catered to them. The British founded virtual colonies in towns like Menton, Nice and Cannes in the south of France, where the British upper classes spent their winters. For decades, Menton had live English theatre, and it still has a statue of Queen Victoria on one of its main boulevards. And of course in Nice there is the Promenade des Anglais. The British coloured red those places on their maps over which the Union Jack flew, and boasted that the sun never set on the British Empire. Justifying the vast sway of their country, those such as Rudyard Kipling spoke of the "white man's burden." To them, they believed, the task had fallen to civilize the lesser peoples of the earth.

Russia, in the days of its empire and in the era of the Soviet Union, displayed a Great Power outlook, as did imperial Japan, Mussolini's Italy and Hitler's Germany.

Today, to be an American is to be special, just as it was special to be a citizen of Rome two thousand years ago. The term *superpower* fails to do justice to the power the United States exercises in the contemporary world. A Great Power mentality has been evident in the United States for at least a century, and never more than today. It has become a commonplace for American political analysts and commentators to make the comparison between America and Rome. And this is a rather remarkable development in a country that was born through a struggle to leave an empire. Until recently, Americans shunned the label *empire* to describe the global sway of their country. Since September 11, the term is being used increasingly, and what is more, it is being used descriptively, without negative connotations.

Among Americans, whatever their position on the political spectrum, the assumption is generally made that the United States is the greatest, most democratic and most freedom-loving country in the world, affording its people the best and most rewarding way of life. These views are nothing more than the daily rhetoric that can be found in any American newspaper or on any American television network. Rhetoric that would seem absurd, grandiose, self-serving and narrow-minded in any other country is completely unremarkable in the United States. Americans believe that their country, as the most advanced, is the natural leader for the whole world. In fact, while there are debates, and sharp ones at that, about this or that military program and about the size of the overall military budget, there is very little dissent about the idea that the United States should spend far more on its military than any other nation on earth.

The Canadian Tory tradition, inseparably linked to the culture, ideas and policies of John A. Macdonald, shaped Canada in direct response to two of these distinguishing factors: revolution and empire. Macdonald was a colonial nationalist, a political amalgam that is unintelligible to an American-style liberal. Macdonald's deepest commitment was to the creation of a Canadian nation that would be able to sustain itself separate from the United States. An American-style liberal would automatically think that the way to achieve this goal would be to continue in the tradition of George Washington and the other leaders of the American Revolution, and to cast off the tie of British colonialism. Latin Americans followed that lead and mounted revolutions against Spain and Portugal. But with the exception of the failed rebellions of 1837–38 in Lower and Upper Canada, Canadians did not. In fact, Canada is the only major country in the Western Hemisphere that did not choose the path of revolution and rejection of Europe.

Indeed, had Canadians taken the path followed by the other nations of the hemisphere, there is every possibility that Canada would never have survived as a great state spanning the continent. Macdonald believed that Canadian survival was not only not threatened by the British tie but depended on it. In a famous wartime speech, Winston Churchill held out the hope to the people of Britain "that the New World with all its power and might will step forth to the rescue and liberation of the old." Macdonald had it exactly the other way around. For him, the Old World was essential to protect Canada from the rising giant of the New. This was no weak-kneed colonialism; it was a profound insight into the realities of power in North America. He saw monarchy as the guarantor of political liberty and feared republicanism as the road to tyranny. While pragmatic and capitalist, his policies contained an element of paternalism and a belief in the large state that was strange on a continent where individualism and the market were the true deities. The state Macdonald constructed was imbued with these Tory notions. To build a railway across the north and to have institutions in place to receive the new settlers would require a strong centre, and Macdonald was determined to succeed where he thought the Americans had failed. The great lesson of the American Civil War was there for Macdonald to watch during the years in which the Confederation idea was born.

The Tory idea proved highly useful to Canadians for generations in their efforts to compete with the powerful nation to the south. In the first decade of the twentieth century, under the leadership of Adam Beck, a manufacturer from London, Ontario, the Province of Ontario drew on the Tory creed when it created a publicly owned hydroelectric system. The inspiration behind Ontario Hydro, at the time the largest public utility on the continent, was the notion that a public corporation could provide electricity at cost to consumers and businesses alike.

To American free market purists and their Canadian disciples, the idea of public ownership being used as a tool to improve Canadian productivity and the viability of the market in Canada is incomprehensible. They cannot help seeing this as a statist heresy, or even as a diabolical leftist scheme. In truth, the idea had everything to do with the Tory view of the proper relationship between the state and society.

While Toryism was present at the founding of English-speaking Canada, an un-American strain of social democracy was later to become a part of the Canadian cultural heritage. It too had British roots. While both the United States and Canada drew much of their founding populations from Britain, the streams of immigration came at crucially different historical periods, and this has had a profound effect on the political cultures of the two countries. There was a great deal of British immigration to the United States after the American Revolution, but once the revolution had occurred, these immigrants were pressured to fit into the values of the new country. North of the border, that was not the case. Between the end of the War of 1812 and 1850, the population of Upper Canada, now Ontario, increased tenfold, mainly through immigration from the British Isles. And because Canada remained in the British Empire, there was no such pressure on newcomers to give up their ideas and culture and to conform to the ways of the new land. British ideas continued to fit, and to be welcome, in Canada. Among the British immigrants were working people imbued with the radical ideas of the Chartists in the 1830s, and later in the century with the ideas of the rising and highly political labour movement in Britain.

Over the course of the next century and more, British immigrants played an essential role in the development of a distinctly Canadian social democratic movement. That movement drew its strength and much of its political program from the social gospel tendency in the Protestant Churches of Canada. Social gospellers such as J.S. Woodsworth, the first leader of the CCF, believed it was the duty of Christians to help their fellow man at a time when industrial capitalism was fostering poverty, unemployment, terrible working conditions and child labour. Canadian social democracy brought the social gospel together with the tradition of British labourism. This important political strain in Canada was central to the building of Canadian social programs, especially medicare.

The historical paths taken by the United States and Canada are fascinating in their own right. However, there is more to it than that. Different histories have shaped societies that are quite unalike in their values and priorities. The Canada–U.S. border draws a line between two societies with strikingly different views on key contemporary societal questions. On guns and capital punishment, the environment and health care, war and peace, Canada and the U.S. march to different drummers.

———

The debate that has loomed over Canada since the American Revolution is about whether Canada can and ought to survive separate from the United States. Never has the position of Canada been more precarious than in the era in which the United States is the world's sole superpower. It has often been said, as for instance by Jean Chrétien in the autumn of 2001, that you don't have to be anti-American to be pro-Canadian. That statement misses the point that Canada is irretrievably intertwined with the United States. The history of North America has left the United States and Canada as nations whose affirmations and rejections have reinforced the line that divides them.

The American Revolution was America's revenge against Europe. Canada is Europe's revenge against America. As the United States has grown into a global superpower, Canada has become the corner of the continent that reveals what America would be like without an empire. Indeed, Canada is the only member of the G8 that has never been an imperial power. It is often supposed that the American Revolution was the most successful in history because it left behind no political force that longed for the restoration of the old regime. While this adage is true enough when we look only at the United States, it falls to the ground when we bring Canada into the picture. The revolutions in France and Russia created a counter-revolutionary France and a counter-revolutionary Russia, both of which have survived to the present day. The American revolutionary war, a civil war within the English-speaking world, had a different outcome. Two nations were to share the continent. Canada, the smaller of the two, was to harbour the counter-revolutionary animus that was born of 1776. Never renouncing its ties with Europe, Canada was to shelter European ideas—ideas that south of the border would have been un-American. In the United States, the ruling ideas of the revolutionary era exclude both the further past and the future. Having escaped the revolution, Canada is a quirky place, where the past and the future cohabit. America, the land of perpetual bourgeois liberalism, is, paradoxically, also a land of stultifying conformity. A fugitive in the United States, idiosyncrasy has found a refuge in Canada. Americans are believers, Canadians sceptics. In the absence of a creed that is a national religion, liberty and personal privacy thrive in Canada. In the United States, freedom is boasted of most when it is practised least. In North America, the smaller nation occupies the larger cultural space. The larger nation is confined in its Lockean compact. The United States espouses equality, but Canada, which has espoused it less, has been more successful in its attainment. Conservative Canada is fertile ground for radical thought that withers in the soil of American liberalism. Although the authors of the American Revolution denounced standing armies, today's American legions have become a global standing army. Canada, once defended by

British imperial regiments and the Royal Navy, is the least militaristic country in the Western world. While America has proclaimed itself a refuge for the peoples of the earth, it is in Canada that Americans have often come to seek refuge—Loyalists, slaves and war resisters. Culturally in touch with the world before the birth of the American republic, Canada is more at home with the wider world of the twenty-first century than its insular neighbour.

In the decades following the American Revolution, culminating in the War of 1812, British North Americans were the first people successfully to resist American expansionism. Today, the Canada–U.S. border is one of the oldest unchanged frontiers in the world. However, a basic question hangs over that frontier in the first years of the twenty-first century. Are Canadians committed to the survival of their country for the long haul?

Chapter 2 | **BOOKENDS: Point Roberts and Campobello**

One enduring image of Canada has it that Canadians live in the southern portion of their vast country, strung out along the Canada–U.S. border. That would make the overwhelming majority of the 30 million Canadians dwellers in the world's longest border town. One might imagine that along the border, Canadian communities on the northern side find themselves cheek by jowl with American communities on the other side. As with many persistent generalizations, there is some truth in this one. Most Canadians do live within a couple of hundred kilometres of the border. And there are some Canadian border communities that are very close to border communities in the United States. Mostly, though, the generalization is hopelessly misleading. A far truer generalization is that the border either follows the course of great waterways that separate the Canadian from the U.S. side or, where there is a land frontier, it typically runs through wilderness, across sparsely populated prairie or over remote mountain ranges.

Yet there are some delightful spots along the border where Canadians and Americans can almost literally open their windows and call across to their neighbours on the other side. One of the most unusual places where a U.S. community abuts a Canadian one is Point Roberts, Washington. Point Roberts is a nodule of land that protrudes south from British Columbia into the Strait of Juan de Fuca below the forty-ninth parallel. As such, it is American territory that can be entered by land only through Canada. Indeed, the Greater Vancouver urban sprawl now extends all the way to the boundary with Point Roberts.

I enter Point Roberts through the sleepy little U.S. Customs post whose main claim to fame is that it is the westernmost land crossing point between Canada and the lower forty-eight U.S. states. The road into this green oasis is the road to nowhere. After a few minutes on it, I arrive at a shopping centre, where there are only a few cars in the parking lot. Inside the large and nearly deserted supermarket, I discover that all of the labelled products have been shipped to Point Roberts from other U.S. points; none of the labels is bilingual, as would be the case in B.C. I drive east a couple of kilometres through wooded country to the other side of Point Roberts and then down to the water on the south side, where there are some new houses being built. It's a strange, funky little world here, with some very comfortable-looking dwellings, modest cottages and lots of green space.

I come upon an attractive, intimate bar at the side of the road, with an outdoor patio, and I pull over. Sitting outside, waiting for the waitress, I am next to a table with two men and a woman, in their late thirties, who have both empty and full beer glasses in front of them. The woman, who is smoking, goes inside and comes back out to report that the Ottawa Senators are leading the Philadelphia Flyers in their afternoon playoff game. I overhear the smaller of the two men saying that he is a dual citizen, was born in Virginia and lives and works now in B.C. near the ferry terminal at Tsawwassen, just a stone's throw from where we are sitting. The big guy, who has broad shoulders and a practised smile, asks his companion: "Why don't you live here?"

"I have to stay six months a year in Canada to keep my health benefits," his friend replies.

"But you'd save so much on taxes."

"Not as much as you think."

Both of them, it turns out, own cottages in Point Roberts. Their female companion having once again gone inside to watch some of the hockey game, the conversation turns to women they have been dating.

The woman comes back to the table and so, at last, does the waitress, who greets the two men warmly and takes my order for a pint of beer. Other people arrive and leave. They all seem to know each other. It's like a little club, off the beaten path. So far, no one has said a friendly word to me, but at the next mention of the Ottawa hockey game I jump into the conversation and they treat me like a bosom pal. The big guy tells me he made it all the way to junior hockey and played in both Toronto and B.C. He says some former NHL players have lived in Point Roberts and that a number of pilots flying out of Vancouver International Airport currently reside here. Singing the praises of this little U.S. enclave, he says it is located in a rain shadow and that this is a sunnier spot than Vancouver—not such a high standard where sun is concerned.

His friend jumps in to say that there are parties here all the time, that in the summer it's a constant round of all-night bashes that migrate from one cottage to another. And it's common practice, I am told, for people to sneak in and out of Point Roberts across backyards in B.C. that butt up against the U.S. enclave. The regulars here, the big guy tells me, get to know the U.S. Customs officers and the local sheriff. "They have to like you," he says. "We had a sheriff a while back who waited outside this bar. When people left in their cars, he pulled them over." He speculates that the sheriff was unhappy to be posted to this out-of-the-way place. But, he says, the customs guys were okay, and once you got to know them, if you crossed the border back into B.C. even for an hour, you could stay for another six months when you came back. (I have trouble imagining anyone actually staying in Point Roberts for six months without ever leaving.)

There are some downsides to life here, I learn. Point Roberts has no public sewage system, which means that if you have a house or a cottage, you have to install or maintain a septic system. And in the immediate aftermath of the September 11 terror attacks, there were two-hour auto lineups to get into Point Roberts. Things are now back to normal and Point Roberts has become a sleepy border crossing once again.

When I pay my bill and finish my beer, my new friends suggest that I spend the night in Point Roberts, making the rounds of the Saturday-night parties. I tear myself away, however, and a couple of minutes later I am back at the border, at Canadian customs. The Canada Customs officer asks me for ID, something the U.S. officer did not do. As I drive away, I notice a local B.C. police car parked right beside the customs post. The car follows me for a few minutes and then turns off and leaves me on my own. Later, I talk to a Canada Customs officer, a man with long experience on the job, who tells me that customs officers often tip off the local police when they think someone has been drinking in one of the bars in Point Roberts. When you think about it, they may have a good bet there. There's not all that much to do in Point Roberts. My customs friend also tells me that customs has kept an eye on Point Roberts for drugs for many years. That's not surprising, since customs on both sides of the border is well aware that the frontier between B.C. and Washington State is a major crossing point for hard drugs heading north and marijuana heading south.

Seattle and Vancouver are the two cities that sit astride the Canada–U.S. border in this portion of the continent. Vancouver is a genuine border city, its southern suburbs now reaching all the way to the U.S. frontier, indeed all the way to Point Roberts.

Seattle, a two-hour drive south of the forty-ninth parallel, while not a border town in the narrow sense, is the American metropolis whose influence is felt throughout the region. The two cities are similar enough in size and climate, and different enough in their economies and ways of life, that they tell us something about life chances on either side of the frontier.

I am staying at the house of friends in Everett, a community about thirty kilometres north of Seattle. It is one of those weird, upper-middle-class exurban spinoffs that has now become a feature of American metropolitan areas. This one has a golf course motif. Large, contemporary houses are located on streets off main drags, all of which appear to go nowhere. The community has no real centre. Instead it has nodal points, where major roads meet, and there are strip malls, some of them with very upmarket stores. A large portion of the American upper middle class is determined to escape from the old cities. The two boys in this household, both teens, go to private schools.

The two great economic forces in the Seattle area are Boeing, the world's largest aircraft manufacturer, and Microsoft, the centre of global software and the creation of the world's richest man, Seattle native Bill Gates. In addition to these two giants, Starbucks and Amazon.com also have their headquarters in Seattle, where they got their start. This is a town of strikingly original entrepreneurs: Bill Gates, of course, along with Howard Schultz at Starbucks and Jeffrey Bezos at Amazon.

In the bad old days, Seattle's economy tracked Boeing's ups and downs quite directly (aircraft manufacturing is notoriously cyclical), so that when Boeing boomed, so did the metropolis, and when Boeing suffered, real estate prices and everything else sagged. The rise of Microsoft changed that, giving Seattle's economy much more buoyancy and balance.

For upper-middle-class Seattle residents, life is suburban, centring on private concerns and private institutions. The kids usually go to private schools. "Public schools are slow to adapt to new ideas," my friend Henry offers. When you go swimming, it is to the private beach on Lake Washington, where you belong to a club, or to a private pool, where you have a membership. Henry hangs out at the Seattle Club, downtown. He takes me along on Saturday morning. There are squash courts, a swimming pool, hot tubs, weight rooms—where I work out—and a deli-coffee bar. The people here are prosperous and the chit-chat is easy. Mike, a doctor who is Henry's friend, tells me, while we are watching a World Cup soccer game between France and Italy on the big-screen TV, that the French unions are crazy if they think they will be able to compete in the world if they insist on working a thirty-hour week.

Missing in Seattle is a sense of common space—space that is there to be used by everyone, from the rich to the not so rich. The upper middle class has its own private institutions and lives its lives in them, scarcely touching the rest of the population in schools, recreational facilities or parks. In Seattle, when you spend time with the well-to-do, it is easy to forget that not everyone is from this part of the social spectrum. But down at Pioneer Square, where there are tours that tell you about the city's early days, plenty of homeless people wander about, being kept on the move by the police.

Vancouver too is a socially divided city. Head east out of Gastown along Hastings and you will discover a Vancouver that is very different from the cheery west end. In part for reasons of climate, Vancouver is Canada's hard-drug-use capital. Among other things, this is linked to the city's high property-crime rate, because there are addicts who finance their habit through crime. How to deal with drug users has become a major issue in city politics. In the November 2002 municipal elections, the high-profile question before voters was whether the city should provide safe injection sites for heroin addicts.

But in Vancouver, public institutions remain stronger than those in Seattle. Private school attendance is much lower for the children of the well-to-do in Vancouver than it is in Seattle. In Vancouver, public parks and recreational facilities predominate. Vancouverites from a very wide social spectrum hang out at Stanley Park and on the beaches at English Bay and Kitsilano. The swimming pools are public and are used by the whole community. People feel free to come to sunbathe, set up nets for their games, have picnics. While downtown Seattle is empty at night, Vancouverites enjoy their public space until late on a summer evening.

––––––

When I think of the West Coast twins, I can't help thinking about Toronto and its unacknowledged twin, Buffalo, New York. Remarkably, the two cities share the same nickname; each is called the Queen City. The two queens have been around for about two centuries. Seventy-five years ago, it would not have been unreasonable to regard them as on a par in terms of wealth, architecture and the quality of life of the people who inhabited them. If anything, Buffalo had the edge over the Canadian queen. When I was growing up in Toronto, Buffalo was a lure, and not just because in those days you could drink beer there when you were eighteen while in Toronto you had to be twenty-one. In recent decades, of course, fate has been much kinder to Toronto than to Buffalo. While Toronto has burgeoned as the most ethnically diverse city in the world, and has mushroomed in population, Buffalo has faced a series of crises and has suffered decline. The story of Buffalo, a cautionary tale about the rise and fall of a metropolis, tells us much about the development of this region of North America, and about the way the border has affected two cities that, as the crow flies, are not more than eighty kilometres apart.

Buffalo rose to metropolitan stature as a consequence of the building of the Erie Canal, constructed as a public work by the State of New York and completed in the early 1820s. By the middle of the nineteenth century, the city had become the greatest grain-handling port in North America. At the end of the century, Buffalo's second great natural advantage was added to the benefits that derived from the Erie Canal. That second advantage was the cheap electric power that flowed from Niagara Falls. Electric power fuelled the rise of Buffalo as a great industrial city, a major centre of the steel industry. Propelled by the explosive growth of an economy focused on heavy industry, Buffalo rapidly became a wealthy American city, famed for the hefty number of millionaires living there and for its fine architecture, including a number of buildings designed by Louis Sullivan or Frank Lloyd Wright.

Then, technology and political economy shifted again, and the fortunes of the two queens diverged sharply. Toronto took off because it was the financial capital of Canada and was located at the centre of Canada's major manufacturing region. A steady stream of immigration brought hundreds of thousands of new residents to the Queen City north of the border. In Buffalo, however, the trend line was remorselessly down. Montreal won its revenge against the Erie Canal with the completion of the St. Lawrence Seaway during the 1950s. Buffalo's commercial and political representatives fought tooth and nail against the Seaway, without success. When the Seaway was complete, Buffalo lost the grain trade, which bypassed it in favour of Montreal. Although Buffalo's industrial production was stoked as a consequence of the Vietnam War during the 1960s, in the following decade disaster struck. First there were massive layoffs at the steel plants, followed by layoffs at auto parts plants. The core of the city's economy was being ravaged.[1] The white middle classes fled from the downtown, leaving it derelict and abandoned. Even the ring of suburbs around the hollowed-out centre failed to grow quickly enough to prevent the population from declining in the metropolitan area as a whole.

Over the past couple of decades Buffalo has experienced one of the sharpest declines in population of any major metropolitan area in the United States. Between 1980 and 1996, the population of the metropolitan area dropped from 1.24 million to 1.19 million. Of 273 metropolitan areas treated in a study by the Bureau of the Census, the Buffalo area was ranked 258th in population change.[2]

Meanwhile, north of the border, the other Queen City was flourishing. Its downtown was alive, its population rising swiftly as a consequence of immigration, largely from Asia, the Caribbean and the Middle East. The patterns of shipping and transport, as well as changes in industry, have affected the two cities in different ways, it is true; but the multi-ethnic faces of the northern twin suggest that national immigration and social policies have a significant effect too.

———

On the East Coast, the counterpart to Point Roberts is Campobello, New Brunswick, an island off the shore of Maine that can be entered by land only from the United States. And Campobello is the easternmost land crossing point between Canada and the United States. Together, Point Roberts and Campobello are the bookends of the Canada–U.S. border.

I had long heard about this enchanted Canadian island off the coast of Maine, so I set out on a road journey to visit Campobello.

Lubec, Maine, is the easternmost town in the United States. It is located in Washington County, known as the Sunrise County. At rest stops on the I-95, the interstate that runs through Maine, the map on the wall appears to show land ending on the eastern edge of Maine. The Atlantic Ocean and Canada are both marked in a watery blue. It seems that the sun does indeed rise first over Maine. The craggy coastline is a natural nesting place for harbours, from which fleets of fishing boats and lobster boats and pleasure vessels head out to sea.

I had been crossing the state for about four hours since I woke up that morning in the Stratton Motel in Stratton, Maine, about a forty-minute drive from the Quebec border. The Stratton Diner, where I ate the night before, was right across the street. The fare at the diner was basic, but it was served cheerfully by a young waitress whose mother ran the place. The chicken was coated with a thick layer of batter, but I tried not to think about that. By the counter, there was a notice for the Building Fund Raffle of Our Lady of the Lakes Churches. First prize was a 30–06 Remington semi-automatic rifle. Second prize was a 12- gauge Stoeger double-barrel shotgun. The Stratton Motel was a plain place, snug up against a small river. The woman who rented out the rooms looked respectable enough, and the whole setting was quiet except for four or five teenagers standing by the river talking in very lively French and throwing stones into the water. I was a bit stunned by the notice on the door of my room. It did not tell me how to flee in the event of fire. Instead it said: "In Case of Any Disturbance or Any Problem You Must Call This Number." Below the number, the notice continued: "After 10 P.M., it is Quiet Time Here."

Stratton seemed like a peaceful little town, but apparently rowdiness ruffles its New England quaintness from time to time. It had certainly appeared to be an oasis to me when I was searching for a place to stay. I was driving across Quebec's Eastern Townships. I started thinking about stopping for the night as I was passing through the vacation country around Magog. Both sides of the border in this region of lakes and hills draw tourists in the summer and winter. As I sat at the wheel thinking fondly of Magog and Lake Memphremagog, which crosses the border to the south, and of the fine cottages, inns and hotels of the area, I found that I had sailed past all the exits to it and was nearing the city of Sherbrooke.

The anchor of the Eastern Townships, Sherbrooke and its environs were settled in the years following the American Revolution as Loyalists trekked north and new settlers arrived from the British Isles. The Eastern Townships became an English-speaking bastion in Quebec. In 1840, Sherbrooke was 90 percent English-speaking. But over the past century and a half, things have changed. The francophone population of Quebec's urban centres has risen sharply—in Quebec City from 60 percent to over 95 percent, in Montreal from 40 percent to 60 percent, and in Sherbrooke from 10 percent to 90 percent. Today, places in the Eastern Townships with quaint English names like Lennoxville, and street names like Dufferin, remembering governors general born in Britain, or Wellington and Waterloo, commemorating victory over Napoleon, have become French-speaking centres.

I have a personal connection to Sherbrooke. It was the unlikely city where my grandfather and grandmother settled in 1900. Getzl and Freda Laxer were young when they decided to leave the eastern reaches of the Austro-Hungarian Empire for a better life in America. They brought with them their one-year-old son, Max, my uncle who was sometimes known as Jack. My grandfather was a penniless rabbi, whose real trade was the art of the kosher slaughter of cattle. When my grandparents disembarked from the ship at Quebec City, my grandfather was on the lookout for a place to practise both the secular and the religious aspects of his trade. He tried New York City first, but finding nothing there, he returned to Canada. To him the distinction between one side of the border and the other was not important. Having been spurned in New York, he chose Sherbrooke. When the family settled there, my grandfather became the first rabbi to ply his trade in the town. The family lasted there for about a dozen years and then moved to Montreal, renting a house in the Jewish ghetto a few blocks west of St-Laurent.

Perhaps I'll spend the night in the Sherbrooke area, I thought. I drove through the city of Sherbrooke and eventually, following a rather circuitous route, ended up in Lennoxville, the small adjoining town where Bishop's University is located. In Lennoxville, with its shaded streets and elegant buildings, I tried for a while to find a motel. After mistaking a retirement residence for a motel, passing the scene of a wedding party exiting from a church and discovering that the motels all appeared to be full, I drove out of town and headed along the highway that would take me due east to the Maine border.

I was driving through a pleasant pastoral countryside, with farms on both sides of the highway. There was very little traffic and I feared that I had shot past the tourist haunts of the Eastern Townships. Far to the northeast, I could see a sombre line of ancient rounded hills, the Notre-Dame mountains. A northern branch of the Appalachians, the oldest mountains on the continent, the range continues south and west into New England and from there across New York and Pennsylvania and down into West Virginia, Kentucky and Tennessee. The town of Cookshire, my next hope for a place to stay, appeared entirely silent on this late afternoon, and there was not a sign of a hotel or motel. Hope flickered briefly about thirty kilometres farther on in the hamlet of La Patrie, where I discovered a pleasant-looking country inn at the side of the highway.

The proprietor told me he was full up for the night but that there was a motel with about twenty rooms in Woburn, the very last town in Quebec before I would reach the Maine border. I had the feeling that Woburn was my last hope. Beyond it, I would be deep in the woods and mountains of Maine. In the mid-nineteenth century, Henry David Thoreau wrote about hiking and canoeing through the Maine woods. The thought came over me that if I didn't find accommodation in Woburn, my fate would be to sleep by a stream in the manner of Thoreau. This part of Maine also made me think about Benedict Arnold. I was retracing in reverse the route he took in the winter of 1775, when he led a scraggly force north along the Kennebec River to invade Quebec. While this invasion by the American colonists did succeed in seizing Montreal for a time and in laying siege to Quebec, in the spring of 1776 a large force of British troops arrived on ships and drove the Americans off.

Woburn is a hilly town. Off in the direction of the border, only a few kilometres away, were vast, empty fields. I found the motel, a stucco building in poor repair, with a big, garish sign for a bar at one end. Fearing that the alternative was a night *à la* Thoreau, I went inside the bar. My arrival brought the jovial gathering in the dark room to a complete halt. Eight or nine faces stared at me as smoke swirled around my head. The woman behind the bar was as startled as the others. When I asked if she had a room for the night, she paused and told me she had one room in the basement. Instantly, I decided that Thoreau and Benedict Arnold were looking better and better. I thanked her and said I'd try elsewhere. As I walked out the door, I could hear the voices rising behind me. Things had returned to normal at the bar.

Five minutes later, I was at the Maine border. The U.S. Customs post was housed in a small white wooden building. There was a stop sign at the side of the road, and a notice informed me that I had to wait to be inspected by customs. A moment later, a pleasant-looking, slightly plump man in his mid-thirties emerged from the building. He was wearing a customs officer's uniform and there was a gun in his belt, but he looked much more cheerful than threatening. He asked me where I was going and I told him Bangor. Why would a Canadian want to go to Bangor, he wanted to know. I explained that after Bangor, I was heading for Campobello. He smiled a broad smile at this and suggested that after Campobello I take the ferry to Deer Island and then a second ferry to the New Brunswick mainland near St. George. I told him that was the route I planned on and asked him if he had any suggestions about where to stop to eat and spend the night.

At this point the customs officer's face lit up with a jovial smile. "I am an immigration officer, not a tourism official," he said, as though he truly wished he could be involved in tourism. "I am going to give you some advice. The town you're looking for is Stratton. It's about a half-hour drive from here. I was born and raised there, lived there all my life!" he exclaimed. "I'll be right back." Abruptly, he disappeared inside the customs post, where he remained for three or four minutes. He came back with a couple of pieces of paper in his hand. When I had arrived at the customs post, there hadn't been another car in sight. By now, though, a line of cars was forming behind me, but the friendly officer took no notice of this.

He handed me a piece of paper with the route to Bangor, and beyond that to New Brunswick, printed on it. He was evidently used to giving advice to itinerant Canadians. The second scrap of paper was written out by hand and for me alone. On it were suggestions about where to eat and stay in Stratton. First on the list were the Stratton Motel and the Stratton Diner, the places I ended up patronizing. There were other choices, listed as more expensive and less expensive.

As I gazed over the list, he remarked rather defensively, "I don't have any connection with any of these places." When he saw that I was delighted and did not suspect him of promoting the interests of his family and friends, he warned me about other establishments in Stratton. "If I didn't mention them, what conclusion do you draw?"

I would have been happy to continue the conversation with the most agreeable customs officer I had ever met, but the line of cars behind me was growing ever longer. I thanked him and headed off into the Maine woods.

With the exception of a soft mattress that pushed my knees and my shoulders into close proximity, my night in Stratton lived up to the customs officer's billing. The next morning I set out for Bangor, and from there along the coast to the easternmost point in the United States. The bridge from Lubec, Maine, to Campobello Island in New Brunswick was constructed in the early 1960s. The span is not a particularly long one, which makes it apparent that Campobello is really an extension of the Maine coastline.

As I gazed at the unspectacular bridge, I reflected on the fact that agreeing on the line of the Maine–New Brunswick border was a politically explosive issue from 1783 to the 1840s—so explosive, in fact, that it almost led to war between the United States and Britain.

Campobello's history has always been intimately connected to that of Maine, indeed to that of New England and the northeastern states. In the last decades of the nineteenth century before air conditioning, wealthy American families were on the lookout for havens where they could spend the summer months away from the sweltering heat. The Muskoka lakes in Ontario were one such locale that drew Americans in large numbers. Many of the historic, luxurious cottages that were really mansions on lakes Rosseau, Joseph and Muskoka were built in this era for families from New York, Cleveland, Detroit and Chicago. By the 1870s, Campobello Island became a similar attraction. Campobello is located on the edge of the Bay of Fundy, a body of water famed for its frigid temperatures. The Bay of Fundy has its own system of "natural air conditioning." I remember a few years ago, on a blistering, hot and humid day in Nova Scotia, I drove to the Fundy shore. A wall of fog sat over the land, covering it for about a hundred metres next to the water. I got out of my car and walked out of the uncomfortable sun into the fog. Along the shore, it was cool and fresh.

In the 1870s and 1880s, Americans built large houses on Campobello. In 1881, the parents of Franklin Delano Roosevelt had a house constructed on the island, a place they could go in the summer when their estate at Hyde Park, New York, was uncomfortably hot. There is a myth that swirls around Campobello that Franklin Roosevelt was actually born there in 1882 and smuggled back across the line by his parents for his "official" birth in Hyde Park, New York. In the upper-class Roosevelt family, the birth of a male always triggered hopes that this could be a future president of the United States. Under the U.S. Constitution, though, presidents must be born in the United States. It's a tantalizing myth that lives on, supported, until now at least, by no actual evidence.

In 1883, when he was only one year old, FDR spent his first summer in Campobello. The family came by train to the nearby Maine coast and from there by boat to the island. The future president spent most of his summers in the two-and-a-half-storey Dutch colonial cottage, which survives today in the form in which it was rebuilt in 1889. When FDR married his distant cousin Eleanor, the couple, and later their children, summered on Campobello. Indeed, one of their sons was born by candlelight in the thirty-four-room dwelling on the island.

Roosevelt pursued a vigorous physical regimen during his summers, sailing and swimming in the frigid waters. He even introduced golf to the island, a pastime that flourishes today on Campobello's nine-hole course. It was on the island in the summer of 1921 that FDR came down with polio, which led to the paralysis that denied him the use of his legs for the rest of his life. After he had lain bedridden during the acute phase of the illness, a boat was brought for FDR and he was carried down to the beach on a stretcher. After the short ride to Maine, he returned home to Hyde Park in a special rail car.

During his presidency, FDR returned to Campobello for two short visits, one in 1933 and the final one in 1939. The thirty-four-room cottage is certainly well appointed—as visitors can readily see—but it is far from luxurious.

Today, the Roosevelt cottage is the centrepiece of the 1,134-hectare Roosevelt Campobello International Park that is maintained by both Canada and the United States. Prime Minister Lester Pearson and President Lyndon Johnson established the park, and both of them visited the island for a ceremony in 1966. Most of the visitors to the park, the day I was there, were Americans.

Today, there are 1,400 residents of Campobello. Many of them, having been born in Maine hospitals, have dual citizenship. During most of the year, their only contact with the outside world is through Maine. The Canadian and U.S. border posts at this frontier point are notably relaxed. They expect the residents at Campobello to hop back and forth from Eastern to Atlantic Time, and to do much of their shopping for food and other necessities in Maine.

From Campobello, the only way to reach other Canadian points directly, and this only in the summer, is by ferry. The morning after my visit to the Roosevelt cottage, I take the car ferry to Deer Island, the next large island north of Campobello. The sign to the ferry directs you to a narrow road leading to a cleared piece of beach. The entrance to the car ferry is rather primitive and disconcerting, considering that you are embarking on a sea voyage with your car, albeit a short voyage in protected waters. I wait about seventh or eighth in the line of cars and watch the small flat barge chug slowly to the landing spot, where the front end was dropped and a couple of vehicles drove off. We all drive on, paying $18 for a car and driver for the short trip. This ferry is privately run.

The ferry ride on this sunny, calm morning takes us close to the Maine shore, past the town of Eastport and then on to Deer Island and another flat landing spot. Deer Island is not as large as Campobello, but it is hilly and beautiful, with twisting roads that provide extraordinary vistas of the sea and the Maine coast. Fine large houses come into view as I drive across the island in the direction of the next ferry I am to take. On the north side of Deer Island there is a ferry departure point for the New Brunswick mainland. The New Brunswick government operates the ferry, a much larger affair than the one from Campobello, and it is free.

———

At Point Roberts and Campobello, the border's bookends, one American and one Canadian, you get a feel for the intimate border life that exists in a few places. In between, while there are other spots where a similar intimacy can be found, such places are very much the exception.

Chapter 3 | **Remote Frontiers**

Overwhelmingly, the Canada–U.S. border runs through remote terrain where you do not come upon charming little Canadian and American communities across from one another. To get the feel not only of the border but of the vastness of Canada and its neighbour, you've got to abandon the Boeing 747 and set out on the road, train or ship to travel the enormous distances that have had so much to do with shaping two similar, but utterly distinct, countries. The key to understanding the settlement and development of the continent is to follow the transportation and communications systems that have linked metropolis to satellite to hinterland. These paths of settlement and commerce have always been pathways for the transmission of culture and political ideas. Mostly, the pathways have moved from east to west, but there have also been south to north pathways, and in the strangest case (which I will come to later), that of the Alaska Panhandle, the initial push was from west to east—from Europe via Asia to America.

I am driving south of Cardeston, Alberta, en route to the Montana border. I feel as if I am approaching the end of the world in this strange country of weirdly sculpted black hills covered in places with patches of snow. The sky is huge. The land feels as if it is being pushed smack up against low clouds. In this corner of Alberta, we are in a landscape that is an amalgam of prairie and foothills. All the way south of Calgary, I have been driving alongside great cattle ranches, which are so big that you are lucky if you get a glimpse of cattle standing together in one corner of the vast domains.

In southern Alberta, the social landscape is as distinct as the physical. In the last years of the nineteenth century, southern Alberta was the "last best West," the frontier that was still open to settlers after the American frontier had been officially designated as closed. A much higher proportion of those who settled in this region of Alberta came from the United States than had been the case in Saskatchewan and Manitoba. After Confederation, Manitoba's first settlers had come from Ontario. To these were added Ukrainians, Icelanders, Finns and Jews from Eastern Europe. In Saskatchewan, the influence of Ontario was not as great as in Manitoba, although it was not inconsiderable. Settlers came from the British Isles, as well as from Western and Eastern Europe. Many of the Americans who settled in Southern Alberta brought with them an evangelical Protestant outlook. That outlook served as the cultural foundation for the development of important political movements that had an impact on Alberta and national politics.

On both the left and the right, Alberta was to have its own brand of populist politics, heavily spiced with the views of American immigrants. One of the first to put his stamp on Alberta farmer politics was Henry Wise Wood, who hailed originally from Missouri. He arrived in Alberta in 1905, the year Alberta became a province. More than any other person, Wise Wood helped shape the philosophy of the Alberta farmers' movement. His critique of Canadian politics was that the party system naturally favoured the wealthy and the powerful at the expense of other segments of society and promoted the domination of the country by Central Canada. Dismissing the Liberals and Conservatives as unprincipled parties seeking power for the sake of power, he called for the creation of a party to represent farmers alone. While his ideas had little impact on the country as a whole, they were ideally suited to the particular conditions of Alberta at a time when the largest single occupational group was farmers who owned their own farms. He was the guiding force behind the United Farmers of Alberta, a movement that became a highly successful political force when it won power in the province and governed Alberta from 1921 to 1935.

The movement that succeeded the UFA in power and then held it for three and a half decades also had important roots in southern Alberta. The charismatic leader of the Alberta Social Credit was William Aberhart, a native of Ontario. Aberhart moved to Calgary, where he taught mathematics in a major high school and then became its principal. What he shared with many southern Albertans was Protestant fundamentalism. With his "Back to the Bible" broadcasts, Aberhart became Canada's most successful radio evangelist in the mid-1920s. In 1932, when Alberta suffered as a consequence of the collapse of grain prices during the Great Depression, Aberhart became a convert to the ideas of a Scottish engineer, Major C.H. Douglas. Armed with the idea that Alberta needed an injection of "social credit," in the form of a dividend to be paid by the government to Albertans, Aberhart built a movement that propelled him into the premier's office in the 1935 election. The former UFA government lost every seat it held in the legislature. Alberta's populism had shifted from the left to the right, where it has remained ever since. With Alberta's major oil discoveries, beginning in the late 1940s, the province shifted from being Saskatchewan's economic twin to becoming a mighty petroleum power.

A new populism, tailored to Alberta's metropolitan stature as Canada's petroleum power, emerged with the election of Peter Lougheed as premier in 1971. From Lougheed, who battled Prime Minister Pierre Trudeau over oil revenues, to Premier Ralph Klein and his struggles against Jean Chrétien over health care and the Kyoto Accord, Calgary and rural southern Alberta have been the locus of power in the province.

And out of the culture of Southern Alberta has come the newest force in Canadian federal politics, the Reform Party, now the Canadian Alliance. Here the link goes straight back to the populism of William Aberhart and the Social Credit. Ernest Manning, a young man from a rural Saskatchewan family, walked into Aberhart's Prophetic Bible Institute in 1927 and enrolled in the Institute's one-year course in Bible studies, becoming its first graduate. It was the most fortuitous choice of a course ever made by a student in Canada. When Aberhart died in 1943, Manning succeeded him as premier and held that post until 1968. His son Preston, a skilled and original political thinker, was the mastermind behind a new political vision of Canada and the place of the West in Confederation. His brainchild, the Reform Party, and later the Alliance, pushed aside the Progressive Conservatives to become the leading vehicle of the Canadian right. It is no accident, given its origins and its history in the "last best West," that the Canadian Alliance is the political party with the most natural affinity for American values, the most pro-American party in Canada.

At last, I see a long hill ahead of me. At its top is the Canada Customs post on the border with Montana. I drive past it in the eerie, early evening light. There is not a single other vehicle in sight. The U.S. Customs post is large and new, with an inviting western motif. A sign on the building warns that this border post is closed nightly from 11 P.M. to 7 A.M.. When I arrive at the customs window, there is no one in sight, only a small sign instructing travellers to wait for the arrival of an officer. After a few minutes, an officer appears and asks in a brisk, professional tone what is the purpose of my trip. I tell him I'm writing a book about the Canada–U.S. border and that I want to visit Montana, where I may take some photographs. He asks me if the photos are to be used in the book. Yes, I tell him, and he waves me ahead.

Down the long hills and into a valley I sail. This is ranch country, and there are some big ranches along the highway to Babb, Montana. I reach Babb just as the sun is setting in a glorious burst of what filmmakers call "magic light," when everything from people to cattle to faded buildings looks better in a glow of bronze and gold. A few minutes later, the magic light is gone and I see Babb in the cool light of reality, a poor and marginal town in a sea of vast hills and valleys.

———

While the crossing between Alberta and Montana showed me just how sparsely populated the border areas can be, and how much physical distance separates Canadians and Americans on either side, two larger journeys were to underline dramatically the remoteness of most of the Canada–U.S. border. In the first of these I drove around Lake Superior, traversing the terrain in northern Ontario en route to Thunder Bay, which I came to see as the hinge of Canada. If you want to understand why Canadian and American conceptions of the settling of the West were so different, you have to travel across Northern Ontario. In the second journey, I travelled by ship from Vancouver up the coast and into the Alaska Panhandle, where the United States and Canada share their strangest and most remote frontier.

The drive around Lake Superior is sixteen hundred kilometres long—a thousand miles for those, like me, who grew up with imperial measurements. I drove what is called the Circle Tour

around Superior—the lake with the dimensions of an inland sea—
in late spring, when the days were long and the sky was achingly
blue. Just getting to the starting point at Sault Ste. Marie,
Ontario, does things to your conception of "the North."
Tradition has long had it that the North in Ontario begins at the
French River, which is about eighty kilometres north of Parry
Sound on Georgian Bay. These days, the Ontario government
officially regards the North as commencing at Parry Sound,
which is a mere two hundred kilometres from Toronto.

I used to think of Sudbury as solidly ensconced in the North.
But there is more territory in Ontario north of Thunder Bay than
south of it. Geographically, that places Sudbury and North Bay
decidedly in the South. Not so socially and politically, of course.
Residents of Northern Ontario are acutely aware of the immense
distances that divide their communities from one another and
from the rest of the province. And they have long harboured the
conviction that they are often treated as second-class citizens in a
province whose political centre of gravity lies well to their south.
When Chapters first opened its bookstore in a mall in Thunder
Bay, its "local interest" section contained books about Muskoka,
the land of lakes that is not much more than 160 kilometres from
Toronto. From Thunder Bay, it is 1,100 kilometres to Muskoka—
hardly a matter of local interest, as residents derisively pointed
out. Chapters soon corrected its error.

En route to Sault Ste. Marie for the start of the journey
around the incomparable lake, I thought a lot about the Great
Lakes and the St. Lawrence River, which provide Ontario with a
"natural frontier" with the U.S., something that is distinctly
absent in most parts of the country. Indeed, from the
Ontario–Quebec border to the frontier between Ontario and
Minnesota, on the shore of Lake Superior, there aren't all that
many crossing points between Canada and the United States.
There are three bridges across the St. Lawrence River connecting

Ontario to New York State. The first is at Cornwall, the second is just east of Prescott and the one farthest west is the Ivy Lea Bridge at the Thousand Islands, east of Kingston. The next bridge to the U.S. is over three hundred kilometres farther west, at Queenston, not far north of Niagara Falls. From there to Lake Erie in the south, there are two more bridges, the last one linking Fort Erie, Ontario, to Buffalo, New York. Again we have to jump more than three hundred kilometres farther west to the next direct link between the two countries, the Ambassador Bridge that ties Windsor to Detroit. A few kilometres along we come to the tunnel between Windsor and Detroit. The next link is to the north on the other side of Lake St. Clair, where a bridge spans the river between Sarnia, Ontario, and Port Huron, Michigan. From Sarnia, we have to go all the way across the immensity of Lake Huron to Sault Ste. Marie, Ontario, where a three-kilometre-long bridge sweeps high above canals and rapids linking the Ontario city with its Michigan sister. The next crossing to the west, I shudder to think as I drive to Sault Ste. Marie, is the border point sixty kilometres southwest of Thunder Bay, en route to Duluth, Minnesota.

The Great Lakes form a series of immense barriers between Canada and the United States that are somewhat similar to the English Channel separating Britain from France. The difference is that the full sweep of the Great Lakes is far longer than the English Channel, and lakes Huron and Superior are wider than the Channel at any point. The idea of natural frontiers has had a long, if not particularly distinguished, history. For centuries, continental European powers fought for what they regarded as their natural frontiers, by which they meant frontiers that could best be defended against invasion. The French long dreamt of making the Rhine their frontier in the north and east, and anchoring it on the Alps farther south. Other powers tried for their own versions of natural frontiers, each of them envious of the unimpeachably natural frontiers bestowed on Britain as an island.

It could be said that Canada paid a very high price for its Great Lakes "natural" frontier with the United States. That's because, at the end of the American War of Independence in 1783, British troops, Canadian fur trappers and their Native allies held on to a considerable slice of territory south of the Great Lakes. This land, much of it traditional Canadian fur-trading terrain in the Ohio Valley and points west, could have remained British soil. In Paris, however, where the American and British negotiators were deciding on the border, the Americans proposed the Great Lakes line. The British, who didn't know that much about the geography of distant North America, went along. Without a shot fired, until 1812 at least, Canada lost a slice of North America that would have changed the course of history had it remained British.

When I get to the city limits of Sudbury, on Highway 69, the only sign that I have entered the nickel capital of the world is Inco's notorious smokestack that stands like a sentinel above the blasted, blackened rocks and the stunted pines. The rocks in the natural depression around Sudbury weren't always blackened. They got to be that way over the course of the past century as a collateral effect of the methods by which nickel was torn from the rock. And the pines around Sudbury are stunted by the toxicity of the soil that surrounds the nickel mines. One theory has it that the nickel was deposited here many millions of years ago when a meteorite crashed to earth and hammered out the Sudbury basin.

At last, I roll into Sault Ste. Marie, Ontario, a city of about seventy-five thousand people, which looks like a major metropolis after the country I've been through. The Soo, as it's familiarly called, is a city whose old commercial downtown has been eaten by a mall. From my hotel room, which is downtown, I face the huge parking lot that surrounds the mall. In the sky beyond, I can see the bridge that connects this city to its smaller sibling, Sault Ste. Marie, Michigan. It's difficult, as I drive across the bridge, not to be distracted by the awesome view below. On the Canadian side, there is a lumberyard and next to it the Canadian lock, which is now closed to major shipping. Then come the rapids and beyond them, on the U.S. side of the line, the four locks that are currently in use as an integral part of the St. Lawrence Seaway.

Both the Canadian and American cities grew up because of their unique locations on opposite sides of the border at a critical point along the Great Lakes waterway. Cheap and efficient water transportation was the key to the development of Algoma Steel, a major operation in Sault Ste. Marie, Ontario. The Soo is just a few kilometres south of Lake Superior and a few north of Lake Huron. Between the Canadian and American cities flow the rapids that made this location a choke point for fur traders in the centuries before locks were built. Today, the waterway houses the four large American locks that move huge vessels between Lake Superior and Lake Huron. The vessels carry the industrial materials and grain that are the lifeblood of the St. Lawrence Seaway. For all its remoteness, the Soo is an ocean port, and that is the key to the life of the cities on either side of the border.

Improvements to the locks on the St. Mary's River, which take a vessel down six metres from the level of Lake Superior to that of Lake Huron, have been going on for 150 years. The first American lock was completed in 1855. From the adjacent observatory, I stand and watch an immense freighter enter the lock from the Lake Superior side, and wait while it drops as the water in the lock lowers to the level of Lake Huron. Sault Ste. Marie, Michigan, has a population of about fifteen thousand. Back from its waterfront, which has been well preserved and boasts one street of trendy shops, the residential districts are filled with modest homes.

An annual ritual highlights the border and the connection between the two cities. Every year, at the end of June, the

International Bridge walk is held. The walk on Saturday, June 30, 2001, began at the Norris Center on the campus of Superior College in Soo, Michigan. The walk, to promote international friendship, took participants across the bridge to the Canadian side and wound up at the Roberta Bondar Pavilion in Soo, Ontario. (Roberta Bondar, who is from the Soo, was Canada's first female astronaut to go into space.) Shuttle buses were in place to take Soo, Ontario, participants to the starting point of the event on the U.S. side.

On the way to the bridge to the U.S. from Sault Ste. Marie, Ontario, I pass the casino. There are casinos in both of these border cities. Indeed, there are casinos in most of the large towns on Lake Superior and in some small communities as well, on Native reserves. Casinos have become an instrument of fiscal and economic policy for the Ontario government in the province's border towns—Niagara Falls, Windsor, the Soo and Thunder Bay. In part, they have been meant to replace declining industry in manufacturing towns. They have also been launched as a way to pull Americans across the border to contribute to the coffers of the provincial government. When I get back to the Canadian side, I'm going to drop into this casino, I tell myself.

The casino in the Canadian Soo boasts a naturalistic motif on its outside walls so that you can imagine you are entering a world inhabited by waterways, trees and canoes. Once inside, I am invited at a reception desk to sign up so I can be issued a card that will allow me to use the five-dollar coupon I have been given at my hotel to get me started on the slot machines. With five dollars of my own, I'm all set. I search out the twenty-five-cent slots, seeing in them a golden mean between the five-cent machines, where you get almost nothing when you win, and the dollar machines, where the whole experience could be over in just a few unlucky pulls of the lever. Even though I am well aware, as a man on the street in Thunder Bay will tell me a few days later, that the only winner at the casino is Ontario's then-premier, Mike Harris, I'm searching for what looks like a lucky slot machine. Should it be one with cherries, lions or sevens? Should it be right next to a chain-smoker? I settle on a machine with a lot of sevens and order a free Sprite from the drinks lady who is making the rounds.

Tonight I'm lucky, sort of. I walk out of the casino with about eight dollars. And since I only invested five of mine along with the five on the coupon, while I actually lost two dollars at the slots, I came out with three dollars more than I had going in. That's a win in my books, and it leaves me feeling feisty and ready for the start of the journey around Lake Superior the next morning.

North of the Soo on the Trans-Canada, the natural world comes alive in spectacular fashion. The highway climbs toward the terrain with the highest altitude in Ontario. On the west side of the road, as I come around a bend or over a hill, vistas of Lake Superior open up. Bays jutting out from the vast lake, with cottages along their shores, alternate with views of the open lake and its deep blue horizon. Tall pines march up and down the hillsides. The country here reminds me of Muskoka, the land of lakes, rock and pines north of Toronto. But this Lake Superior country is like Muskoka on a much grander scale. About half of Canada is composed of country in the Canadian Shield, the terrain of Precambrian rock that dominates Ontario and Quebec, and the northern Prairies, and sweeps north into Nunavut and the Northwest Territories. There are bits of Michigan, Wisconsin and Minnesota that jut north into the Shield, but it is overwhelmingly Canadian, and this terrain on the shore of Lake Superior is one of the most impressive stretches of it.

One of the great challenges of building the Canadian Pacific Railway was the construction of the track through the sixteen hundred kilometres of the Shield. In the course of railway construction, the discovery of nickel in the Sudbury basin opened people's eyes to the fact that this land was a motherlode of resources.

If the Canadian Shield is a barrier, it is also in fundamental ways the essential Canada. The Precambrian rock is the oldest on the continent, two billion years old. Indeed, it is the ancient core of North America. Across its face are the scars of the ice age, when glaciers scraped and twisted the land and left it with its myriad waterways, most importantly the Great Lakes, the remnant of a giant glacial lake of long ago.

The Shield and the Great Lakes–St. Lawrence waterway are the brute physical facts out of which the history of Central Canada has been wrought. The Shield covers most of Ontario and Quebec, pressing down close to the southernmost regions of the two provinces. The good arable land in Central Canada forms a fairly narrow band along the St. Lawrence and the northern shores of lakes Ontario and Erie. Only from Toronto west to the Michigan border does this stretch of first-class farmland widen to more generous proportions. By the end of the 1850s, the best land in Central Canada had been occupied. Indeed, the pressure for more arable land helped provide the energy for Confederation in the 1860s. Before the Pacific railway was completed in 1885, hundreds of thousands of Canadians migrated to the United States, especially in the bad economic times of the early 1880s. Many from Quebec went south to New England, to factory towns where there were jobs. For Ontarians, the western frontier of the day was across the border in Michigan, where there was land for would-be farmers.

———

I am thinking about Wawa, which means "wild goose" in Ojibwa. It is the first place of any size north of the Soo on the Trans-Canada. Many years ago when I drove to Wawa, I stopped to see the giant statue of the Canada goose that dominates the entrance to the town. Wawa, just off the highway, and not on Lake Superior, is in the centre of a large region of hunting and fishing.

Over a hill, I pull into a zone of construction on the highway and slow to a crawl in the midst of tractors and blasted pines and rocks. The long line of travellers comes to a stop. After a few minutes, I climb out of my car and join two men and three boys who have got out of a station wagon bearing Indiana licence plates. The older man, a fit-looking guy in his mid-forties who is wearing a baseball cap, tells me they have driven through the night from Indianapolis, and that the battery of their vehicle died in Sault Ste. Marie. They had to spend several hours getting a replacement. He explains that they are en route to Wawa, where a private plane will fly them in to a remote lake, where they will spend three days fishing and camping.

By the time you get to Wawa, you are off the shore of Lake Superior for close to two hundred kilometres. Communities and amenities are pretty basic in this stretch of the Trans-Canada. There is the occasional hamlet, with a gas station and a small private outlet, licensed by the Liquor Control Board of Ontario (LCBO), that sells liquor and wine. White River, far from the lake, is the only fairly big town on this leg of the journey. It was founded as a railway town, like many of the towns in this part of the province. These remote communities were created as points where trains could be serviced with coal and water. Today, White River is mostly strung out along its main street, on both sides of the highway. Unlike the houses in White River, the institutional buildings are large rectangles, with no embellishment of any kind.

I'm happy to reach Marathon, an hour out of White River, because now I'm free of the endless woods on both sides of the road and back on the rugged shoreline of Lake Superior. Marathon, Terrace Bay, Schreiber and, at last, Nipigon slide by— all basic towns, these, some of them heavily afflicted with the acrid scent of sulphur, the telltale companion of the pulp mills. Some of these communities look as if they were designed by the Soviets at the height of the artless architecture of the fifties and sixties.

I roll into Thunder Bay, the city that is really two cities, with its unparalleled location on the northern shore of Lake Superior. The city faces the lake, and lying across the entrance to the harbour is one of the most remarkable physical features in the world. The Sleeping Giant, so called because it resembles a recumbent figure, is part of a peninsula that juts out into the lake from a forested area to the northeast of the city. The subject of Ojibwa legend, the Sleeping Giant is eleven kilometres long and over three hundred metres high.

The twin cities of Port Arthur and Fort William are still clearly etched in the now united municipality of Thunder Bay. Here at the Lakehead, western and eastern Canada meet. When Sir John A. Macdonald launched the National Policy in 1879, he was initiating a set of integrated plans to make Canada one country from coast to coast and to draw a very clear line between Canada and the United States. In 1879, Macdonald made the momentous decision to raise the level of Canadian tariffs to the point that they would become overtly protectionist. The tariff would increase the price of U.S. imports and would thereby encourage Canadian manufacturing. The key to the success of the strategy was to link the West, particularly the Prairies, to Central Canada by means of a transcontinental railway on Canadian territory. The railway would carry to the prairies immigrants who would become the farmers who would grow the wheat that was to be the great Canadian export, on which the whole economic strategy depended. Western farmers, though they came to detest it, were pressured by the tariff to buy finished products manufactured in Ontario and Quebec instead of across the border in the United States.

The wheat was transported east on the railway to the Lakehead on Lake Superior, and from there it was shipped to eastern markets and to Europe by ship. Thunder Bay is the point where western wheat arrives by rail to be stored in giant grain elevators. From there, the wheat is loaded on the ships that ply the Seaway.

If the Lakehead was the hinge of the Canada designed by Sir John A., it was also the stamping ground of an American immigrant who became one of the most influential Canadian politicians of the twentieth century. Clarence Decatur Howe was born in New England. With a degree in engineering, he immigrated to Canada as a young man. He ultimately settled in Port Arthur and went into the grain shipping business, where he was highly successful. Prior to the federal election of 1935, Liberal leader William Lyon Mackenzie King, who was then in opposition, recruited Howe to run for the Liberals. Howe won the Port Arthur seat and went straight into the cabinet as a member of the new Liberal government.

The only businessman in the cabinet, Howe over time became Mackenzie King's economic czar. He presided over the creation of Trans-Canada Air Lines, the forerunner to Air Canada, in the late 1930s. Although he was an entrepreneur to the core, Howe was perfectly prepared to create a Crown corporation, such as TCA, to do a needed job if the private sector wasn't up to it. He referred to TCA as "my airline." Howe's power expanded greatly during World War II. It was his job to shift the economy to the production of bombers, naval vessels, tanks and military vehicles. He coaxed the brightest private sector executives to come to Ottawa to help with economic mobilization. For this, they won the title "the dollar-a-year boys," because that's how much the federal government paid them.

During the war, Canada industrialized and even became less dependent on U.S. investment, though not for long. C.D. Howe supervised the transition to peace as minister of reconstruction. Many Crown corporations were sold off to the private sector. To keep the economy humming, Howe looked south to the United States, which produced half of the entire world's economic output in 1945, to encourage American investment in the manufacturing and resource sectors of the

Canadian economy. And to fend off the threat from the political left—the CCF predecessor of the NDP, was rising in the polls—the Liberal government established the family allowance, a small monthly payment allocated to every mother to help support each of her children. The age of the welfare state was getting under way.

Howe remained in the Liberal cabinet until 1957, when he came up against a remarkable foe who helped wrest his parliamentary seat away from him. In many ways Cyrus Eaton was much like Howe, except that he was a Canadian who immigrated to the United States. Eaton was born in Pugwash, Nova Scotia, put aside his boyhood aspiration to be a Baptist minister, set out for the U.S. and amassed a great fortune. He was active in public utilities and eventually went on to form the Republic Steel Corporation.

Cyrus Eaton, who loved horses as well as yachting, was an optimistic, self-confident man who could charm Communist dictators as well as capitalist political leaders. In 1956, he established the Pugwash Conferences, held at an estate near his birthplace, to which he invited scientists, intellectuals and politicians from both sides of the Iron Curtain to meet in the informal setting of his home. His efforts on behalf of peace and understanding with the Soviets did not endear him to Western leaders. Nor did his standing with them improve when Soviet authorities awarded him the Lenin Prize in 1960. Nevertheless, his dealings with Communist leaders—he was on close terms with Nikita Khrushchev and Fidel Castro—did nothing whatsoever to shake his faith in capitalism.

I spent two days as the personal guest of Cyrus Eaton at his estate near Chester, Nova Scotia, in the spring of 1968. Eaton, then in his mid-eighties, was a little perplexed about what was on the mind of the younger generation in the turbulent 1960s, which is why I received the invitation.

As Eaton explained to me as we drank tea in his extraordinary study in the main house—it was piled with books on shelves that soared to the high ceiling—Communism was a dead end, a system that could never compete successfully against capitalism. Like other self-made, super-rich individuals, Cyrus Eaton exuded the confidence that was the product of all he had achieved. He did not doubt that the way he had built his empire pointed the way for others with imagination and energy. Capitalism was the superior system. To think anything else was naive, at best a symptom of youthful inexperience. After explaining why Communism could never work, he told me he had just sent a prize bull to Castro to help Cuba develop better herds of cattle.

In the 1950s, Cyrus Eaton became embroiled in a power struggle with C.D. Howe. Eaton had business interests in Northern Ontario, and Howe had used his vast governmental power to cross him. Not accustomed to losing, Eaton was determined to get back at the haughty cabinet minister. To strike at his foe where it mattered, Eaton sent a journalist friend to check out the political terrain in Howe's constituency in Port Arthur. Soon Eaton received a message from his scout informing him that Douglas Fisher, a young schoolteacher who was running for the left-wing CCF, was politically talented and could make a good show against Howe in the election. But Fisher needed support, Eaton's source told him. He got the support, Eaton intimated.

Howe lost his seat to Doug Fisher, the first time he had ever been defeated at the polls. In a way, he was fortunate. The Liberals also lost office after holding it for twenty-two years, a record in Canadian political history. Thus, Howe never had to sit on the opposition benches, for which he was not much suited.

———

I check into a hotel not far from the airport, which is located on the Fort William side of Thunder Bay. Across the bottom end of the city, there is a rather unseemly gap between the old heart of Fort William and that of Port Arthur. On one side of the road there is an endless rail yard with huge stretches of boxcars bearing the insignia of the Government of Canada. These are the cars that haul the wheat to Thunder Bay. Beyond the rail yard, in the distance, I can see the grain elevators with the names of the wheat pools of Manitoba, Saskatchewan and Alberta. There are one hundred million bushels of grain stored in the elevators. On the other side of the road is the entrance to a large modern mall.

Port Arthur's old downtown is a little livelier than its counterpart in Fort William. The railway station, which lies between the downtown and a waterfront area where dozens of pleasure craft are tied up, is now rather forlorn. The Canadian, the transcontinental train, once the pride of the Canadian Pacific Railway, used to stop for close to an hour at Thunder Bay every day of the week. I can remember climbing out of the train, which I took many times from Ottawa or Toronto to Winnipeg, Regina or Calgary, to take a quick walk by the station at Thunder Bay. Today, no passenger trains run through Thunder Bay. The Canadian, now sustained by Via Rail, still operates from Toronto to Vancouver three days a week, but it takes the CN route, that of the old Canadian National Railways, which runs through towns north of Thunder Bay. The station in Thunder Bay is now shut down.

The next day I get a more cheerful look at downtown Port Arthur. It's a perfect Saturday morning in June. My destination is Bay Street, the heart of the Finnish community in Thunder Bay. The Finns have lived in the Lakehead, and in other northern Ontario towns, for a century. They worked in the bush, on the trains and in the local industries of the region. They have left an indelible mark on Thunder Bay.

Bay Street is a happening place. Up and down the street and at the intersections, there are places that sell sauna equipment. If Thunder Bay has a rather daunting climate—one woman I met said there is winter ten months of the year and two months of bad skiing—the ubiquity of the sauna is a big help. Several groups of men, most of them over sixty, are lounging at various points along the street, chatting in Finnish and enjoying the fine weather. The centre of this hive of activity is the distinctively dome-peaked Finnish Labour Temple, constructed in 1910. Today, the building houses, in addition to the Labour Temple, the Finlandia Club and the Finnish Building Company. But what has drawn a crowd, as it does every weekend morning, is the Hoito Restaurant.

The Hoito Restaurant (Hoito means "care" in Finnish) started as an idea among Finnish bush workers at a camp near Nipigon during World War I. A founding meeting to establish the restaurant was held in March 1918. Within a few days, the organizing committee had collected enough money in small loans from prospective customers—three hundred dollars in total—to hire a cook and some waitresses to open the restaurant. The restaurant, which is in attractive but plain quarters in the basement of the building, seats 110 people. It is not unusual for patrons to stand in line for fifteen minutes to half an hour to be seated. The place is a hubbub of pleasant conversation. Waitresses are carrying trays bearing generous servings of food and refilling coffee cups.

The menu arrives, and it is immediately apparent to me that this is not a low-fat restaurant. If it is nouvelle cuisine you're looking for, the Hoito is not the place for you. The restaurant prides itself on providing hearty food in large portions at the same time as it pays its staff competitive wages. A special on the blackboard that is not in the menu is a plate of perogies for $3.95. I see a number of patrons washing down the filling perogies (potato and cheese dumplings), smothered in sour cream, with gulps of coffee. For $7.50, I could order salt fish, potatoes and *viili* (clabbered milk). There is a lengthy list of breakfast items, which are served to 7.30 P.M. Putting thoughts of bacon, ham, sausages and eggs out of my mind, I opt for a salt fish (fresh salmon) sandwich for $4.25. It is delicious.

Later on Saturday, I get together for coffee with some long-time residents of Thunder Bay. Mark Niesenholt, his wife, Marianne, and their twelve-year-old son, Isaac, have a house in Port Arthur. Mark, who teaches art at Lakehead University, was born in Winnipeg. He feels at home in Thunder Bay. He's somewhat rueful about the fact that most of his relatives, from Winnipeg and Toronto, rarely make it to where he lives. Instead, he tells me, "They fly over my head in their visits to each other." Marianne, who once owned a house in the trendy Beach area in Toronto, tells me that having sold a house in Toronto many years ago, she cannot think about ever owning one there again. That's because house prices in Toronto have skyrocketed while those in Thunder Bay have stayed flat.

We get into a discussion about my present journey around Lake Superior. Mark tells me he thinks I'm going to like Duluth, Minnesota, the next major stop on my trip. Duluth has a more successful downtown than Thunder Bay, he says. Thunder Bay has two old downtowns, while Duluth, with a smaller overall population, has a denser, single urban core. Even Duluth, the American town-next-door, comparatively speaking, is more than three hundred kilometres away, in this region of vast distances. Mark and Marianne like Duluth and the drive along the shore of Lake Superior to get there, but they seem to feel much closer to Winnipeg and Toronto. In some ways, I think, the whole logic of Thunder Bay is historically and today inextricably tied to the east-west venture of a Canadian nation. It is a city where metropolitan-satellite linkages tie it to the Prairies, to Winnipeg and to the whole of the St. Lawrence Seaway.

Mark studied at a university in the U.S. several decades ago, where, remarkably, he met a young man with exactly the same name as his—Mark Niesenholt. Not surprisingly, given the rarity of the surname, the two turned out to be distant relatives. Everywhere Mark went in the university town, it seemed he was encountering a kind of doppelgänger. When he tried to have a phone installed, he was asked: "Haven't you already done this?" On one occasion, Mark and his namesake, who was a U.S. citizen, were travelling together and crossed the border from Canada to the United States. The U.S. Customs officer asked them for their names and their citizenship. When one of them said "Mark Niesenholt, Canadian" and the other said "Mark Niesenholt, American," the officer was puzzled and not pleased. He pulled them over for questioning, which went on for some time before the two men were allowed to continue their trip.

————

I head southwest out of Thunder Bay, past the airport on the highway to Duluth. On the short drive to the border, only sixty kilometres away, the terrain becomes more gentle. There is farmland here, something I didn't see between the Soo and Thunder Bay. There are actually cattle in the fields!

At the border, the U.S. Customs officer asks me where I'm going and I tell him Duluth. "You came all the way from Toronto to go to Duluth?" he queries. I explain that I also visited Thunder Bay. When I tell him I teach political science at a university in Toronto, he loses interest and waves me through.

I'm just getting used to the idea that Ontario has a border with Minnesota. I see a sign welcoming me to the state where Jesse Ventura, the former professional wrestler, is the governor. As a kid, I thought of Ontario as having a border with New York. It was a stretch for me to think of a border with Michigan. Now I'm having the same reaction to Minnesota, which I think of as a place far to the west.

There's no denying that this border point between Ontario and Minnesota has the feel of a break in the terrain. Just past the customs post, the highway climbs and climbs to a great height and then comes down the other side as the deep blue water of the lake comes into view. On this very hot day, a dense wall of fog sits atop the frigid water for long stretches.

The Minnesota shore of the lake is much more commercially developed than the Ontario. There are a lot of lodges and summer homes. The towns along this stretch are tarted up with gift shops, trendy food outlets, clothing stores and commercial places where you can purchase collectibles. These establishments clearly play to people in the twin cities of Minneapolis and St. Paul as well as Milwaukee, Chicago and Detroit. Within five to seven hundred kilometres of the shore is an American population base far larger as a support for tourism than on the Canadian side.

It is pleasant rolling into Duluth along the shoreline of the lake. A big, wide street lined with leafy trees takes me past upper-middle-class homes with SUVs and trailers carrying motorboats in the driveways. And Mark was not wrong. Ahead, I see a compact knot of buildings. Duluth appears to have a downtown, something I have not seen yet in my drive around the huge lake.

Superior Avenue, Duluth's main drag, boasts five or six blocks of commercial buildings about five to seven storeys high. The whole stretch has an attractive, dense feel about it. Above the street-level restaurants, shops and businesses create a series of enclosed overhead walkways over the street. I can imagine that in winter it would be very pleasant to take the walkways and avoid the outdoors in what must often be a frigid town. Up behind Superior Avenue, the cross streets climb to the summit of a steep ridge that sweeps along the whole centre of the town.

The trendiest place to go, I soon discover, is the other way, toward the water. Duluth, like Thunder Bay, is a great port, with dozens of kilometres of wharves used to service ships carrying wheat, iron ore, industrial products and semi-processed raw materials. The city is located right at the southwestern tip of the lake on its north shore. On the other side of the tip is the state of Wisconsin. Two enormous bridges curl up over the corner of the lake to carry traffic to Superior, Wisconsin, Duluth's much smaller cousin across the water.

Duluth has been smart about its waterfront, seeing potential here for pleasure and tourism in addition to the traditional storage and shipping. I head for an area not far from the downtown called Canal Park, directly adjacent to a canal lock that has been completely redeveloped. An old warehouse district is alive with shops and restaurants, from a Burger King to a rather snooty-looking Italian bistro with seating outside as well as inside. A huge throng of people mill along the streets here on this hot afternoon. A pier juts far out into the lake, and children and their parents are out playing in the public area beside the canal. I take a drive out onto the island beyond the canal, accessible over a lift bridge that can be raised when high vessels need to pass underneath. The narrow, flat island pokes several kilometres out into Lake Superior. On both sides of the single road through it are highly desirable houses, with those on the north side looking out on the open lake while those on the south have a view of the inner harbour and the bridges to Wisconsin. A curious feature of this long, narrow island is that it has its own natural air-conditioning system. The day is hot and sunny, but the water of the lake is so cold that the temperature here and in the warehouse district is at least five degrees cooler than in downtown Duluth. At the end of the island is a park where people from the city come to play with their children.

When I get back to the warehouses converted to shops and restaurants, I settle on a place that serves Mexican food. I sit outside where I have a great view of people enjoying the early evening.

The good weather has come to an end when I leave at dawn for the drive back to Sault Ste. Marie. I take the innermost of the two bridges to Wisconsin in driving rain, and soon I am on the other side of this triangle of water, with Duluth behind me. Superior is a small town that looks pretty dismal on this wet morning. I quickly get to open highway and find myself traversing flat land that alternates between forested stretches and farms with drenched cattle standing in the fields. It is a striking contrast to the hilly bedrock that lies on the other side of the lake. Wisconsin is America's dairy state, famous for its cheeses—Green Bay Packers fans call themselves "cheeseheads"—as well as for breweries associated with the state's large population of German origin. Milwaukee, far to the south of where I am, is home to Miller, Pabst and Schlitz. The highway here is not as good as the Trans-Canada, and in the rain, pools of water have collected on the pavement. As my tires hit them, I have to take care that the car does not plane out of control.

Ninety wet minutes later, I am in Michigan on a similar highway, still vigilantly controlling the car on wet pavement. The terrain in this part of Michigan is flat, much like that in Wisconsin. The country I am passing through is mostly thickly covered with woods. From time to time along this route, I come upon casinos, which seem to provide much of the live entertainment here. Some kilometres back, there was a casino in Bad River, Wisconsin, and now I am passing another one in Christmas, Michigan. As you can imagine, on its large and rather ancient sign, the largest motel in this hamlet features reindeer and a giant Santa.

The Canadian and American shores of Lake Superior are two different worlds. All the way from Sault Ste. Marie to Thunder Bay, the Canadian shore is rugged, remote terrain where the small communities are transportation centres, jumping-off points for wilderness tourism, or pulp and paper towns. The American shore, by contrast, is flatter, often agricultural, more tamed by settlement.

————

The second of my long journeys along the remote frontier took me to Alaska, the one portion of America where the European conquest of the territory of Aboriginal peoples came from the west rather than the east. While Russian America has left relatively few cultural traces, that fact of Russian America was to have an immense impact on the Canada–U.S. border.

———

I'm in downtown Sitka, Alaska, looking at the city's masterpiece, St. Michael's Cathedral, a Russian Orthodox church with copper domes and a twenty-five-metre-tall bell tower. Sitka was the capital of Russian Alaska when Russia sold Alaska to the United States in 1867. Alaska was the farthest point reached in Russia's eastward expansion. Russian fur traders had pushed across Siberia, just as French and British fur traders had carved out an empire in Canada. In 1741, Vitus Bering, the Danish navigator who believed that Kamchatka, on the Pacific coast of Russian Asia, was close to America, made a historic voyage to Alaska in the service of the Russians. It was this voyage that brought the existence of Alaska to the attention of the European world.

After Bering, the Russians created a maritime fur-trading realm in Alaska. For the next half century, while the Russian state showed little interest in Alaska, fur merchants dispatched men and ships to the Aleutian Islands to procure the pelts of sea otters, for which there was a market in China. Not themselves adept at the quest for the animals, the Russian adventurers forced the native Aleuts to do the hunting. Several Aleut revolts were suppressed with much bloodshed.[1]

The pattern of the Russian trade was to move eastward along the chain of the Aleutian Islands, exhausting the fur supplies in the first islands and then shifting their interest to others. The original capital of Russian Alaska had been on Kodiak Island, located south of the main body of the territory. When the supply of furs ran low in Kodiak, the Russians pushed farther east, establishing Sitka (first called Novo-Arkhangel), and in 1808 it became the capital. By that time, the Russian state had become much more involved in the Alaskan colony. In part, this was in response to ventures into the region by the Spaniards, the British, the French and ultimately by American fur traders. Faced with the potential for a challenge to Russian control, the authorities invested more resources in securing their hold on Alaska.

While few Russians actually settled in the Alaskan colony—only about seven hundred at its peak—Sitka became its jewel. For a time in the nineteenth century, it was the largest town on the west coast of North America, and was known, in a spirit of wanton exaggeration, as the "Paris of the Pacific." Today, Sitka, population nine thousand, about 20 percent of it Native, lives off its extravagant natural resources and setting as well as its romantic past. This is a town of fishermen, who fish for salmon, halibut, black cod, crab and herring. It is also a town where government services employ many—teachers in public schools and colleges, health care workers and civil servants. And tourism is huge here. Thousands arrive in Sitka annually and hire locals to take them out fishing or guides to help them explore the spectacular surroundings. Sitka is a rainy place, with a gentle climate, considering that it is located over seven hundred kilometres north of Vancouver.

Each year, about 200,000 people arrive in Sitka as I did, on a cruise ship. The harbour is too shallow to allow the giant cruise ships to come ashore, so a couple of kilometres offshore the ships drop anchor. They lower a few of their life boats into the sea and use them as tenders to ferry the passengers into Sitka and to bring them back again a few hours later in time for departure.

The cornerstone for St. Michael's Cathedral was laid in 1844 and the building was dedicated in 1848. In the winter of 1966, when fire swept through the heart of Sitka, the cathedral was destroyed. Vigilant residents of the town managed to save many of its most prized ornaments and icons, including silver vessels and vestments made with Chinese silk. Reconstruction on the same site, and using the original blueprints, this time with fireproof materials, resulted in the new structure being consecrated in 1976.

I find it a little distasteful that at this cathedral you have to pay an admission fee—only two dollars—rather than deciding how much to contribute, as in most other places of worship. Once inside, I discover that St. Michael's is a not altogether comfortable hybrid of a museum and a church. A few people are praying, and a bearded Russian Orthodox cleric is sitting on a bench with his hands folded and his eyes shut. But most of those inside—like me—have climbed off a cruise ship and are checking the place out in less than reverent fashion.

My cruise ship has been sailing north from Vancouver up the Inside Passage along the coast of British Columbia and into the Alaska Panhandle. The Panhandle is a beguiling maritime region that stretches along the coast from just north of Prince Rupert, B.C., to the Yukon. The Panhandle, the southeastern portion of Alaska, which borders on B.C. and the Yukon, is a realm of islands and bits of mainland invaded by long fjords, which are called canals. It is a mysterious territory where black mountains rise sharply out of the misty sea and climb to snow-streaked peaks. Marking off the Panhandle from Canada is a range of mountains that makes the interior of B.C., although only a few kilometres distant, much more remote than Seattle or San Francisco.

For Americans, Alaska looms in the imagination as the "last frontier." Playing heavily on this notion, a number of cruise lines offer week-long trips north through the Inside Passage, with stops at several points in the Alaska Panhandle. I'm on the *Sea Princess*, a four-year-old luxury vessel that carries two thousand passengers. On board for several hours before the ship sails away from the dock at Canada Place in Vancouver, the passengers check out their staterooms. These range from a simple room with a bathroom and shower (such as mine) to much more luxurious quarters, in which a large room with a sliding-glass door opens onto a balcony above the sea. Then there is a rush for the buffet, which is open twenty-four hours a day. Located on the ship's top deck, the buffet dispenses hot and cold foods, shrimp salad, roast beef, chicken of all kinds, salads, breads, desserts, coffee and tea. Many of the passengers are heaping huge portions of food on the oversized plates, as though they fear that once we get to Alaska we will be rationed. Later in the week, when it becomes clear that the bounty will flow without interruption, the rush to the buffet is a little less frantic.

Almost everyone is out on the top deck, where the swimming pool and the mammoth hot tub are located, as we sail under the Lion's Gate Bridge and out into the strait between Vancouver Island and the mainland of B.C. It is brilliantly sunny. I am struck by how quickly the metropolis of the Lower Mainland of B.C. is left behind. On both sides—on Vancouver Island and the mainland—we see few buildings, docks, power lines or roads. The shores are rugged, with fir trees marching up the great slopes to majestic heights. There is not a trace of the pastoral in this landscape.

Next morning, there is no hint of the sun, nor is there a view of land to either starboard or port as we steam north. It is a cool morning, and a high wind has whipped the sea into deep furrows of white-topped waves. The ship is rolling appreciably and more than a few of the passengers are a little green around the gills. Some of them have had a little circular patch stuck against the bone behind their ear by the medical staff to help ward off seasickness. All day we sail on through grey seas. There are few people outdoors on deck, and only a few hardy souls venture into the swimming pool and the hot tub. Life on board is kept cheerful despite the grey skies. In the casino on deck eight, the slot machines, and the blackjack and craps tables, are fully engaged. The shops on deck five are doing a brisk business, selling jewellery and knick-knacks. The cinema on deck six is showing *Gosford Park*. On deck twelve, the fitness rooms are full of people taking turns on the treadmills and the step machines and trying their hand at the weights. Some masochists are being given fitness and body reviews by the professional staff.

At dawn the following day, there is general excitement on board as we sail up the fjord toward Juneau, Alaska's capital city. On the east side of the vessel, the landscape is more spectacular than on the west. Mountains, their lower reaches cloaked in fir trees, reach up out of the sea to bare, black peaks laced with snow. Deep valleys laden with snow are carved into the sides of some of the mountains. Low-lying clouds cling to the mountain valleys. From the promenade deck, I see three fish jumping side by side in the green water. A few minutes later, the black fin of a humpback whale skims along the water's surface. I see a road at the base of a mountain and a few buildings along its route at the edge of the water. We are passing white fishing vessels that are trailing nets about thirty metres long. Propeller aircraft with pontoons are taking off from the water on our port side.

At last, the *Sea Princess* ties up at the Cruise Ship Terminal. A flood of passengers head down to deck five to go ashore. As we are processed off the ship, we have to present our plastic smart cruise card to a ship's officer, who enters the card into a terminal to note that we are going ashore. The smart card—the size of a credit card—is used to trigger all our on-board personal data. When we first came on board, a photo was taken of each passenger. At every stop during the cruise, when a passenger re-embarks, the card is inserted into the terminal, which flashes the photo on the screen so that the crew knows this is a legitimate passenger. All purchases of alcohol on board the *Sea Princess* are handled through the card, as are purchases of the many photos taken to commemorate your formal evening, happy moments sitting on deck, or when you stood in line to get back on board the ship and had your picture taken with your arm around someone dressed as a bear or moose.

It's good to be back on terra firma. It's a cool, misty day in Juneau, and it looks like rain. Many of the passengers have signed up for various adventures while they are ashore, including a heli-copter outing to the nearby Mendenhall Glacier. I haven't signed up for anything. I walk past the lineups of *Princess* passengers who are waiting to climb on a *Princess* bus to take them to the glacier. A few metres farther on a young woman is standing at a booth selling bus rides to and from the glacier for five dollars a person, a fraction of the cost of the *Princess* tour. She tells me that the bus departs every half-hour from downtown Juneau, a few blocks away, at the Red Dog Saloon.

The city of Juneau is flush up against a mountain. From the tiny, flat downtown area, the streets climb very steeply both to the east and the north. Wooden staircases are built into the side of the slope to take pedestrians from one street to the next. In part because of the compressed space, the city's centre has a great sense of energy. This is also because of the daily influx of thousands of people from the cruise ships during the summer season. People are milling everywhere along the streets and in and out of the shops in the commercial area next to the waterfront. Shops selling jewellery, T-shirts and Alaska memorabilia dominate this part of town.

With a population of about thirty thousand, employment in Juneau is focused on government and tourism. In 1900, the U.S. Congress decreed that Alaska's capital should be moved from Sitka to Juneau, when suitable grounds and buildings were in place. As it turned out, the move was not made until 1908. Juneau got its start when gold was discovered there in 1880. Later, the city's rise was closely linked to the Klondike gold rush of 1898 that resulted in a large increase in Alaska's population, particularly in the Panhandle, the region whose strategic location held the key to access to the Yukon and the gold deposits.

Juneau became the capital at a time when Alaska was a district with very limited powers of self-government. As the white American population grew in conjunction with the rise of mining, fishing and the lumber industry, so too did the demand for self-government, but the struggle was to be long, convoluted and at times seemingly hopeless. It was to continue until the summer of 1958, when President Dwight Eisenhower signed into law the bill that made Alaska a U.S. state. On January 3, 1959, Eisenhower signed the proclamation admitting Alaska as the forty-ninth state.

Alaska was the first American acquisition of territory that was not contiguous to the lower forty-eight states. The U.S. purchase of Alaska was by no means a bolt from the blue. For three-quarters of a century prior to the purchase, Americans had been involved in Alaskan commerce, in the fur trade and in whale hunting. Much of the U.S. relationship with Russia had turned on questions arising out of Alaskan commerce. As early as the 1840s, the U.S. government queried Russian officials about rumours that Moscow was considering selling the Alaskan colony. In the following decade, the Crimean War between Russia and an Anglo-French coalition posed a potential threat to Russian Alaska. A deal reached between the Russian-American Company and the Hudson's Bay Company to keep their territories neutral in the event of war was honoured by London and Moscow. Had Britain, the world's leading naval power, sent a fleet to Alaska, the Russian colony could easily have been seized.

In the 1860s, the Russians were preoccupied with railway construction and efforts to modernize their industries and society. In that context, Alaska seemed nothing but a burden. Indeed, the Russian colony had really touched only a small part of Alaska, centred as it was on the Aleutians and the islands and mainland of the Panhandle. The prospect of actually receiving payment for the colony was tempting. In December 1866, top Russian officials, including Czar Alexander II and Baron Eduard de Stoeckel, the Russian ambassador to the United States, met in St. Petersburg and decided to offer to sell Alaska to the United States. When Stoeckel landed at New York the following March, he immediately contacted William H. Seward, the U.S. secretary of state, to begin negotiations about Alaska.[2] After a brief discussion about fishing rights in Alaska for Americans, which led nowhere, Seward asked Stoeckel if the colony was for sale. When the secretary of state received an affirmative reply, the two sides came to be nub of the matter. Following hurried consultations with both governments, the price agreed on was US$7.2 million.

For this sum, which appears so paltry to us, the U.S. acquired Alaska and the Russian-American Company, a private fur trade business that had been established in 1799 on the model of the Hudson's Bay Company. The question of why the Russians gave up so vast and potentially valuable a territory for so little cannot be avoided. As they were under pressure to develop their own vast realm and facing upheaval at home, Alaska seemed more a burden than a blessing. Some in the ruling circles in Moscow believed that it was likely that in the long run the Americans would acquire Alaska anyway, and therefore they might as well gain some welcome cash for the transfer. In the United States, there was little enthusiasm for the purchase. For many the acquisition of a distant northern territory in a period when Americans were dealing with the aftermath of the Civil War seemed an act of extravagant foolishness. The purchase was commonly referred to as "Seward's folly."

For Canada, the long-term consequences of the transfer of Alaska to the United States have been immense. In the mid-nineteenth century, three possible outcomes for Alaska seemed conceivable: the territory could remain Russian; the United States could acquire it; or it could pass into British hands. Beginning in 1839, the Hudson's Bay Company leased a large portion of the mainland of southeastern Alaska. A British Alaska would likely have become part of Canada at some future date. During the Cold War, that would have put Soviet Kamchatka cheek by jowl with Canadian Alaska. The pressure on Canada from the U.S. to allow for a permanent military base in Alaska under such circumstances would have been considerable. For that reason, the American purchase of Alaska can be seen as a piece of very good luck for Canada.

In the 1880s, as the mining boom began in Alaska, the number of white miners in the territory rose rapidly. With the influx came a growing demand for self-government. In 1884, the U.S. Congress passed the Organic Act, which gave Alaskans an extremely limited form of civil government. Under the act, Alaskans were not entitled to elect their own legislature. Instead, the president appointed the officials of the government, subject to the approval of the Senate. Alaska was designated a "district" rather than a "territory," to squelch pretensions to self-government. In keeping with the most basic principle of American government, Alaskans, having no right to political representation, paid no taxes.[3]

It was the discovery of gold in 1896 in the Klondike, in Canada, that was to motivate thousands of Americans to flood north to Alaska. While the gold rush was only a brief episode in the history of Alaska, it proved a catalyst to the founding of towns and to economic development. With the region much more prominent in American thinking, Alaska won the right to send a non-voting delegate to the U.S. Congress. In 1912, this was followed by the Second Organic Act, which allowed Alaskans, for the first time, to elect their own legislature. Despite this step toward self-government, however, Washington still held the whip hand in terms of decision-making power. The U.S. government reserved for itself control over decisions concerning Alaskan resources, the incorporation of its towns, gambling and the sale of liquor. The Alaskan legislature was allowed to collect only very limited tax revenues, and the governor was still appointed by the president of the United States.[4]

Alaska developed at a tepid pace through the 1920s and during the Great Depression of the 1930s. It was the Japanese attack on Pearl Harbor on December 7, 1941, and the threat of Japanese military moves against the Western Hemisphere that made Alaska strategically important to the United States. Indeed, in 1942, Japanese forces were to occupy Attu Island and Kiska Island in the

Aleutians. The occupations did not involve strategic plans for the Japanese to attempt landings on the mainland of Alaska or elsewhere on the west coast of North America. The effect, however, was to steel Washington's determination to buttress the defence of Alaska and the links between the territory and the lower forty-eight states. In November 1942, the Alaska–Canada Military Highway from Dawson Creek, British Columbia, north to Whitehorse in the Yukon and from there to its terminus in Fairbanks, Alaska, was completed. The road, though extremely rough when first opened, allowed the U.S. military to transport weapons and other goods to Alaska. The Alcan Highway became one of the routes by which the U.S. supplied *matériel* to the Soviet Union during World War II.

Thirty years ago, when the road was more primitive than it is today, I drove the Alaska Highway from Dawson Creek, B.C., to Whitehorse, a distance of about fourteen hundred kilometres. It was mostly a dirt road, and in the dry conditions of mid-July there was a constant swirl of dust and dirt in the air. I was driving a ten-year-old station wagon with no air conditioning. Although the days were hot, I could not bear to open the windows because so much dirt and sand blew in. Even with the windows shut, the dust and grime were everywhere. I could taste it in my mouth and I had to rub it out of my eyes. Often on that drive, I passed fancy RV rigs with U.S. licence plates that had broken down by the side of the road and were waiting for tow trucks from service stations as far as 120 kilometres away. That said, the countryside in northern B.C. and the Yukon is unmatched. Range after range of mountains come into view, covered with a flower that gives the peaks a shade of purple that is brighter in the sun, darker under cloud, and shifts as the ranges grow closer or more distant. It is a land of cold mountain lakes with clear blue or blue-green water. In July there are only a couple of hours of darkness each day in this heavenly country. When I got to Whitehorse, I had to pull the blinds shut in my motel room to get any sleep. In town, ten-year-olds played baseball on the street at one o'clock in the morning.

By August 1943, the Americans had succeeded in retaking the Japanese bases in the Aleutians, and from that point on, the military presence in Alaska declined sharply. After World War II, however, the U.S. faced a new foe only a few kilometres across the Bering Strait from Alaska: the Soviet Union. During the Cold War, Washington dispatched thousands of troops and spent hundreds of millions of dollars on Alaskan bases. In 1947, the U.S. began the construction of what was to be—in its day—the largest airfield in the world, Eielson Air Force Base, about forty kilometres south of Fairbanks. Spurred by military expenditures, Alaska's population grew rapidly. The increase was mostly on the Alaskan mainland rather than in the islands or the Panhandle. Between the end of World War II and the 1980s, the population of Anchorage—now Alaska's largest city—grew from 8,000 to more than 200,000.[5]

In the age when the threat from Soviet manned bombers carrying nuclear weapons was foremost in the thinking of the Pentagon, Canada joined with the U.S. in the construction of the Distant Early Warning (DEW) line, a radar system that stretched across the continent, including installations in Alaska and the Canadian Arctic.

Paralleling the development of Alaska was the road to statehood, which proved to be long and arduous. In 1946, after a report favourable to statehood was distributed throughout the territory, Alaskans supported the move by a three-to-two margin in a referendum. Turnout for the referendum was a dismal 23 percent of eligible voters, however, and the margin in favour was not the landslide for which proponents had hoped.[6]

Holding up progress toward statehood over the next decade were regional rivalries within Alaska, as well as sectional and partisan concerns in U.S. politics. Military spending in Alaska promoted the rapid growth of Anchorage and Fairbanks, while there was almost no growth in the older established centres such as Juneau and the rest of the Panhandle. With a close balance between Republicans and Democrats in the U.S. Congress, it was feared that the admission of Alaska and Hawaii could tilt the balance. The debate was also sidetracked for a time by consideration of the idea that Alaska and Hawaii could become commonwealths, as Puerto Rico did in 1952, rather than states.

The final drive for statehood began in the late fifties. By this time, leading figures in Congress and in the Eisenhower administration had come round to full support. In May and June 1958 respectively, the House of Representatives and the Senate at last passed bills authorizing Alaskan statehood.

The tale of Alaska's long journey to statehood ought to be a salutary lesson to those Canadians who believe that Canada should opt for some form of political community with the United States, or even should attempt to join the American republic. This is not an easy tribe to join.

———

I wait outside the Red Dog Saloon, which is jammed with tourists from the cruise ships. Behind the two swinging doors at the front that allow you a good look inside is a very tall doorman-bouncer, dressed in a gold-rush-period costume. Inside, a singer bangs out honky-tonk tunes that celebrate the glory days of a century ago.

A faded blue bus pulls up across the street. I climb aboard along with a man and a young couple, who I later learn are also from Toronto. The male member of the couple has a patch discreetly tucked behind his ear, the hallmark of the queasy cruise ship passenger. Our driver, a dark-skinned man with a wrinkled face, climbs back on the bus and collects our tickets. As soon as he sits behind the wheel, he announces that his name is Marvin and that he is a Tlingit. The Tlingits are the largest Native tribe in this area. He was born in Haines, which is not far from here.

As we head northwest out of the centre of Juneau, Marvin gives us a running patter about the city, its people and their way of life. We are traversing a flat area of land next to the water. Marvin tells us about the decline of the local fishery, and jokes that to find work these days you have to get a job either with the government or in tourism. We are driving along Juneau's only expressway, a four-lane highway that takes you out of town. Just in case we are getting carried away with the idea of driving to distant places, Marvin points out that there are only sixty-six kilometres of road in Juneau and its environs. You can have a car or an SUV here, but there's nowhere to go. On paper, the boundaries of the city of Juneau extend all the way to the British Columbia border, only a few kilometres from here. But there is no road to B.C. Indeed, B.C. feels completely remote from this coastal city.

Only twenty-two kilometres from the centre of Juneau, we arrive at the parking lot from which it is only a short walk to a spectacular view of the Mendenhall Glacier. It is raining lightly as I walk up to a viewing area. Across a small lake is the glacier, an endless field of triangular ridges of blue-and-white ice. The great valley of ice is a snapshot frozen in time. The most recent bits of ice that have broken off the glacier are 200 to 250 years old. Everywhere great chunks of ice, some of them six to nine metres long, in a myriad of shapes, are floating on the surface of the lake. Most startling are the blue icebergs, chunks of ice that retain their spectacular colour for only a few days after the fall from the glacier.

Later in the cruise, we visit the Hubbard Glacier at Yakutat Bay. This time, the *Sea Princess* does not land. Instead, we sail into the great bay that leads to the glacier, the ship slowing to a crawl as it makes its way through a vast field of icebergs. Off the starboard side, mountains covered with evergreens rise steeply from the sea, stretching to bare and snow-covered peaks. On the port side, the land is less spectacular and more distant. As in the case of the Mendenhall Glacier, the icebergs here have recently fallen into the sea from the immense Hubbard, the largest tidewater glacier in Alaska. Some of the icebergs are blue, others white. A few of them are shaped above the water like spectral boats, with bows and sterns, and they rock eerily to and fro, washing into other icebergs in their path.

Ahead of us, I see another cruise ship that is closer than we are to the glacier, cutting a graceful, deliberate arc through the field of floating ice. At our closest point, we are several kilometres from the edge of the glacier, which is shaped like the top half of a flattened sphere. Over the course of centuries, the Hubbard has alternated between periods when it pushes forward, such as now, and periods when it retreats. Here we are catching a momentary glimpse of an immense creator of the natural world at work. Glaciers and icebergs reshape the landscape over the course of thousands of years. As rocks are carved away, the ice forges new fjords in the valleys between the mountains, into which the sea will flow. The landscape and seascape of the Alaska Panhandle is the creation of earlier glaciers and their iceberg offspring.

Recent reports find that Alaska's sixty-seven glaciers are melting at more than twice the rate previously thought, a consequence of rising temperatures. Using airborne laser measurements, scientists have concluded that the glaciers are melting at an average rate of two metres a year, and in extreme cases a hundred metres. In the past seven or eight years, the pace of melting has increased appreciably. The consequence is that the Alaska melt has been adding about two-tenths of a millimetre annually to sea levels. Over time, this seemingly small rate can contribute to flooding in coastal areas and on Pacific islands.[7]

The morning after our visit to Juneau, I awake early in my little stateroom on the *Sea Princess* and flip on the television above my bed. I switch to the channel that gives a live view from the ship's bridge and see that we have already tied up in the harbour at Skagway, where we are to spend about fourteen hours. This is the stop on the tour I've most anticipated. This time, I've booked a seat on a tour that will take me by bus through Skagway and up the White Pass, where we will cross into a tiny corner of British Columbia and then on into the Yukon. We will have lunch in the Yukon and return partway by bus, coming back the rest of the way on the fabled White Pass and Yukon Railroad.

Skagway is a narrow little town, overwhelmed by surrounding mountains. It sits at the head of the Lynn Canal, making it the nearest point where adventurers could land by sea to go in search of the gold of the Klondike. On August 17, 1896, when George Carmack and two Native companions, Skookum Jim and Tagish Charley, found a nugget of gold at Bonanza Creek in the Yukon, they set off one of the world's greatest gold stampedes. What was to follow was the Trail of '98, the race to the Yukon that was to make Skagway, Alaska, and Dawson City in the Yukon names that resounded the world over. Tens of thousands of would-be gold miners came through Skagway en route to the White Pass, the Canadian border, and the harrowing trek from there to the goldfields of the Klondike. It was a drama that made the Canadian boundary with Alaska a critical issue. It was the drama out of which the Yukon was created as a territory separate from the Northwest Territories, in June 1898.

There are about twenty-five of us sitting on the tour bus, on a cool, rainy morning in Skagway. A fair-haired woman—she looks about twenty years old—climbs on board and sits down in the driver's seat. She announces that her name is Suzy and that she is our driver and guide. A few of the passengers exchange concerned looks—the average age on the bus has to be sixty—but within a few minutes Suzy has won us all over. This is Suzy's second summer working in Skagway. Last year she graduated from the University of Washington in Seattle, but when she couldn't find a job, she decided to come north again to spend another summer in

Skagway. She drives the tour bus three days a week and the rest of the time she works at a café in town. Last summer, she informs us, she met a young man named Matt, and he is a major reason she is back this year. In fact, Matt is also driving a tour bus, and we are likely to see him today at one of the stops.

The route we are taking is one of the two main ones followed by the miners of '98, the climb out of Skagway up the White Pass. The other route taken was out of Dyea, just northwest of Skagway, up the shorter but steeper Chilkoot Pass. At the top of the passes, the miners encountered the Canadian border. The North West Mounted Police, confronted with this American invasion into Canadian territory, were determined to keep the peace in a remote place and to ensure that the miners were well-enough supplied for them to survive in the forbidding climate of the Yukon.

As a consequence of the invasion, the population of Dawson City surged to a peak of eighteen thousand, making it for a brief time the largest city in Canada west of Winnipeg. Eighty percent of Dawson City's turbulent residents were U.S. citizens. Tension between an American populace and Canadian law enforcement sometimes threatened to boil over. Dawson was a city of saloons, bawdy houses, hotels and an endless stream of colourful characters. One might have expected lawlessness in the heady days of '98, but under the steady hand of Superintendent Sam Steele, the Mounties kept order in Dawson. In 1898, there was not a single murder there, and very few instances of major theft. In his excellent book on the Klondike, Pierre Berton writes: "It was possible to leave one's cabin or tent wide open, go off on a six-week trip, and return to find all possessions intact."[8] Steele was a judicious man who knew how to deal with the mass sentiments of the people of Dawson City. For instance, he declared both Dominion Day, July 1, and the Fourth of July holidays so that Americans could celebrate Independence Day on Canadian soil.

The Mounties established a rule that any miner entering the Yukon had to bring with him two thousand pounds of supplies, enough to survive through a frigid winter. Since the miners could carry only between forty and fifty pounds on each ascent up the White or Chilkoot Pass, they had to make between forty and fifty trips up the perilous trails to meet the standards set by the Mounties. At the end of each trip, they left the supplies they had carried and then returned to Skagway or Dyea for the next load. For the American adventurers who constituted the vast majority of the stampeders, the arrival at the frontier must have been something of a shock. Here the stern, and not wholly welcome, Mounties met them, the law enforcement arm of a distant Canadian government in Ottawa.

The contrast with Skagway, on the U.S. side of the line, was pronounced. When the gold rush began, Skagway was a lawless place in the manner of the American Wild West. With so many newcomers, it quickly exploded to become Alaska's biggest town. Jefferson Randolph "Soapy" Smith was the gangster who dominated Skagway. In a town that was described by a visiting Mountie, who had no authority there, as just "about the roughest place in the world," Soapy Smith made himself the boss. Smith assembled a private army that cowed the local militia. He had the civil authorities in his pocket, along with merchants, businessmen and journalists. His power extended all the way to the Canadian border, where the Mounties mounted Maxim guns to make sure his hoodlums didn't stray across. Smith's gang set up bogus businesses in Skagway to swindle the prospectors out of their money. For instance, they ran a fake telegraph company, promising to send a telegram anywhere in the world for five dollars. There was, in fact, no telegraph line to Skagway in 1898, but newcomers eager to reach their families didn't know that. A couple of hours after a telegram was "dispatched," a faked return telegram would arrive collect so that the sucker could be bilked out of more money.[9]

Smith's demise came when the mood in Skagway shifted against the local dictator and his gang of swindlers. A vigilante group was formed to seize power back from Smith. Frank Reid, the toughest of the vigilantes, was the man who shot Smith dead one sunny evening in July 1898. But Smith managed to take Reid with him with two shots from his Winchester. Both men are buried in Skagway's Gold Rush Cemetery, the gravesites now a local tourist attraction.[10]

As we curl up the side of the cliff on the bus, we see an immense drop below us into a vast canyon with a river flowing down its centre. The miners had to climb from Skagway, at sea level, to the White Pass Summit—the border with Canada—at an elevation of 873 metres. The route they took was barely a path; in places it straddled the edge of cliffs where a misstep meant a plunge to the canyon below. Not surprisingly, many of the miners were prepared to pay a considerable sum to buy a pack horse to help them make the repeated journeys to the summit and beyond. Seventeen kilometres up the trail, we look down at a forbidding valley called Dead Horse Gulch, named in memory of the three thousand pack animals who went to their doom, victims of heavy loads and brutal treatment. By no means all of the prospectors mistreated their horses. Many of them were inexperienced with animals, however, and the trail was narrow, slippery and strewn with boulders.

The bus pulls over at a spectacular viewpoint and we all climb out. A young man comes over from the adjoining bus and enfolds Suzy in a rapturous embrace. Everyone is delighted to see the fabled Matt.

Before we reach the summit, the bus passes the U.S. Customs post, which is located thirteen kilometres miles inside U.S. territory because the actual border point at the summit of the White Pass is such a forbidding, desolate, windswept place. At the summit, Suzy tells us that we are now crossing into British Columbia. It is several kilometres farther before we reach Canadian customs.

Suzy collects our passports and takes them inside the customs post, while we remain on the bus. A few minutes later she returns and we proceed without having seen a Canada Customs officer.

We have now reached the point where the adventurers on the Trail of '98 were required by the Mounties to leave their loads and return with their next loads until they had their full ton of equipment. Once these journeys were done, the miners were allowed to move their supplies forward another thirty kilometres to Bennett, B.C., on the southeastern tip of Lake Bennett. Thirty thousand prospectors spent the winter of 1898–99 building makeshift rafts and boats at Bennett so that in the spring they could float their supplies across the lake and from there sail down the Yukon River to the goldfields. The feat of the prospectors is almost unimaginable. These were, after all, amateurs, not trained triathletes. They were the members of the last great army of the nineteenth-century gold seekers, in the mold of the Forty-niners who had blazed the trail in California's gold rush. In 1859, the same breed of men had gone in search of gold in British Columbia. Now, in the most romantic gold rush of them all, thousands of them did things that would make all the exploits of survival television look tame by comparison.

Few of the stampeders got rich. In the end, the miners spent about as much money getting to the Klondike and out again as they extracted in gold. The gold rush inspired the building of the unique railway we will be taking on our journey back to Skagway, after we have lunch and pay a visit to the little settlement of Carcross, Yukon.

The White Pass and Yukon Railroad was built in a remarkably short time. Construction began on May 28, 1898, and the railway reached Bennett, B.C., on July 6, 1899. The White Pass is a narrow-gauge railway, with its tracks set only three feet apart, compared with the regular gauge of four and a half feet. The narrow gauge meant that the rail bed could be ten feet wide instead of fifteen, and this cut construction costs very considerably. In

addition, the narrow gauge made it easier for the train to negotiate the tight curves of the White Pass. Under extremely difficult
conditions, the completion of the railway in such a short time,
including a tunnel blasted through mountain three hundred
metres up a sheer cliff, was an extraordinary achievement.
Ironically, however, by the time the railway was finished, so too
was the gold rush. None of the stampeders on the Trail of '98 rode
up the White Pass in the comfort of a train.

The rail journey back to Skagway is spectacular. In the early
days, steam engines hauled the loads. Today, diesel and electric
locomotives pull the passenger cars, which are outfitted with high
windows that make for a completely unobstructed view. The first
few kilometres downward are fairly gentle, but soon we are on the
edge of the mountain, staring straight down at the canyon more
than hundreds of metres below. We cross from one ledge to the
next on a giant trestle, then plunge into the black of Tunnel
Mountain. Out of the tunnel, the canyon opens up below us, the
stream running beside the boulders and the narrow path of the
Trail of '98. Tall evergreens reach upward beside the trail.

Out of the train, I take a look around Skagway, whose population year-round is now about eight hundred, double that in the
summer. With about six thousand people from the cruise ships
roaming the streets today, the little place is overrun. But I suppose
the whole history of Skagway has had to do with being overrun,
first by the prospectors in the days of Soapy Smith and now by the
tourists, hungering for an authentic taste of the Trail of '98.

I find a little bar between the downtown and the dock where
the *Sea Princess* is tied up. As the waitress puts a cold beer on the
table in front of me, I ask her what it's like to have all these outsiders around throughout the summer. She looks at me for a
moment, not wanting to offend one of those outsiders. The real
townspeople, she says, wait until evening, when the cruise ships
leave, to come out and party.

On the final two evenings aboard the *Sea Princess*, there is a festive air. The first evening, it's the second occasion for formal attire at dinner. Out come the tuxes and the kilts. At dinner's end, with the lights turned down, all the waiters and chefs parade around the dining room, carrying trays of baked Alaska with liquor on top that is set ablaze. It is the end of June. Attention is focused on the fourth of July and the patriotic feelings of the fifteen hundred Americans on board. Outside the clothing shops on deck five, a brisk business is being done selling shirts emblazoned *Princess 2002*, with the rest of the shirt in the form of a wraparound U.S. flag. The *Sea Princess*, and most of its passengers, ignore Canada Day as we slide down the B.C. coast.

Chapter 4 | **Seeking Refuge**

I n mid-December 2002, the American dream, as fervently espoused by thousands of illegal Pakistani immigrants to the United States, turned suddenly into a nightmare. The U.S. government announced that within three months, all men sixteen years of age and older from a list of Arab and South Asian countries had to register with the Immigration and Naturalization Service (now a part of the newly created Department of Homeland Security). Registration meant that illegal immigrants who had been making new lives for themselves and their families faced the threat of jail or expulsion. Up against this predicament, thousands of Pakistanis flocked north to seek asylum in Canada.

Many had calculated that as long as they behaved themselves, they would never be noticed or challenged among the 9 to 11 million unlawful immigrants in a vast and open society like the United States. If they found employment, worked hard and raised their children to become Americans, they would be able to achieve what generations of immigrants before them had.

Thirty-one-year-old Raza Kibriya was one such Pakistani who came to the U.S. in 1998. He entered the country with a three-month visitor's visa in his passport. "In my mind, I was not going back," he said in a newspaper interview. "I knew that America is a free country, and nobody throws anybody out." Kibriya found work in construction in small-town Delaware, saved his money and in a couple of years owned a brand-new Honda Civic. His hopes for a new life crashed, however, on the shoals of the September 11 terrorist attacks. The order to register confronted him and others like him with a terrible choice. If they registered, they could immediately face incarceration and expulsion. Some of the Pakistanis reported that for them the order to register had been the final blow, that after September 11, confronted with hateful looks and racial slurs, life in New York had become unendurable.[1]

In the first two months of 2003, thousands of Pakistanis headed across the border to customs posts in Ontario and Quebec to make their claims. Doing so, they placed themselves in a highly precarious position. Instead of interviewing the claimants immediately, as they had in the past, officials of the Canadian Department of Citizenship and Immigration, under a controversial new policy, sent many of the refugees back across the border, setting up appointments to interview them weeks later. Nearly two hundred men, directed back to the U.S. from the LaColle border crossing point south of Montreal, were jailed, and some of those were deported to Pakistan.

Based on the record of Pakistanis seeking refugee status in Canada in 2002, the odds of winning approval from Canada's Immigration and Refugee Board were just over 50 percent. For some who were granted admission to Canada, especially children and teenagers, there was great sadness at leaving behind friends and neighbourhoods in the U.S. One fourteen-year-old girl, now with her family in Toronto, told a reporter that life in Canada was okay, "but it's kind of boring." She missed her Queens neighbourhood in New York City. "I don't want to live here. I'm hoping we'll go back to New York soon. If not move there, then visit a lot," she said.[2]

Like other international frontiers, the Canada–U.S. border has often afforded opportunities for those who needed to escape from the government of the day and its policies. Having a border handy to allow for flight has always been valued by freedom seekers (and by criminals) the world over. Sometimes, over the course of the past two centuries and more, it has been residents of the United States fleeing north, other times Canadians fleeing south.

The northward migration of Pakistanis was emblematic of the new era that began on September 11, 2001. In what now feels like the distant past, a great debate raged about globalization and its highly unequal effects on the peoples of the world. And that debate drew thousands of Americans into Canada in the spring of 2001. I was on hand to witness the arrival of one contingent of young Americans who came up with a variation on the theme of crossing the border in search of refuge. They crossed from the United States to Canada through the Akwesasne Reserve, just south of Cornwall, Ontario. They were seeking not asylum in Canada but passage through a place whose inhabitants defined their territory as a refuge, claiming rights that flowed from a time that long predated the Canada–U.S. border.

At the Summit of the Americas in Quebec City in April 2001, government leaders committed themselves to launching a hemispheric Free Trade Area of the Americas, the FTAA, by 2005. The heads of government of all the countries in the hemisphere, with the exception of Cuba, were meeting in a fenced-in enclave in the old city as tens of thousands of demonstrators protested against the FTAA. Police hurled hundreds of canisters of tear gas over the fence at the protestors. Even blocks away from the fence, I had to cover my face with a handkerchief to keep from choking. Clouds of tear gas drifted down the steep streets of the city, driving people out of their apartments, causing deep distress to the elderly and to the parents of babies and young children. From Tierra Del Fuego to the Arctic, a great power struggle had begun over whether the free trade deal should go ahead and what should be included in it. Both sides in the debate set out to do all they could to recruit people, communities and interest groups to their cause.

Among these communities are the Aboriginal peoples of the hemisphere, who are being courted by the contending forces. Living on islands and pieces of the mainland in and next to the St. Lawrence River in Ontario, Quebec and New York State, the Mohawks of Akwesasne have been drawn into the debate because of the strategic terrain they occupy right along the Canada–U.S. border. For years, the reserve was the site for large-scale cigarette smuggling between the United States and Canada.

Indeed, the people of Akwesasne get their own first-hand view of protestors and police on the eve of the Quebec City Summit. At noon on April 19, 2001, I arrive on Cornwall Island, the Ontario piece of the Akwesasne Reserve, to find that the Canada Customs post there has been transformed into an armed camp. For several weeks, there have been stories that American protestors, en route to Quebec City, intend to cross the border into Canada through Akwesasne.

A phalanx of Ontario Provincial Police (OPP) and Native police officers are lined up next to the customs post across the only road into Akwesasne. When I explain that I want to drive down that road into the reserve, a member of the Akwesasne police force tells me that it "is not advised," and that I will have to proceed over the bridge to the U.S.

On the U.S. side, I find another customs post in a state of alert. As an excuse to hang around there, I ask if there is a washroom I can use. As I go inside, the large steel door clicks shut behind me. When I try to leave, I find that the door is locked. For ten minutes I bang on it until I hear a key turn. As the door opens I find myself facing two armed customs officers.

Before I get back to my car, a guy hanging around U.S. Customs tells me that the protestors are expected to arrive at a wooded grove about a kilometre away. Next to the trees, in an open area, fish, venison and bread simmer in large steel trays over gas burners. Stacey Boots, who introduces himself as a member of the Akwesasne community, tells the assembled Canadian and U.S. media that he believes the North American Free Trade Agreement (NAFTA) has not been beneficial to the Mohawk people. He says he fears that the new hemisphere-wide agreement will do serious harm to the environment. Because he opposes the free trade deal being hammered out at the Summit, he intends to welcome the protestors to Akwesasne, and to provide food for them before they march peacefully to the border.

An hour later, a caravan of about seventy-five cars and an old bus from Palm Springs, California, roll into the open area and close to four hundred young people climb out, to be greeted by Stacey Boots and a few other Mohawks. Almost all of the protestors are in their early twenties, and they are dressed in what has come to be the attire of the anti-globalization movement: bulky jeans with big pockets and long, loose-fitting dresses. Many of those here, I soon discover, have been involved in other demonstrations and have faced the police before. They line up for ample portions of food and exchange greetings with one another. They do not seem fazed by the prospect of marching to the border of another country where they will face a massive police mobilization. This is a crack regiment in the new movement.

I cross back over the bridge to the Canadian side so I can watch the protestors approach the border. This time I manage to park my car off the main road, inside the reserve. Awaiting the arrival of the Americans over the top of the bridge ahead are customs officials, riot police, OPP officers and their dogs, members of the Akwesasne police force and hundreds of members of the community. This is enough muscle to turn back a band of armed marauders. For the unarmed young people who are coming, this is massive overkill.

I find myself standing with two men and a woman about a hundred metres behind the customs post. Together we watch the riot police and the stretch of concrete ribbon that climbs to the high point of the bridge. My three companions are wary about this event. The woman, who I later learn is a chief of the Mohawk Council of Akwesasne, says this kind of thing is not good for the community; it reinforces the idea that this is a place where trouble happens. The three of them recall earlier times of trouble for Akwesasne—the crisis a few years ago about whether spent nuclear material should be shipped through the reserve, and the explosion of 1990, when Mohawk factions fought each other in armed battles.[3]

Stacey Boots may share the goals of the protestors, but these three leaders—the men are also chiefs, I learn—are worried about trouble that could imperil the shaky autonomy enjoyed by the Mohawks. Akwesasne is a natural flashpoint along the Canada–U.S. border. Many of the Mohawks here regard themselves as members of an Aboriginal nation and reject the notion that they are citizens of either Canada or the United States. Having to deal with separate band councils and provincial and state governments in Ontario, Quebec and New York, as well as authorities in Ottawa and Washington, makes this divided community a tinderbox.

Here at Akwesasne, one is reminded that to the Native peoples of the continent the Canada–U.S. border is a relatively recent creation not of their making. A map of North America depicting the territories of the First Nations prior to the first European settlements would graphically represent the entirely different political space that then existed. Native peoples have always claimed the right to cross the Canada–U.S. border as they choose, taking with them their goods, which they believe should not be subject to the customs regulations of the two countries.

Akwesasne police officers break the mood of tense expectation as they tear back and forth around the sides of the bridge and up the main road on noisy all-terrain vehicles. At last, we witness a strange American invasion of Canada as the protestors come over the summit of the bridge on foot, followed by a long procession of cars. The riot police are lined up across the road. Off to the side I find a lacrosse field, where hundreds of residents of Akwesasne have assembled to watch the confrontation between the protestors and the police.

The protestors stop about fifty metres from the police and Stacey Boots addresses them. While he is taking the side of the young Americans, he ends his speech by urging them to go through customs peacefully, either on foot or in their cars. As many of the protestors head back to their cars, a couple of young Mohawks call out disgustedly that they are "wusses."

The riot police pull back to one side, and the protestors who have stayed out of the cars proceed to the wickets to be questioned by customs officials, one at a time. Soon they are walking across the main intersection of the reserve and up the hill to the second bridge, which will take them to Cornwall, Ontario.

Reporters, huddled together at the side of the road, call out questions to the protestors as they pass. Some members of the community shout insults about how the protestors are dressed and tell them to "keep moving." One young woman, asked why she opposes free trade, stops and gives a highly articulate three-minute answer on how globalization widens the gap between rich and poor.

This confrontation has ended peacefully—if in apparent incomprehension among its various actors. Many of the people of Akwesasne seem uncertain about whether to extend hospitality in their refuge on the St. Lawrence to the young Americans who are passing through. Only time will tell what role indigenous peoples will play in the battles that lie ahead over the free trade pact of the Americas.

As for the protestors, they are birds of passage, on their way to the main demonstrations in Quebec City. That makes them different from Americans and Canadians who have crossed the border in earlier times not to make a fleeting political point but in a deadly serious quest to find a refuge for themselves and others.

———

In September 1851, a young black woman who was a determined fighter for the abolition of slavery in the United States paid a visit to Toronto. Mary Ann Camberton Shadd was nearly twenty-eight years old when she came to get a first-hand view of the opportunities in Canada for blacks who were fleeing slavery in the United States. Shadd had been born into a free black family in the slave state of Delaware. In Wilmington, the prospects for an education for a free black child were very poor. By the time Mary was ten years old, her family had moved to West Chester, Pennsylvania, not far from Philadelphia. According to the story passed down from her family, Mary was educated by Quakers.[4]

During her decades-long struggle to educate blacks and to free them from slavery, she showed herself to be the most remarkable member of an exceptional family. Her father, Abraham Shadd, a shoemaker, fought actively for the cause of abolition. Dangerous though this was, he made his house a way station on the Underground Railroad, the route by which slaves who had escaped were helped on their way to freedom in Canada. For a time, he was the president of the National Convention for the Improvement of Free People of Color in the United States. Later, he was the first black person to be elected to public office in Canada West (Ontario).[5] After slavery was abolished, during the brief period of Reconstruction before the political rights of blacks were once again stamped out, Mary Shadd's brother Isaac served in the Mississippi legislature, between 1871 and 1874, part of that time as speaker of the House. Her brother Abraham was a lawyer in Mississippi and Arkansas.

After she finished school, Mary Shadd returned to Wilmington, Delaware, to open a school for black children. She also taught school for a time in Trenton, New Jersey, and New York City.[6]

It was her continuing work for the liberation of her people that brought her to Canada West in 1851. At a meeting in Toronto she heard prominent abolitionists, as well as Henry Bibb, the founder of *Voice of the Fugitive*, a newspaper that was published in the little community of Sandwich, near Windsor. Mary Shadd liked what she saw in Canada and she wanted to play a direct role. After a visit to Buffalo, she travelled by steamer to the Detroit–Windsor area. In Windsor, then a tiny hamlet with a population of about two hundred, she got a first-hand view of the wretched conditions faced by runaway slaves at this terminus of the Underground Railroad.

The blacks who arrived in the Windsor area faced not only rising prejudice against them, but poverty, poor housing and disease. It was an uphill struggle for the freed slaves to adapt to the climate and laws of Canada West. For Mary Shadd, the most appropriate way to help this struggling community was to establish herself as a teacher. Overcoming the problems that stood in her way, including her unwillingness to teach in a racially segregated school, she managed to set up a private school. Initially, she charged four shillings a month, but later she was forced to drop this to three shillings. She carried on, raising money where she could, despite the fact that she had become embroiled in a bitter factional dispute with Henry Bibb and his wife, who also ran her own school.[7]

A year after her arrival in Canada, Mary Shadd wrote and published a forty-four-page pamphlet, *Notes of Canada West*, on the possibilities for blacks north of the border. Of the alternatives, she wrote that tropical Africa was "teeming . . . with the breath of pestilence, a burning sun and fearful maladies . . ." In the slave-owning

South, she commented that blacks confronted "the probability of worse than inquisitorial inhumanity." In Canada, while blacks would confront prejudice, she wrote, they would find conditions that were superior to the alternatives:

> Coloured persons have been refused entertainment in taverns, (invariably of an inferior class,) and on some boats distinction is made; but in all cases, it is that of distinction that is made between poor foreigners and other passengers . . . It is an easy matter to make out a case of prejudice in any country. We naturally look for it, and the conduct of many is calculated to cause unpleasant treatment, and to make it difficult for well-mannered persons to get comfortable accommodations. There is a medium between servility and presumption, that recommends itself to all persons of common sense, of whatever rank or complexion; and if coloured people would avoid the two extremes, there would be but few cases of prejudice to complain of in Canada. In cases in which tavern keepers and other public characters persist in refusing to entertain them, they can, in common with the travelling public, generally, get redress at law.[8]

Mary Shadd was promoting the option of black immigration to Canada during a period when desperate efforts were being made by political leaders south of the border to find a compromise that would prevent the secession of the slave-owning states from the union. In 1850, the last great compromise to stave off the conflict was cobbled together. It included the notorious Fugitive Slave Act, which was passed by Congress and signed into law in September 1850. The act allowed slave owners to send human hunters into free Northern states to track down runaway slaves and to forcibly return them to their masters.[9] Not only were slaves returned, often to a terrible fate, but in many cases free blacks were seized and carried south as well.

There were times when the slave hunters ignored the border and tried to seize blacks on Canadian soil. On one occasion, hunters tracked a black youth into Chatham, in Canada West, where they seized him. Mary Shadd burst upon the hunters and tore the boy away from them. She then ran and rang the bell of the courthouse. The townspeople crowded into the street to see what was going on, and the hunters, without their prey, made their escape.[10]

By the time Shadd had become a prominent advocate of blacks leaving the United States for Canada, she had also made herself the driving force behind the *Provincial Freeman*, an abolitionist paper published in Canada. Although for a time, while she was actually editing and raising money for the newspaper, the nominal editor of the publication was a male, she eventually became the editor in name as well as practice. When she was on a tour in the United States to raise funds for the newspaper and to promote the cause of black immigration to Canada, she was feted in Philadelphia as the first black woman in North America to edit a newspaper.[11]

In 1855, Mary Shadd married a Toronto barber by the name of Thomas Cary. She and Cary had two children, a daughter and a son. By the time her husband died in November 1860, war was in the air south of the border. That was the month Abraham Lincoln was elected president. The next few months brought the secession of the Southern states and the outbreak of the Civil War. Mary Shadd managed to play her own distinct part in the conflict. Beginning in early 1864, she helped recruit blacks in Canada to enlist in the Union army. After the war, she returned to the United States. She taught in Detroit and then in Washington, DC. In her later years, she was deeply involved in the women's rights movement, giving an address to the national convention of the Women's Suffrage Association in 1878. She died in Washington, DC, in 1893.[12]

It is natural to compare Mary Shadd's remarkable career to that of the much better known Harriet Tubman, who was often called the Moses of her people during the perilous decades of the struggle of American blacks for freedom during the mid-nineteenth century. Tubman, born into slavery in Maryland in 1825, was a contemporary of Shadd, born two years earlier. The circumstances of the two, however, differed dramatically. Unlike Shadd, who received an education and became highly literate, Harriet Tubman was never able to write.[13]

As a teenager who was accustomed to working in the fields, on one occasion Tubman tried to stop the beating of a fellow slave and was struck on the head with a two-pound weight. The blow broke her skull and left her semi-conscious and near death for weeks. In his book on political leadership, American political analyst Garry Wills points to this episode as the turning point in Harriet Tubman's life. "Harriet lay ill, after the blow," Wills wrote, "reciting feverish prayers for her master's conversion to loving ways. She would suffer the rest of her life from catatonic spells she connected with the long semiconsciousness of her convalescence . . . The blow that cracked Tubman's skull struck off her psychic chains. She had already died once; she had nothing to lose."[14]

Escaping from her master, Tubman made her way north to freedom. But having found freedom herself, she was determined to lead others to it. Many times, she returned to the South to organize other slaves to make their escapes. Having learned the routes and the techniques for evading the slave hunters, she led parties of slaves north, using the North Star to guide her by night and hiding by day. Once they reached the North, Tubman received aid from abolitionist Quakers who helped the fugitives make it to the Canadian border.

Tubman's exploits won her fame and respect among those who were fighting for the freedom of the slaves. John Brown, who attempted to trigger an armed slave revolt and who was hanged on the eve of the Civil War, came to Canada in 1858, where he met Harriet Tubman. Brown referred to her as "the General."[15]

Though she was slight in stature, barely five feet tall, Harriet Tubman exhibited immense physical courage, returning to slave-owning areas where she could be recognized. A high price had been placed on her head, and slave owners and their minions were on the lookout for her. She would lead runaway slaves who could not swim across rivers, heading out first to show the others they could make it. On one extraordinary occasion, she happened to be in Troy, New York, when she saw a former slave she had led to freedom in the hands of guards. The intention of the authorities was to return the man to his owner under the powers established by the Fugitive Slave Act. Tubman rushed forward and seized the man. Guards beat her, but she wouldn't let go of the former slave. With the aid of a crowd of bystanders, she and the freed man made good their escape. It was said of Harriet Tubman that she never lost a slave whom she had set out to free.[16]

Mary Ann Shadd and Harriet Tubman played complementary roles in the freedom struggle. Shadd was an educator, writer and newspaper editor who promoted the cause of black immigration to Canada. Tubman was the greatest "conductor" on the Underground Railroad, personally leading about three hundred blacks to Canada. Over the decades of its operation, the high point being the period from 1840 to 1860, about thirty thousand black Americans found freedom in Canada.

A century after the slaves were freed, Martin Luther King reflected on the role of Canada in the struggle of black Americans:

> Deep in our history of struggle for freedom Canada was the North Star. The Negro Slave, denied education, dehumanized, imprisoned on cruel plantations, knew that far to the north a land existed where a fugitive slave, if he survived the horrors of the journey, could find freedom. The legendary Underground Railroad

started in the South and ended in Canada . . . Our spirituals, now so widely admired around the world, were often codes. We sang of "heaven" that awaited us, and the slave masters listened in innocence, not realizing that we were not speaking of the here-after. Heaven was the word for Canada and the Negro sang of the hope that his escape on the Underground Railroad would carry him there. One of our spirituals, "Follow the Drinking Gourd," in its disguised lyrics contained directions for escape. The gourd was the big dipper, and the North Star to which its handle pointed gave the celestial map that directed the flight to the Canadian border.[17]

The best-known migration of refugees to Canada prior to the flight of Vietnam War resisters in the 1960s and 1970s, the Underground Railroad stopped running with the abolition of slavery in the United States. Just over a decade after the end of the Civil War, a veteran of that war who had fought at Gettysburg led U.S. troops into a battle that was ultimately to drive a desperate band of American Native people to look to the north for refuge.

On June 25, 1876, Lieutenant Colonel George A. Custer led his 7th U.S. Cavalry to annihilation against Sitting Bull's Sioux at the Little Bighorn River in the Montana Territory. At the time of the battle—a synonym for military catastrophe ever since—the North West Mounted Police was less than three years old. Ottawa had founded the NWMP as a force whose job was to keep the peace in the vast western territory that had been transferred to Canada from the Hudson's Bay Company in 1870. The summer following "Custer's last stand," the undermanned Mounties came face to face with Sitting Bull on Canadian soil. Even before the Battle of the Little Bighorn, the Mounties realized that the Indian Wars being fought on U.S. soil were likely to drive desperate Native bands north into Canadian territory.

In May 1877, NWMP Major James M. Walsh, a sergeant and three troopers encountered the Sioux about eighty kilometres north of the U.S. border. Walsh was the commander of a ninety-man Mountie unit based at Fort Walsh. Located fifty-five kilometres south of the present-day Maple Creek, Saskatchewan, in the Cypress Hills, the unit had the job of maintaining law and order in a large part of what later became southern Saskatchewan and Alberta. For a time, Fort Walsh was the most populous settlement on Canadian soil between Winnipeg and Vancouver. The location of the fort in the Cypress Hills was no accident. The slaughter in the Hills of several Native men, women and children by whisky traders and wolf hunters in June 1873—known as the Cypress Hills Massacre—had spurred the federal government to establish the NWMP.

Having spotted mounted Sioux lookouts posted on hilltops, Walsh and his men rode past the sentinels, encountering more Sioux, until the small Mountie patrol was surrounded. Soon they found a large Native camp before them. Reining in their horses, Walsh and his men were met by a Sioux war chief. The Mountie said he wanted to meet Sitting Bull.

Informed by the Sioux party that they were the first white men to dare to ride up to Sitting Bull's camp so fearlessly, Walsh and his men soon were joined by Sitting Bull, who approached at the head of a group of chiefs. Walsh and Sitting Bull studied each other warily. Growing more comfortable, they headed into the Sioux camp, where they spent the day in conversation. Walsh asked the Native leader why the Sioux had come to Canada. Sitting Bull replied that they had been fighting on the defensive for years south of the border, and that they had suffered greatly at the hands of the U.S. army. They hoped they would be granted sanctuary north of the border.

Walsh replied that as long as the Sioux obeyed the laws of the land, did not make war against other tribes and did not use Canadian soil as a base for carrying out raids south of the border, they could remain in the country. To Sitting Bull this was a reasonable deal. He requested ammunition for his people to hunt buffalo. Walsh agreed, with the proviso that the ammunition not be used for military operations across the line in the United States.

The relationship between Walsh and Sitting Bull had been cemented, which was a good thing, because there were to be tricky problems in the future. The federal government in Ottawa did not want the Sioux to remain in Canada permanently, fearing that this could cause friction with other First Nations groups, and could threaten the viability of the remaining buffalo on the Prairies as a food source for Native peoples. At the behest of Ottawa, the U.S. government sent a mission to Canada to negotiate with the Sioux. In October 1877, U.S. Brigadier General Alfred H. Terry, who had been Custer's superior at the time of the Battle of the Little Bighorn, met with Sitting Bull at Fort Walsh. Prior to the meeting, the Sioux leader was very negative about even talking with the Americans. In the end, he was coaxed to change his mind by Major Walsh. The meeting went nowhere, however. Not trusting the U.S. general who had dispatched Custer to his doom at the Little Bighorn, Sitting Bull refused to consider returning with his people to the United States.

Newspapers on both sides of the border played up the story of the meeting for their readers, predicting trouble from the Sioux whether they returned to the U.S. or stayed in Canada. For a time tensions mounted, but for the present at least, the Sioux were staying in Canada.

The following spring, Walsh, now famous in the U.S. as "Sitting Bull's Boss," travelled to Ottawa via railways in the northern U.S. (The transcontinental Canadian Pacific Railway was not completed until November 1885.) On his journey south of the border, Walsh repeatedly had to quash rumours that the West was about to explode as a consequence of a great Native confederation to be led by Sitting Bull and the Sioux.

Walsh was also forced to deal with a nemesis of the Canadian government from the past, Louis Riel. Riel had been the leader of the uprising of the Metis at Fort Garry (now Winnipeg) in 1869–70, at the time when Rupert's Land, the territory of the Hudson's Bay Company, was transferred to the Dominion of Canada. Riel's rebellion had threatened the fledgling Dominion only a few years after the conclusion of the American Civil War, which had left a strong aftertaste of hostility toward British North America in Washington. Now Riel was living in Montana. His dream was to forge a great alliance of peoples of Native blood in order to reclaim the plains of North America from both the U.S. and Canadian governments.

Faced with this threat, Walsh crossed the border and rode down to Wolf Point, on the Missouri River, where he talked the Assiniboines out of joining with Riel in his push for a great rising of Native peoples. Back in Canada, he met with Sitting Bull and other Sioux chiefs to remind them that they had agreed to abide by the law as their condition for remaining in Canada.

Despite Walsh's diplomacy, tensions grew between the Sioux and the Canadian authorities. Ottawa's policy remained what it had been from the start: Sitting Bull and the Sioux must eventually return to the U.S. The Sioux, having hoped for the grant of a reserve on Canadian soil, became restive. For a time there was even tension between Sitting Bull and Walsh, although their friendship survived.

By the end of the 1870s, Sir John A. Macdonald, who had established the Mounties in 1873, was back in power as prime minister of Canada. Concerned that Walsh had grown too close to Sitting Bull and that the Sioux were never going to return to the U.S., Macdonald had Walsh transferred to Fort Qu'Appelle, a long-time Hudson's Bay Company trading post. Sitting Bull, saddened that his old friend was leaving, asked Walsh if he would plead the case of the Sioux to Ottawa. Walsh told him that there was no hope that the government would grant the Sioux a reserve in Canada.

If Walsh could do nothing for the Sioux in Ottawa, what about in Washington, Sitting Bull wondered. Could his Mountie friend go to the White House to negotiate on behalf of the Sioux? Walsh responded that since he had some leave coming, if Ottawa would allow it, he would go to Washington to try to obtain assurance that Sitting Bull and his people would not be punished for their victory at the Little Bighorn.

On his subsequent leave, Walsh returned to his hometown of Brockville, Ontario. He was granted an interview with the prime minister in Ottawa, only a short distance away. At their meeting, Macdonald turned down Walsh's request that he be allowed to go to Washington to make the case on behalf of the Sioux. Stymied by the prime minister, Walsh proceeded to Chicago, where he met with a friend in the U.S. Indian Bureau who promised that he would contact people of influence in Washington to get them to speak up on behalf of Sitting Bull.

By this point, the Sioux leader had effectively lost much of his former power. Most of the members of his band had slipped back across the border to the United States. In April 1881, Sitting Bull travelled to Fort Qu'Appelle with the destitute, hungry Sioux who remained with him—two hundred to four hundred of them—in search of Walsh. Still in Ontario on an extended leave, Walsh sent a message to Sitting Bull through an intermediary, urging him to lead his followers back to the U.S. to surrender to American authorities.

In July 1881, Sitting Bull and the small band of Sioux headed south to the United States. They had concluded that in Canada they were condemned to poverty and hunger. On their journey out of Canada, not a single member of the NWMP accompanied them. On July 19, Sitting Bull and those with him surrendered to the U.S. military at Fort Buford, Dakota Territory. Now a prisoner of war, Sitting Bull was transferred to Fort Randall, Dakota Territory.

The last days of the Sioux leader were a sorry sequel to the career of a man who had been a leader of Indian resistance on the Great Plains. Two years after his surrender, the authorities released Sitting Bull. He settled on the Grand River in present-day South Dakota. Although he led a quiet life, his name still resonated across the continent. He spent one season as a major attraction in the touring Buffalo Bill Cody Wild West Show.

The end came for Sitting Bull in 1890, at a time when tension flared among the Native peoples in the Dakota Territory. With the government pushing for the acquisition of yet more Indian land, a new movement of Native resistance sprang into being. Anxious that Sitting Bull might be recruited and galvanize the movement, about three dozen Indian police came to arrest him at his cabin. In the shootout that ensured, Sitting Bull, his teenage son and a dozen other Sioux were killed.

As for his old friend Walsh, the struggle with John A. Macdonald had ruined his career. In 1883, he was forced to resign from the Mounties. When he learned of Sitting Bull's death, Walsh wrote:

> I am glad to hear that Bull is relieved of his miseries, even if it took the bullet to do it. A man who wielded such power as Bull once did, that of a King, and over a wild spirited people, cannot endure abject poverty . . . without suffering great mental pain, and death is a relief. I regret now that I had not gone to Standing Rock and seen him. Bull had been misrepresented. He was not the bloodthirsty man reports made him out to be. He asked for nothing but justice. He was not a cruel man. He was kind of heart. He was not dishonest. He was truthful. He loved his people and was glad to give his hand in friendship to any man who was honest with him.[18]

The most recent major exodus of American refugees to Canada occurred during the 1960s and 1970s, when the Vietnam War resisters crossed the border. Because I was involved in the anti-war movement and the New Left during those years, I remember many young men who came to Canada to evade the draft or as deserters from the U.S. forces. I met them in Toronto, Montreal, Ottawa and Kingston, where I was a graduate student at Queen's University.

The best estimate is that there were about sixty thousand Americans who headed north during the Vietnam War. About half of them were men, half women. When the opportunity to return to the U.S. arose, half of these migrants returned home and the rest stayed in Canada. On January 21, 1977, President Jimmy Carter issued an amnesty for draft evaders. Later, there were amnesties for deserters.

It is easy to understand why most of those wanting to escape from the U.S. chose Canada as their refuge. It was close, much of it was English-speaking and Canada did not have a policy of extraditing draft evaders and resisters. That is not to say that the Americans who fled to Canada were treated with uniform kindness by Canadian authorities. In an interview for this book, I was told by a retired Canada Customs officer in British Columbia that he knew of cases in B.C. where customs officers rounded up a number of those on the run from the U.S. and returned them to U.S. Customs on the other side of the border. This was done, my informant told me, despite the fact that these actions were without authorization and in violation of the policy of the Canadian government.

The Americans who came to Canada during the Vietnam War were of many types. Some of them were strongly political and became active in the anti-war movement in Canada. Others were apolitical, simply wanting to be left in peace and not forced to fight in a war in which they did not believe.

Some of the Americans who came north remained deeply American in their values, while others came to idealize Canada and to make a concerted effort to take on the values and outlook of their adopted country. I remember a number of the more political of the refugees from the U.S. believing that they would make natural leaders for the anti-war movement in Canada. After all, they reasoned, they had been face to face with the American state and had stood up for their beliefs; now they could teach the lessons they had learned to Canadians. During this era, there were some rather farcical demonstrations on Canadian university campuses in opposition to the war in Vietnam, which featured Canadians shouting the slogan, "Hell no, I won't go." Since no one was proposing to draft Canadians to serve in Vietnam, it was a simple case of people adopting someone else's political slogan.

Others among those who came north saw Canada as an innocent country, populated by people who displayed values these disillusioned Americans believed had been abandoned south of the border. For some, Canada was a kind of true America. This is a theme that has recurred over the long course of the relationship between Canada and the United States. Just as Europeans were once delighted to regard Americans as plain-spoken founts of popular wisdom who could teach the old continent a thing or two, Americans have often seen Canadians as exemplars of lost American virtues. For instance, Michael Moore, the radical American filmmaker, regularly depicts Canadians as folks who endlessly exude common sense. In his film *Bowling for Columbine*, Canadians are depicted as people who leave their front doors unlocked and who manage to own guns without shooting each other. While I'm flattered by the attention Moore gives us, his view of Canada always seems simplistic to me. Moore has said that he purposely uses Canada as a foil for the U.S. because his intention is to explore American problems, not Canadian ones.

In October 1970, those who subscribed to the notion of Canada the innocent received a terrible blow when the government of Prime Minister Pierre Trudeau proclaimed the War Measures Act in response to actions of the Front de la libération du Québec (FLQ). U.S. draft evaders and deserters had tended to regard Trudeau and his predecessor, Lester Pearson, with favour.

After all, it was these Liberal leaders who had kept the door open for them to enter Canada. In 1970, in a speech to Mennonite and United Church leaders, Trudeau had declared: "Those who made the conscientious judgment that they must not participate in this war . . . have my complete sympathy, and indeed our political approach has been to give them access to Canada. Canada should be a refuge from militarism."[19] But suddenly, the FLQ kidnapping of the British trade commissioner, James Cross, and the kidnapping and murder of Quebec labour minister Pierre Laporte had provoked Trudeau into making use of an act that suspended civil liberties in Canada.

The Americans who came north to evade military service often failed to understand the crucial role of Quebec in the calculus of the Liberal governments of those days. I remember young Americans who had fled the draft predicting to me that Lyndon Johnson would not stand for Canada remaining on the sidelines during the war. What they didn't appreciate was that with its staunch opposition to Canadian participation in foreign wars, Quebec made it very difficult for the Liberals even to consider entering the war. The opposition of Quebeckers to conscription in the two world wars had been the principal reason that Canada was the only major country in the West without compulsory military service in the decades following World War II. Similarly, these young Americans did not understand just how far Pierre Trudeau would go to counter the Quebec separatist movement.

Many of the American war resisters who had come north to Canada were permanently disillusioned as a consequence of the invocation of the War Measures Act with the country they had adopted. One American refugee, who is now a freelance writer, penned his thoughts many years after the event:

> When the Canadian government brought in the War Measures Act, and was arresting people into the small hours of the

morning, people whose only crime was to have spoken publicly in favour of Quebec independence, I said, "I want no part of this." That was for me as galvanizing an event with regard to Canada as the Vietnam War was for the United States.[20]

A study of Vietnam War resisters concluded that those who arrived in Canada in 1970 were the most affected by the imposition of the War Measures Act. Those who had been in the country a year or two before the October Crisis were not as deeply affected by it.

———

Canadians are familiar with the idea of Americans seeking refuge here at various times over the past two centuries. Less well known is that there were times when Canadians crossed the border to seek refuge in the United States. One such case—hardly a staple in the popular telling of Canadian history—unfolded during World War II. Those on the run from Canada were the leaders of Canada's Communist Party. The stage for this remarkable drama was set in the geopolitics of Europe as the continent lurched toward war.

In the years following Adolf Hitler's accession to power on January 30, 1933, a three-way struggle developed in Europe as Hitler moved from triumph to triumph, casting off the limitations imposed on Germany in the Treaty of Versailles after World War I and rebuilding his nation's armed forces. It was apparent that Hitler was driving toward war—but war against whom? As Germany rearmed and threatened its neighbours, the Third Reich clashed with both the Western powers, Britain and France, as well as the Soviet Union.

Under the direction of Soviet leader Joseph Stalin and the Comintern, Communist Parties throughout the world adopted a political line whose essence was to forge alliances with anti-Nazis and anti-Fascists to help ensure that when war came, the Soviet Union would not be involved in a conflict against Germany without the assistance of Britain and France. Communist Parties, including the Communist Party of Canada, sought to build "united fronts" against the Fascists. The high point of this struggle came in 1938, when Communists fought against the appeasement policies of the British and French governments.

Germany swallowed Austria in the *Anschluss* of March 1938. Then came Munich, the darkest hour of all, when British prime minister Neville Chamberlain and French premier Édouard Daladier met Hitler and Mussolini in September 1938 and agreed to let the Germans march into the Sudetenland and thus dismember Czechoslovakia. To Communists, it seemed perfectly obvious that the ruling classes and leaders like Chamberlain were hell-bent on encouraging the Nazis to attack the Soviet Union, and thereby to obliterate the world centre of Bolshevism. In the months following Munich, the Communists pushed ahead with their effort to build united fronts against the Fascists. But the struggle to which they had dedicated their lives did not turn out as they had expected.

In March 1939, when Hitler occupied the rump of Czechoslovakia, the Chamberlain government warned that Britain would guarantee the territorial integrity of other states that stood in Hitler's path, chief among them Poland. For the next few months, the Western powers and the Soviet Union carried on negotiations to forge an alliance against Nazi Germany. The alliance was to go into effect if Hitler invaded Poland. But the alliance between the West and the Soviet Union was not consummated.

Instead of such an alliance, a diplomatic revolution occurred as a result of a startling initiative from Berlin. On August 22, 1939, the world was stunned by the news that the two implacable ideological foes, Nazi Germany and Soviet Russia, had signed a non-aggression pact. Not only did Hitler and Stalin agree not to go to war against one another, but they also made a sweeping secret deal to divide Eastern Europe between them. Germany was to be allowed to invade Poland and to occupy most of the country, up to an agreed line east of Warsaw; the rest of Poland would go to the Soviet Union. For their part, the Soviets were to be allowed to occupy the Baltic republics of Latvia, Lithuania and Estonia. In addition, they were permitted to seize strategically important territory from Finland and Romania.

At dawn on September 1, Hitler launched his blitzkrieg offensive against Poland. Two days later, Britain and France declared war against Germany. Following a parliamentary debate, Canada declared war on September 10. The United States stayed out of the war until Japan attacked Pearl Harbor on December 7, 1941.

Communists in the Western democracies found themselves in a predicament they would not have thought possible only a few weeks earlier. The three-way poker game of the thirties did not end as Communists had feared, with the Nazis fighting the Soviets while the West stayed on the sidelines. Instead, the West was at war with Hitler and it was Stalin who was standing on the sidelines.

The Nazi–Soviet pact and the invasion of Poland left the world's Communists in disarray. The first instinct of the French, British and Canadian Communist Parties was to endorse the war efforts of their countries. But on September 18, 1939, Stalin issued a directive to all Communist Parties ordering them not to support the war against Hitler. In the directive, the supreme leader of the world's Communists proclaimed:

> The present war is an imperialist and unjust war for which the bourgeoisie of all the belligerent States bear equal responsibility. In no country can the Communist Parties or the working class support the war. The bourgeoisie is not conducting the war against fascism as Chamberlain and the leaders of the Labour Party pretend. War is carried on between two groups of imperialist countries for world domination.[21]

By the end of September, every single Communist Party in the world had adopted the line laid down by Stalin. While in a few cases there were some dissidents who refused to go along with the new orthodoxy, the Canadian Communist Party went over to Stalin's position without dissent. The U.S. Communist Party was even quicker in its conversion, adopting the new Stalin line on the basis of a broadcast from Moscow that predated Stalin's actual directive by a few days.

Shockingly, Communists in Canada, who had spent years complaining that the social democrats were not standing up to Hitler, now condemned them for their treachery in backing the war against Hitler. After the fall of Poland, the strange time of the so-called phony war got under way, with the Western allies and the Germans staring at each other across no-man's land while neither side took the offensive. During these months of apparent non-conflict, the Communist Party remained legal in Canada. Canadian Communists denounced the war and demanded that Canada withdraw from it. Far from being in the vanguard of the struggle against Hitler, Communists became the allies of those, such as French-Canadian nationalists, who wanted to stay out of the war.

During the wartime federal election in March 1940, the Canadian Communist Party campaigned for Canada's withdrawal from the conflict. The party's election manifesto included this message: "In this war the Canadian capitalists plan to revel in luxury at home, raking in the mounting piles of profits, while sending our sons to rot and die in the trenches of someone else on a far-off continent . . . A degenerate, besotten, parasitical class, they are carrying on a traffic in death."[22]

With the Canadian election over, the phony war was succeeded by Hitler's assault on the West. On June 6, 1940, the government of Mackenzie King, by Order-in-Council, making use of the War Measures Act, designated the Communist Party and fourteen "auxiliary" organizations illegal.[23] A few days later, the RCMP began to round up Communists, dispatching them to internment camps in which Nazis and Fascists were also present.

Top leaders of the Canadian Communist Party went into hiding and were successful in dodging the police. The Political Bureau of the party decided that while many of the party's leaders would remain in Canada, three would go into exile. Party leader Tim Buck, along with Charles Sims and Sam Carr, succeeded in crossing the border and making it to New York City. In New York, they were housed and protected by the U.S. Communist Party.

Tim Buck and his associates remained in New York until August 1941. By that date, the world situation had again altered dramatically. On June 22, 1941, Hitler's armies invaded the Soviet Union. Instantly, the Communist Parties of the world dropped their opposition to the war. They now became the most ardent advocates of the military struggle against the Nazis. Although it would take the Communists many more months to convince the King government to lift the ban on the party and to allow Communists to enlist in the Canadian forces, Tim Buck returned to Canada along with Sims and Carr. Just over a year earlier, they had denounced those who favoured Canada's participation in the war. Now they turned their rhetorical weapons against those who failed to give the war 100 percent support.

———

The flight of Communist leaders from Canada to the U.S. was not the only time that Canadians, embroiled in a political struggle, sought refuge south of the border.

At the end of the unsuccessful armed rebellions against the British crown in Upper and Lower Canada in 1837–38, the leaders of the rebellions, as well as many followers, fled across the border to the United States. While a number of the leading figures involved in the armed struggle were hanged by the British authorities, and others were imprisoned and exiled, both Louis-Joseph

Papineau and William Lyon Mackenzie made it to the United States. For a time after the uprisings had been crushed, efforts continued to regroup the forces of rebellion on American territory. Funds were raised at public meetings in Detroit, Cleveland, New York and other cities to support the continuation of the struggle against the British crown in Canada. Americans and Canadians volunteered to establish new units to pursue the battle.

Several unsuccessful armed incursions were mounted on Canadian border points from the U.S. The most noteworthy of the cross-border assaults was led by a Polish revolutionary democrat who had participated in the failed Polish rising of 1831 against Russian rule. Nils Gustav Szoltewcki, known as Von Schultz, took up the cause of the Canadian democrats against the British colonial regime. In November 1838, a force of about seven hundred men assembled to carry out an assault on the town of Prescott on the St. Lawrence River in Upper Canada. From there they intended to move on Kingston, the key base of the British army in the region. As a consequence of military mismanagement, the British found out about the planned attack, and most of the band of seven hundred were left out of the action. Von Schultz carried out the attack with only about 170 comrades.

The rebels seized a stone windmill near Prescott and held out there against British troops for four days. Up against superior numbers and firepower, they surrendered. Brought to trial for his role in the unsuccessful invasion, Von Schultz was defended by a young Kingston lawyer by the name of John A. Macdonald. The Polish revolutionary was found guilty, though, and was hanged in Kingston on December 5, 1839. Ten others were also executed.[24]

Three decades later, John A. Macdonald was the prime minister of the new Dominion of Canada. Britain was transferring Rupert's Land, the vast territory of the Hudson's Bay Company, to Canada. It was the intention of the Macdonald government to administer the territory, comprising the present Prairie provinces and the northern territories, from Ottawa.

The inhabitants of a corner of the territory had other plans. Under the leadership of Louis Riel, the Metis of Fort Garry formed a provisional government with the support of the Native peoples of the area. Riel's regime demanded that Ottawa create a new province that would mean self-government for the people of Fort Garry and the surrounding region. Having no way to dispatch the militia to put down the rebels at Fort Garry, Macdonald was forced to make a deal with them. The prime minister feared that without a deal, the whole territory on which Canada's future rested could be occupied by the United States, whose Civil War had ended only a few years earlier. In 1870, the new province of Manitoba was established. Initially, it included only Fort Garry and a relatively small area around it.

Louis Riel was elected to Parliament from the new province. He travelled to Ottawa and paid one visit to the House of Commons. Fearing arrest, he left the capital and did not return. He went to the United States. In 1885, Riel returned from the U.S. and organized a great movement of Native resistance in opposition to the occupation of the land by settlers from the East. By this point, the transcontinental railway was nearing completion, and it was evident that the days of the buffalo-hunting Indians and Metis were numbered. As in 1869–70, Riel led an armed rebellion on the Prairies, this time centred in territory that was to be a part of the future province of Saskatchewan. Amid fervent patriotic displays in Central Canada, the militia set out for the West, able to make most of the journey on the new railway. Captured once his rebellion had been stamped out, Riel was put on trial for murder.

He was tried for a murder committed long before. In 1870, when Riel was leader of the provisional government in Fort Garry, during the Metis rebellion, he ordered the execution of

Thomas Scott. An Ontarian, Scott had been an obstreperous opponent of Riel's regime. Now, fifteen years later, Riel was on trial for the killing of Scott. When Riel was sentenced to hang, Canada was divided in two over the verdict. Ontario cried out for Riel's head, while French-speaking Quebec, seeing in Riel a defender of francophone rights, demanded clemency. In November 1885, a week after the completion of the transcontinental railway, Riel was hanged in Regina. From there, his body was transported for burial to St. Boniface, Manitoba, the little French-speaking town across the Red River from Winnipeg. Today, a statue of Riel stands in Winnipeg in front of the Manitoba legislature, and there is another statue in St. Boniface, next to his grave.

Macdonald, who had tried to save the life of Von Schultz, decided that this rebel, who had also entered Canada from south of the border, would be executed.

———

From the time of the Loyalists, the first northward refugees, there has been a long tradition in Canada of providing sanctuary. At times, as well, the United States has served as a sanctuary for Canadians. In all of this, there is perhaps a warning against the tyranny implicit in the idea of a universal state. Borders act as brake points that limit the power of the state. For those who care about freedom, that is not a bad thing. In the eighteenth century, Voltaire, always wary of the wrath of the French government because of his satiric crusades, lived a couple of kilometres from the border with Geneva. When he received word that the king's minions were coming to get him, he simply crossed the border and waited on the other side until things calmed down.

Chapter 5 | BORDER RICHES: Customs and Smuggling

I n one important respect, the old cliché about the undefended border between Canada and the United States is patently untrue. While the last military fortification built in Canada to protect the nation against American invasion was constructed in Lévis, Quebec, in the early 1870s, over the course of more than two centuries the customs service has risen from rudimentary beginnings to become the transcontinental operation it is today. "We *are* defended at our border," wrote Dave McIntosh in his history of Canada Customs, "against illegal importation of firearms and narcotics, diseased plants and foreign criminals, professional and amateur smugglers, and other artful dodgers."[1]

Customs posts, where the state collects duties on legal imports and bars illegal imports, have existed for centuries. In Canada in the era before the creation of the income tax, duties collected on imports were the lifeblood of the state. In the early days, customs posts along the Canada–U.S. border operated in a haphazard fashion. They often kept shoddy records. In the early 1840s, customs collectors in Canada West (Ontario) kept as a part of their salaries 50 percent of collections valued at up to £200, and a smaller percentage for collections valued between £200 and £4,500. Maximum wage for a collector was pegged at £300 a year. On top of that, collectors were allowed to keep one-third of the money raised in auctions where seized goods were sold—half if the seized goods yielded £40 or less.

In those days, many customs posts in Canada were located at a considerable distance from the frontier. In the 1840s, importers often picked the customs post where they could get the lowest valuation on their products. And since collectors' incomes were linked to the business they attracted, there was much competition among collectors to entice importers to frequent their particular post.[2]

Despite its idiosyncratic features in the early days, the collection of duties and excise was deadly serious business as far as the government was concerned—and that was equally true for the United States government. Prior to the establishment of the income tax in 1917, customs and excise duties accounted for three-quarters of the revenues of the Canadian government. The same had been true for the colonial regimes in British North America that preceded Confederation. After Confederation, the collection of customs and of inland revenues were administered by separate government departments. Then, in 1927, the Department of National Revenue was established, with two separate components, taxation and customs and excise. With one minister, each of these components had its own deputy minister and departmental organization. On November 1, 1999, the Department became the Canada Customs and Revenue Agency.[3]

Because the collection of customs and excise duties on imported goods was so crucial to government coffers, Canadian customs collectors were given extraordinary powers. Today, Canadians are at least vaguely aware that the penalties for bringing goods into the country without declaring them are potentially severe. Under current law, evading customs can mean the forfeiture of the vehicle in which the undeclared goods are conveyed. In the customs act passed in the Province of Canada in 1847, the same regulation was in effect, except that it applied to ships and their rigging and tackle, and to horses, carriages and harnesses. Prior to Confederation, customs officers were allowed to stop and board all manner of vehicles—boat, canoe, carriage, wagon, cart or sleigh—anywhere in the province, to search for smuggled goods. And a writ of assistance, which, once issued to a collector, remained in force for the full reign of the current sovereign— Queen Victoria reigned for over sixty years—allowed the collector to search virtually any building. Where necessary, collectors were permitted to break down doors and open chests and other containers. Not until 1976 did the federal government declare a moratorium on the use of such writs. All use of customs writs has since been withdrawn.[4]

It was in the decades following Confederation that the federal Department of Customs and Excise grew into a standardized, continent-wide operation. At the end of the nineteenth century and the beginning of the twentieth century, the federal government built elegant customs houses in the major cities. They were often neo-classical edifices with fluted stone columns. Built to last, they remain monuments to the architecture of the time. But the construction of customs houses did little to keep the department abreast of the problems it confronted collecting revenues on imports. In the days when trains and ships were the main ways of undertaking lengthy journeys, it was relatively easy for customs officials to set up their operations so they could check the goods being shipped. But the advent of the automobile and the building of hundreds of driveable or semi-driveable roads across the border changed that. The automobile quickly made cross-border smuggling a major problem. It was a case of new technology doing an end run around customs.

Early on, customs officers in Canada found themselves being forced into the ticklish position of acting as moral arbiters. The first recorded case seems to have been in 1853, when a customs collector at Port Hope, Canada West, by the name of Marcus Fayette Whitehead, wrote a letter to the Commissioner of Customs seeking his instructions:

> I beg to report to you that I seized a number of pamphlets and small books of a most obscene, immoral and disgusting description, not fit for the gaze of the most licentious or accomplished libertine, much less to be circulated in a civilized community, and in the event of my own modesty being questioned, I have called to my aid and counsel a very virtuous and pious old Baptist who has pronounced the whole "too abominable to be even looked at." I have therefore placed them under lock and key and await your instructions.

The commissioner instructed Whitehead to destroy the offending material at once. This being done, we have no record of the titles of the lascivious works in question.[5]

For decades, Canadian customs officers played the role of moral guardians, blocking shipments of written and pictorial materials coming into Canada from south of the border. Today the Internet brings pornography to computer screens in Canada from all over the world, and the flow of printed pornographic materials across the border has declined appreciably. In other ways, however, Canada Customs remains the front line against the entry of unwanted people and illegal weapons, toxic waste, explosives, and food and plants that could transport disease into the country. From coast to coast, where roads and highways cross the frontier, at ports and at airports, Canada Customs is in place.

Wherever there are borders and customs, it is axiomatic that there will be smuggling. The golden age of smuggling across the Canada–U.S. border, if that is not too grand a term, followed World War I.

During the era of Prohibition in the United States, from 1920 to 1933, Canada provided a refuge for Americans that was very different, and rather less heroic, from the refuge during the time of the Underground Railroad. It was the powerful temperance movement in the United States, a remarkable amalgam of social reform zeal and puritanism, that convinced the American people and lawmakers to undertake an extraordinary experiment. Proposed in December 1917, the Eighteenth Amendment to the U.S. Constitution was ratified by the necessary thirty-six states in January 1919. The amendment declared that "the manufacture, sale, or transportation of intoxicating liquors within, the importation thereof into, or the exportation thereof from the United States and all territory subject to the jurisdiction thereof for beverage purposes is hereby prohibited." Once the Volstead Act, enforcing the Eighteenth Amendment, came into effect in 1920, the great American social experiment was in full force.

Canada too had gone through a period when its temperance movement had briefly prevailed, during World War I. But in 1919, the federal government allowed the expiration of its wartime Orders-in-Council enforcing Prohibition. It was now up to the provinces to chart the course in Canada. And the course moved Canada ever further from Prohibition. In 1920 and 1921, Quebec and British Columbia pioneered what was to become the Canadian alternative when the two provinces established government-operated liquor stores. During the 1920s, the other provinces followed suit. The Ontario Temperance Act was repealed in 1926. The following year Queen's Park created the Liquor Control Board of Ontario, whose mandate was to allow the sale of liquor to Ontarians, but to do so in a restrained and careful manner that respected the sentiments of temperance advocates. By the end of the decade only Prince Edward Island remained dry.[6]

With the U.S. dry and Canada wet, the scene was set for the massive smuggling of Canadian booze into the United States. If there was ever a truly porous border in the physical sense, it was in the 1920s and early 1930s, when smugglers found a myriad of ways to move their contraband. All along the border, there were routes south. Favourites were by sea from the east coast of Canada to the New England states, by boat across the Great Lakes, from Windsor to Detroit, and by bridge from Niagara Falls, Ontario, to New York State. The most heavily travelled route was across a stretch of the St. Lawrence River from Cornwall, Ontario, to Rock Island, Quebec, two hundred kilometres to the east. Along this part of the border were dozens of small, unguarded roads leading to New York State and Vermont.[7] In 1924 alone, about five million gallons (nineteen million litres) of liquor was smuggled into the United States, principally from Canada, Havana, Nassau and the tiny French islands of St. Pierre and Miquelon. That year, in their effort to thwart the trade, U.S. officials seized 753 American vessels, mostly motor launches, and 39 foreign ships.[8]

The Canadian government did not seem much concerned about the smuggling. Sounding rather philosophical about it in 1929, when he addressed the issue in the House of Commons, Revenue Minister W.D. Euler said: "It is impossible to have wet and dry countries adjacent to each other without a flow from the wet to the dry." In fact, however, the rum-runners directly victimized Canada as well. The federal government collected a $9-per-gallon excise tax on liquor sold in Canada, but the tax was not collected on liquor that was exported. Smugglers had the option, if they chose not to try to get their contraband into the U.S., to land it instead in Canada, thereby avoiding the tax and the $10-a-gallon additional customs duty.[9]

At times, smuggling could be a highly dangerous affair. In 1929, two U.S. Coast Guard vessels sank a Nova Scotia schooner, the *I'm Alone*, provoking a furor in Canada. The schooner had been built in Lunenburg, Nova Scotia, five years earlier and had earned its owners about $3 million during its darkly glorious career.

Big business, organized crime and corrupt officials on both sides of the border played their parts in making sure the booze flowed south to the speakeasies, where thirsty Americans went for a drink during the years of Prohibition. A major beneficiary of the American demand for liquor was the Bronfman family, who began in Saskatchewan the accumulation of what was to be their stupendous fortune in the booze business. The Bronfman brothers, Harry and Sam, from an immigrant Russian Jewish family that settled in Saskatchewan in the 1890s, got their start through a mail-order liquor business during World War I. With the onset of Prohibition in the United States, the Bronfmans saw their great opportunity, and they moved with alacrity into whisky manufacturing, setting up the Yorkton Distributing Company. Producing whisky in Yorkton, Saskatchewan, they set out on a course that would lead ultimately to the creation of the Seagrams liquor empire. The Yorkton operation was highly profitable from the start. With sales from the plant of between 8,000 and 10,000 cases a month—two gallons to a case—the Bronfmans managed a profit of $39.50 a case. This worked out to between $316,000 and $395,000 a month, a profit reduced only a little by office and sales expenses. From the plant, the booze was purchased by the rum-runners who shipped it to the United States.[10]

Taking advantage of corrupt customs officials on both sides of the border, the rum-runners drove north into Canada from the U.S. in high-powered touring cars that featured concealed compartments. On their journeys south, these cars carried shipments of liquor. In an article in the historical periodical *The Beaver,* Lita-Rose Betcherman commented that "the customs station at Rouses Point, New York, was so understaffed and corrupt that smugglers drove brazenly and openly past it, giving the highway the name of Rum Row."[11]

By 1924, the smuggling generated by Prohibition had become a highly profitable two-way flow. For their northward journeys, rum-runners from the United States filled their empty cars with high-value consumer items—silks, jewellery, radios, cigarettes, drugs and clothing. In those days of high tariffs, the contraband entered duty-free, thereby robbing the government of millions of dollars. In addition, the smuggled goods turned up in bargain retail outlets in Montreal and Toronto, where they sold for prices that undercut Canadian manufacturers, who complained bitterly to the authorities.[12]

The combustible ingredients were all in place for what blew up as the customs scandal of 1926. At the centre of the scandal was Jacques Bureau, the customs minister in the Liberal government of William Lyon Mackenzie King. Bureau, an alcoholic who was being supplied with illicit booze by a Montreal customs officer, presided over a department that was rife with corruption. The chief preventive officer of Canada Customs in Montreal was one J.A.E. Bisaillon, who, while a regular customs official, had trafficked in liquor and automobiles that had been seized by customs for non-payment of taxes.[13]

Bisaillon was a central figure in the so-called Barge Tremblay Affair of November 1924. Liquor from a Belgian ship was transferred to a barge in the St. Lawrence River that was owned and operated by a certain Captain Tremblay. With two New York bootleggers on board, the barge was to unload the booze in Montreal and then to smuggle it across the U.S. border—all this with the connivance of Bisaillon. The plan went awry, however, when police from the Quebec Liquor Commission, who had been tipped off, seized the cargo and arrested everyone on board. Bisaillon then arrived on the scene and took control of the operation in the name of the federal government, allowing the rum-runners to leave and to sail off on a waiting yacht.[14]

Criminal charges were laid as a result of the affair. Tremblay, the barge captain, was charged with smuggling but got off with a fine. Bisaillon, who was charged with conspiracy, was acquitted.

During his trial, Bisaillon admitted that the customs duties he collected were deposited in his own bank account. With a salary of $2,300 a year, he had a bank balance of $65,000.[15] Bisaillon took full advantage of his position as a customs officer to line his own pockets. When he confiscated illicit liquor, he would then turn around and sell it himself through a dummy company. A motor launch he seized soon turned up in a lake in the Laurentians where he had a cottage. The resourceful Bisaillon even owned a farm at Beebe, Quebec, that straddled the Canada–U.S. border. Clothing products were shipped through his farm from the U.S. side, thereby entering Canada duty-free.[16]

The exploits of Bisaillon, who was part crook, part government official, were exposed by Walter Duncan, an investigator hired by the Commercial Protective Association, an organization set up by Canadian manufacturers to fight the smugglers. According to these manufacturers, smuggling was driving many domestic concerns out of business, especially those in the textiles sector.[17] Armed with the facts turned up in Duncan's investigation, R.P. Sparks, the chairman of the Commercial Protective Association, took the squalid story to the prime minister. The ever cautious Mackenzie King told Sparks that if the association would make charges against Bisaillon, the government would appoint a Royal Commission to investigate them. Enraged at the idea that the government would not move unless his organization took the first step, Sparks handed over the information to H.H. Stevens, a populist Conservative MP from Vancouver. In a fiery four-hour speech in the House of Commons in February 1926, Stevens put the whole story into the public domain. He claimed that Customs Minister Jacques Bureau had destroyed incriminating documents, and he accused the prime minister and four of his ministers of covering up the scandal.

King, who headed a minority government with the backing of western Progressive MPs, stalled for three days and then agreed to set up a special nine-member parliamentary committee to investigate the administration of the Department of Customs and Excise. Four days later, the committee heard the first of 224 witnesses. When the committee's report was made public in June 1926, it exposed a story of sensational smuggling, of evasion of the law, and of incompetence and direct complicity in illegal activities by the customs department. In its report, the committee concluded that the Department of Customs and Excise had been "slowly degenerating," and that the minister had failed to discharge his duties properly. The report called for the criminal prosecution of Bisaillon and the firing of six Quebec customs officers, as well as the immediate retirement of the deputy minister of the customs department.[18]

The committee report was far from the end of the scandal. Indeed, it was only the beginning of a political earthquake. Prodded by the Conservatives, who sensed that the scandal could propel them into power, the House of Commons unanimously passed a resolution calling for the appointment of a judicial commission with the power to complete the investigation of the Department of Customs and Excise and to prosecute the offenders. As the three-member Royal Commission began its hearings, Conservative H.H. Stevens moved a motion to censure the Liberal government for the customs scandal. Debate raged around the Stevens motion, and when Mackenzie King concluded that his minority government faced certain defeat in the House, he went to Lord Byng, the governor general, and asked for a dissolution of Parliament and an election. In one of the most controversial decisions ever made by a governor general, the British nobleman who had been appointed by the government at Westminster refused King's request.

At this point King resigned and Byng called on Conservative leader Arthur Meighen to form a government. The hapless Meighen went ahead and did so, but the wily King outsmarted him. The Liberals came up with a motion that challenged the makeup of the new government, and it carried in the House by one vote. This time, the governor general granted a dissolution and an election was called. The Conservatives tried to make the customs scandal the main election issue, while King focused on the constitutional crisis that he insisted had been created when Lord Byng refused to grant him a dissolution. King's spin on the crisis prevailed, and the Liberals won enough seats that along with ten Liberal Progressives, they were assured of a majority in the Commons.

With the Liberals safely back in power, the Royal Commission issued a series of interim reports that detailed widespread fraud and smuggling in the liquor business. One report stated that "enormous quantities" of liquor had been shipped from the ports of Vancouver and Victoria with no duty having been paid. In a later report, the commission found that many roads that crossed the border from British Columbia into the United States had no customs stations. One report revealed that a company that was supposedly acquiring alcohol to produce vinegar was actually manufacturing booze to be smuggled out of the country—thereby depriving the federal government of the excise tax on liquor. And in a special section added to one of the reports, the commission outlined the prodigious illegal activities of the Bronfman family empire, including evasion of taxes, smuggling and bribery. The commission recommended the firing of the customs collectors at Windsor, Toronto, Vancouver and Regina in a subsequent report on the grounds that there was a "great deal" of smuggling and undervaluing of goods at these operations. The commission cited a long list of companies in the liquor business that had engaged in various illegal activities to evade the payment of excise taxes and customs duties.[19]

The final report of the Royal Commission was an indictment of the customs department, whose headquarters operations were said to be weak and outdated. The commissioners reported that they had discovered smuggling operations from coast to coast, that there was no efficient border patrol, and that in many places customs posts were "not located in strategic positions to give the officers reasonable opportunity of detecting or preventing smuggling."[20]

Canada's career as a supplier of illegal booze south of the border ended only with the repeal of Prohibition in the United States. As it was proposed on February 20, 1933, and adopted on December 5 of the same year, the U.S. Constitution was once again amended. The Twenty-first Amendment repealed the Eighteenth Amendment. The social experiment in which a great nation attempted to outlaw the consumption of alcohol on its territory was at an end. North of the border, a government had very nearly been brought down and fortunes had been made. The name Bronfman would be renowned in Canadian and global business circles long after Prohibition was no more than grist for the mill of Hollywood gangster films.

Chapter 6 | Modern-day Rum-runners

O f course, smuggling survived the end of Prohibition and is
alive and well in our own time. Seventy years after
Prohibition, smuggling in illegal drugs and cigarettes keep
both Canadian and U.S. authorities busy, but it is the smuggling of
human beings that has occupied the attention of governments on
both sides of the border. And as was the case with booze, the traffic
in human smuggling flows from north to south. The most important routes to the Canada–U.S. border begin in Asia. Indians,
Pakistanis and Chinese who desperately want to enter the United
States pay large sums of money to gangs who undertake to transport them first to Canada and then to the United States. A second
significant stream is made up of people from the Middle East.

In the late 1990s, the public in Canada and the United States,
as well as in Australia and New Zealand, was treated to a rash of
media stories about human smuggling rings based in China's
Fujian province. The smugglers, known as snakeheads, charged
would-be migrants to the First World sums ranging from
US$25,000 to US$40,000 to transport them to their destination

and the promise of a better life. For those travelling in rusty freighters, the journey was indescribably miserable, leading to the deaths of more than a few of the migrants. Often they were hidden deep inside cargo ships, sometimes housed in containers, with a pail for a toilet and a small quantity of food and water to see them through what could be a month-long voyage. For the smugglers, the business of moving desperate people was exceptionally attractive because the costs of the enterprise were low compared with the very high prices being charged.

In the summer of 1999, the issue blew up into a political storm as six hundred illegal migrants from Fujian province arrived on Canada's west coast in four rusting, barely seaworthy ships and sought refugee status when they were picked up by Canadian authorities. A pilot flying a Canadian Forces CP-140 Aurora aircraft on a patrol flight over the Queen Charlotte Islands spotted more than one hundred Chinese nationals climbing out of the cold water of the north Pacific and onto the rocks. The hot summer of concern in Canada about these "boat people" stirred political controversy about the adequacy of the nation's coastal patrols and the wisdom of its refugee system. Opposition politicians used the issue to bash the Chrétien government in Ottawa and to stir up concern about an uncontrolled influx of Asians into Canada. South of the border, U.S. authorities were also anxious about what was happening along the coast of British Columbia, because the final destination of many of the migrants was the United States. The Americans wanted Canada to speed up the processing of refugee claimants and to toughen up the rules to make Canada a less attractive entry point for migrants intent on making it to the U.S. Even in these pre–September 11 days, the U.S. government was worried about Canada as a potential gathering point for terrorists.

The passion of people to migrate from poor countries to wealthy ones is driven by a number of motives. For many the goal is a better way of life and a higher standard of living for themselves and their families. Wars, political repression and religious strife drive others to set out on their perilous journeys. Of great importance as well is the fact that the advanced countries have been bolting their doors to migrants. A century ago, a poor European family had a very good chance of immigrating to Canada or the United States. Today, the educational and monetary requirements for immigrants to countries like Canada are prohibitively high for all but a few. The ancestors of most Americans and Canadians would never have made it to North America if standards comparable to today's had been in place in the nineteenth and early twentieth centuries. That said, in comparison with other developed countries, Canada's immigration policies are relatively open. It remains Ottawa's goal to welcome newcomers equivalent in number to up to 1 percent of the country's population—about 300,000 people—each year.

Estimates of the number of migrants throughout the world today range as high as 200 million. A United Nations estimate has it that 15 million migrants were transported by professional smugglers to the countries where they now reside. Pino Arlacchi, an Italian sociologist who is the UN's director general for Drug Control and Crime Prevention, has stated that the fastest-growing business for organized crime syndicates is human trafficking. Worldwide, human smugglers are estimated to make about US$9.5 billion annually. A smuggling enterprise can charge as much as US$70,000 to transport an illegal migrant to North America.[1]

The RCMP Immigration and Passport (I&P) Program is the criminal enforcement arm of the Department of Citizenship and Immigration Canada. The program is responsible for investigating and combatting migrant smuggling. Officers in the program, who work with domestic and foreign agencies, seek to combat criminal organizations involved in smuggling illegal migrants into Canada, as well as to counter unscrupulous or unlawful activities carried out by professional immigration facilitators. An operation in 1988 resulted in the arrest of smugglers who were moving between 100 and 150 Chinese migrants a month through Canada to the United States. The smugglers were charging each migrant US$47,000, and stood to make a profit of as much as $84 million a year.

For most of the migrants, the pot of gold at the end of the rainbow was the United States, not Canada. While many smuggling rings brought people directly to the U.S. from their country of origin, the route through Canada was favoured by some rings because of their particular connections, or because they believed initial entry into Canada would be easier.

Methods used to transport aliens into Canada and then into the United States vary. Receiving the greatest media attention has been the smuggling of people into the country in cargo containers or in rickety vessels that make the long and dangerous voyage across the Pacific to Canada's west coast. More often, though, the migrants enter Canada by air, having been provided with counterfeit or altered travel documents. At the airports, smugglers meet the illegal migrants, take the documents from them—often to be reused—and get them ready for the next step, the journey across the Canada–U.S. border. Many of the migrants who are unable to come up with the full payment to the criminal syndicate that transported them end up indentured to the traffickers on their arrival in North America. They are forced to work for less than the minimum wage and are charged usurious interest rates on what they owe. Girls and women are often forced into prostitution. The smuggler gangs use violence and intimidation to control their victims, who are unable to speak English and are afraid to run off and inform the police.

In October 2002, a joint Canadian-American police operation cracked a human smuggling operation that was ferrying migrants from Pakistan and India into the United States. Outfitted with forged Canadian, Indian and Pakistani passports, and posing as members of tour groups, the migrants arrived by air in Toronto, Vancouver and Montreal. From the airports, they were taken to safe houses or hotels. The 80 percent of the migrants who wished to continue across the border to the U.S. made the last leg of the trip hidden in tractor-trailers, in car trunks or in boats that ferried them across the St. Clair and Niagara rivers. The favoured crossing points by road were at Windsor, Fort Erie and Niagara Falls. The illegal aliens, who included people of all ages, paid up to US$40,000 each to be shepherded on their hazardous journey. The ring, which operated for twelve years, was thought to have made multi-million-dollar profits over its time in operation.[2]

Those arrested in a co-ordinated operation in Toronto, Hamilton and Windsor were accused of being the smuggling ring's overseers, the brokers who financed the operation and the drivers who escorted the migrants across the border. The suspects were charged with belonging to a criminal organization and with two counts each of conspiracy to violate U.S. immigration laws. This was the first time Canada's organized crime law was used to charge people allegedly involved in human smuggling. The investigation that led to the arrests involved the Royal Canadian Mounted Police, the Ontario Provincial Police, Toronto police, Citizenship and Immigration Canada, and the U.S. Immigration and Naturalization Service.[3]

In recent years, smugglers have also used even more challenging ways to cross from Canada to the United States. The St. Clair River, which runs from north to south from Sarnia, Ontario, to Lake St. Clair, freezes over in the winter. The river forms the boundary between rural Michigan and rural Ontario, and has been used as a route for the stout of heart to cross the border. According to papers filed in court in Detroit, a criminal ring that linked Chinese smugglers with Native people from Walpole Island, Ontario—located at the mouth of the St. Clair River—ran the operation. The migrants, mostly Chinese or Korean, walked across the river at night, accompanied by Native guides. Those buying the service paid between US$20,000 and US$50,000 to get from their home country to New York City.

According to U.S. border patrol officers in Michigan, in 1999 about one hundred people were detected crossing from Canada to the U.S. at this point. Previously, virtually no crossings had been detected in the area. U.S. authorities made the assumption that the majority of those crossing the ice on the St. Clair River were not being caught.[4] Crossing the border at this point is not for the faint of heart, because the river's current causes the ice to creak, groan and crack. Migrants, led across by guides who tapped a steel pole on the ice, were described as terrified during the crossing by U.S. authorities who apprehended them.

The Indian reserve on Walpole Island is not the only one close to the border that has been used as a launch pad for human smuggling. At the Akwesasne Reserve near Cornwall, Ontario, there has been a human smuggling operation that at times has ferried as many as two hundred illegal migrants a week across the St. Lawrence River to New York State. From China and Pakistan, these migrants have often endured a long illegal voyage across the Pacific followed by the journey across Canada. Some of these migrants have prepaid a smuggling ring for the whole of their odyssey. Others show up at Akwesasne on their own and hand over up to US$4,000 for the last leg of the journey.

From Akwesasne, the migrants are whisked across the river at night in a powerboat driven by a masked Mohawk runner. The deal is that on the other side they will be met by a driver, whose cut is US$250. The driver is supposed to take them to their destination, possibly a safe house in New York State. In many cases, however, the migrants are dropped off on the American shore and no driver is there to meet them. Meanwhile, their boat runner has sped off back to Akwesasne. The hapless newcomers end up on the streets of the reserve hoping to find a taxi or rent a limousine.

Wandering about, sometimes with a suitcase in hand, the migrants look completely out of place and are often picked up by Mohawk Tribal Police.

Sometimes illegal migrants attempting to enter the U.S. do so without the aid of a smuggling ring. The consequences can be deadly. On New Year's Day, 2001, U.S. officials revoked the business visa of Andrew Mazanembi, a thirty-six-year-old Zimbabwean who had been working in the United States for the previous eighteen months. Two days later Mr. Mazanembi, who had been visiting Canada, tried to cross from Fort Erie, Ontario, to Buffalo, N.Y., by hiding in the service hatch at the back of a Greyhound bus. After the bus driver drove his vehicle across the Niagara River and stopped at U.S. Customs, he tried to park the bus while his passengers were talking to customs officers, but something appeared to be wrong with the transmission. The bus driver got out and checked the rear of his vehicle, where he found a shoe and, on closer inspection, a pair of legs under the rear bumper. The bus was towed to a municipal garage. It took several hours to remove the mangled body of Mr. Mazanembi from the vehicle's undercarriage.

In some cases, the goal of human smuggling operations is to get migrants into Canada so that they can claim political asylum. A pre-sentence hearing at a court near Heathrow Airport in London, England, in September 2002 shed light on how such a smuggling operation works. Having already pleaded guilty, Anthony Krieger, a thirty-eight-year-old security supervisor at Initial Aviation Security, explained his role in a human smuggling scheme. Krieger's role, which he played along with two other Heathrow guards, was to allow migrants holding bogus or stolen passports to board Air Canada flights to Montreal, Calgary, Vancouver and other Canadian destinations. While most of the illegal migrants were from India, the ring also handled people from Algeria, Romania, Rwanda, Lebanon, Iraq, Sri Lanka,

Pakistan and Afghanistan. The way the system worked was that Krieger would receive a call on his cellphone up to a week ahead of departure giving him a description of a person he was to enable to board a specific Air Canada flight.

During the check-in period for the flight, someone with a valid ticket, a valid passport under the same name and luggage would check in at the Air Canada counter at Heathrow. This person would be issued a boarding pass, which he or she would then hand over to the migrant. Armed with the boarding pass, the migrant would head for the security checkpoint and from there to the flight gate. Krieger or someone else involved in the scheme would be at the gate to check the migrant's papers—usually a stolen or badly faked passport without the proper visa. The migrant would be allowed to board the aircraft. While in the air, the migrant destroyed the passport and any other tags or documents indicating that he or she had been on an Air Canada flight. Upon landing in Canada, and without documents, the migrant would arrive at customs in a general line that included passengers from a number of flights. Having reached the officer at the desk, he or she would claim political asylum.

After the authorities broke this operation, the number of passengers arriving in Canada from Heathrow without documents dropped sharply. During the ten months prior to the bust, 110 passengers arrived from the British airport with no papers.[5]

In October 2002, Citizenship and Immigration Canada launched Project Identity, a pilot project at Toronto's Pearson International Airport to detain arrivals, mostly refugee claimants, whose identities could not be ascertained. The goal of the project was to detain migrants without valid documents, who might have destroyed or hidden papers such as passports and other forms of identity. A key feature of the program was that it allowed a fair degree of discretion to immigration officials to determine if a migrant was behaving evasively or unco-operatively. The operating procedures issued to officers advised that "failure to provide information or lack of co-operation should be carefully recorded in the file as future grounds for continued detention." A month after the program went into effect, thirteen people were being held at the immigration centre near Pearson Airport, known as the Celebrity Inn. Those being held did not include obvious security threats or criminal cases, who were sent instead to the Metro Toronto West Detention Centre. The program was also not meant to include children or the elderly.[6]

A spokesperson for Citizenship and Immigration said the purpose of the project was to "find out who these people actually are." Réjean Cantlon said the project could "be used as a strategic deterrent" to discourage those whose goal was to enter the country illegally. Others took a darker view of what was afoot in Ottawa's new program. "The point of it is that they are very much interested in a new enforcement climate, they are very much interested in showing off to Big Brother in the United States how tough they are," said Toronto immigration lawyer Marshall Drukarsh. Janet Dench, executive director of the Montreal-based Canadian Council for Refugees, shared this view. "People are worried about harmonization with U.S. policy. The U.S. does a lot more detaining people on the basis of ID," she said. "This is more than a bit worrisome. It is deeply disturbing, particularly for its impact among refugees. Those detained are potentially people who have been tortured and for whom being put into detention retraumatizes them and reminds them of the experiences that they had fled."[7]

While the number of migrants smuggled into Canada by criminal gangs cannot be known exactly, broad estimates exist. Official government figures estimate that at least 8,000 people entered Canada illegally in 1998 as a consequence of criminal operations worth between US$120 million and US$400 million.[8] To put the human smuggling issue into perspective, in 1999, of the 1.6 million people caught crossing illegally into the United States, all but 42,000 were intercepted on the Mexican border.[9] What is happening on America's southern border is a migration of historic dimensions. By contrast, on America's northern border, there is something very different: a significant law enforcement problem.

In the minds of U.S. authorities, the human smuggling issue on the northern border is linked to the terrorism question. If people can be successfully smuggled across the border to gain a better life for themselves in the United States, they can also be smuggled into the U.S. to carry out acts of terror, the reasoning goes. Added to the issues of human smuggling and terrorism, a third issue now embroils the Canadian-American border regime—that of drug smuggling.

———

Particularly since the terror attacks on September 11, there has been a dramatic increase in the number of drug seizures along the Canada–U.S. border. And while Canadian official attitudes toward narcotics and drug addicts have become more tolerant, with the Republicans in office in the United States, American policy remains implacably hard-line on drugs. For some, what is happening along the border may be reminiscent of what took place during the Prohibition years, with Canadians supplying marijuana to Americans the way they once supplied booze to their thirsty southern neighbours.

What has American authorities most concerned is the rising traffic across the border of marijuana that goes by the name B.C. Bud, grown in hydroponic houses in British Columbia. Alarming to the Americans is that B.C. Bud is a particularly potent drug, with a THC content as high as 25 percent, compared with the typical 2 percent for the pot of the 1970s. THC—tetrahydrocannabinol—is the active ingredient in marijuana.

The amount of B.C. Bud seized by American border authorities has been increasing dramatically over the last several years—

from 2,648 kilograms in 2000, to 3,400 kilograms in 2001, to a rate expected to have hit 7,300 kilograms by the end of 2002. To put these numbers in perspective, along the border with Mexico in 1998, U.S. authorities seized 450,000 kilograms of illegal drugs.[10] As is the case with illegal border crossings, the problem faced by the United States on its southern frontier is enormously greater than that on the northern border.

Increasingly, criminal gangs have been involved in the Canada–U.S. cross-border marijuana trade. B.C. Bud turns up right across the continent. For instance, U.S. Customs in Buffalo, New York, has been seizing an increasing amount of it. Part of the rise in drug busts at the border can be attributed to heightened U.S. Customs security since the September 11 terror attacks.[11]

What especially alarms U.S. authorities are signals that Canadian and U.S. official attitudes toward drugs, particularly marijuana, are diverging. In the spring of 2002, a controversial report from the Senate of Canada concluded that the criminalization of marijuana has been a monumental failure and proposed that Canada move toward decriminalization. "Canada is a sovereign country," said Robert Maginnis, an adviser to U.S. government drug czar John Walters, "but there are consequences when neighbours cannot cooperate on serious issues and this is a very serious issue. It appears as if it's a trend going in the wrong direction and it is incumbent on the U.S. administration and the U.S. Congress to communicate that this is a key concern."[12]

The ultimate nightmare for U.S. authorities is that Canada could become a North American version of the Netherlands, where soft drugs can be consumed free from the threat of criminal prosecution. American authorities have made it clear that they intend to lobby Ottawa vigorously on the issue, holding over the heads of Canadians, if necessary, the stick of tougher border controls, always a threat to Canadian exports.

In addition to high-grade marijuana, there has been traffic through Canada to the United States of high-purity heroin, originating in South Asia and shipped across the border by ethnic Chinese criminal gangs.

The traffic in illegal drugs across the Canada–U.S. border is by no means a one-way flow. From south of the border, the principal drugs being smuggled into Canada are cocaine, liquid hashish and marijuana. The cocaine that is shipped into Canada is often controlled by Italian or Colombian criminal syndicates, as well as by outlaw motorcycle gangs. Marijuana grown in the U.S. Southwest or smuggled across the southern U.S. border is also frequently smuggled into Canada. Smugglers use many methods to get their contraband to its destination. For instance, in 1997, Canada Customs in Montreal found 350 kilograms of cocaine hidden within a shipment of coffee. The contraband had originated in Brazil, and after being shipped to the east coast of the United States in a freighter, it had been transported to Canada in a tractor-trailer.

While drug smuggling has become a much hotter border issue in recent years, cigarette smuggling also continues to concern Canadian authorities. The threat Canada has faced for more than a decade is of Canadian cigarettes being exported to the United States and then smuggled back into Canada.

In the 1980s, in an effort to drive down the smoking rate in Canada, particularly among teenagers, Canadian lawmakers adopted a strategy of dramatically increasing cigarette taxes. By 1991, as a consequence of how tax increases pushed up the price of a package of cigarettes, per capita consumption had declined by 40 percent compared with 1982. In the case of teenagers (aged fifteen to nineteen), the drop in per capita consumption was an even more dramatic 60 percent. Higher prices, it turned out, really did work as a way to drive down cigarette consumption.

To defend its domestic market position, the tobacco industry tried to lobby against the rapid tax increases and to win public sympathy for Canadian tobacco farmers. These stratagems failed, however, so the tobacco companies came up with a new one: they warned Ottawa that because Canadian tobacco prices were so much higher than those south of the border, the country was courting a serious risk of large-scale smuggling of U.S. cigarettes into Canada. That threat too also proved hollow, however, because Canadians and Americans smoke different blends of cigarettes. Despite the price differential, the demand for U.S. cigarettes did not increase appreciably in Canada.

The matter did not end there. Powerful actors within the tobacco industry were not willing to watch their Canadian market erode. They came up with a direct strategy to ensure that Canada would indeed have a smuggling problem. In the early 1990s, the Canadian subsidiaries of multinational tobacco companies started exporting huge quantities of Canadian cigarettes to the United States. But just as Canadians had little taste for American cigarettes, Americans had no desire for the Canadian product. The only legitimate market for Canadian cigarettes south of the border was snowbirds and other Canadian tourists on vacation in Florida and other southern climes during the winter months. Despite that, by 1993, exports to the United States had soared to about 20 billion cigarettes a year, or forty times the level needed to meet the demand of Canadian winter sojourners.

The excess export of cigarettes to the United States did not generate a market for the product among Americans. Instead, the cigarettes found their way into the U.S. black market. From there they were smuggled back into Canada. The smuggling threat that the tobacco companies had warned about had now come into being.

Here's how it happened.

In the early 1990s, as exports of Canadian cigarettes to the U.S. increased, so too did the smuggling of these cigarettes back into Canada. In February 1992, in an effort to stifle the smuggling, the federal government imposed an export tax of $8 per carton on cigarettes. As a consequence of intensive lobbying by the tobacco industry, though, the export tax was repealed two months later, in April 1992. The door was now wide open for smugglers to thrive.

As early as January 1992, Leslie Thompson, an executive with RJR Macdonald and its parent company, R.J. Reynolds, began the sale of large shipments of Canadian cigarettes to a smuggling ring in upstate New York. Later that year, R.J. Reynolds created a new subsidiary, Northern Brands International, whose publicly stated rationale was to promote the sale of Export "A" cigarettes—a Canadian brand—in the United States. Thompson, later imprisoned for his role in the smuggling, said in an interview with *60 Minutes II* that R.J. Reynolds established Northern Brands for the purpose of smuggling cigarettes into Canada, and that the parent company was fully aware of its subsidiary's role in the smuggling operation. Thompson stated that Northern Brands shipped billions of cigarettes per year to the outskirts of the New York State part of the Akwesasne reserve, directly across the St. Lawrence River from the Ontario part.

Because the Canadian cigarettes were exported, they were exempt from a federal tax that had pushed up the average price of a pack of cigarettes from $2.64 in 1984 to $5.65 in 1993. Tony Laughing, a Mohawk who was accused of smuggling cigarettes through Akwesasne, explained in a media interview that he and fellow Mohawks would pay $8 for a carton of cigarettes on the New York side of the reservation and sell it for $18 on the Canadian side. Shipped out to Canadian cities, the cigarettes were sold for $22 a carton, a huge bargain next to the $40 to $60 a carton for legally bought Canadian cigarettes.[13]

During the period of his active smuggling, Laughing said, he had met Leslie Thompson at Akwesasne. "They knew exactly what business we were in," Laughing said of the R.J. Reynolds management. "They knew their product was going to my warehouse and to other Indians who were taking it across the river [into Canada]." Along with Larry Miller, another accused smuggler, Laughing was flown on an all-expenses-paid visit to Winston-Salem, North Carolina, where the headquarters of R.J. Reynolds Tobacco is located. There, he said, they received the royal treatment—a tour of company facilities and lots of goodies to take back home with them.[14]

Between 1990 and 1993, the volume of cigarettes being exported to the U.S. increased elevenfold. According to a Canadian government estimate, the smugglers were making a profit of half a million dollars per truckload on the contraband. In 1993, just over two million Canadians purchased approximately 90 to 100 million cartons of smuggled cigarettes, whose legal retail value would have been about $4.5 billion. In Quebec, where the problem was most severe, up to 60 percent of the cigarette market had been taken over by the smugglers. In other regions of Canada, contraband accounted for between 15 and 40 percent of the market.[15]

In January 1994 in Quebec, the media ran a series of stories about an apparently spontaneous tax revolt by convenience store operators, who openly sold smuggled cigarettes in order to exert leverage in support of a tax reduction. In Montreal, the daily newspaper *La Presse* soon unearthed close ties between the organizers of the tax revolt and an association of convenience store owners that was partially funded by the tobacco industry.

On February 8, 1994, the Chrétien government knuckled under to the pressures from the smuggling of Canadian cigarettes into Canada. Ottawa announced that it was rolling back the tax on cigarettes, something that was matched by Quebec and soon followed by the governments of Ontario, New Brunswick, Nova Scotia and Prince Edward Island. In Quebec the price of a carton of cigarettes plunged from $47 to $23 as a consequence of the tax cut. Having caved in to the smuggling generated by the tobacco industry, the federal government reimposed the 1992 tax on cigarette exports. Under the circumstances, it was like closing the barn door after the horse had fled. The tobacco companies had engineered the tax rollback they wanted. From their point of view it didn't matter all that much if some of those involved in the smuggling were hung out to dry.

In November 1998, following a long investigation and a series of plea-bargain deals with the prosecution by his accomplices, Larry Miller, the head of a smuggling network in New York State, pleaded guilty to criminal charges and undertook to testify against his suppliers in the tobacco companies. A month later, Northern Brands International, the subsidiary of R.J. Reynolds, pleaded guilty to evading U.S. taxes and agreed to a payment of US$15 million as one of the conditions of its plea bargain. In March 1999, Leslie Thompson, the former senior executive with R.J. Reynolds and Northern Brands International, pleaded guilty to a smuggling conspiracy in the U.S. district court in Syracuse, New York. It was estimated that the smuggling operation in which he was involved had defrauded the Canadian government of more than US$650 million.

In December 1999, the government of Canada filed a suit in a U.S. court against R.J. Reynolds Tobacco and the Canadian Tobacco Manufacturers Council, seeking $1 billion in damages. Ottawa was accusing them of undertaking a vast smuggling scheme in the wake of Canada's increase in its cigarette taxes. In June 2000, New York judge Thomas McAvoy ruled that the Canadian government was using its lawsuit as a way to collect taxes owing to it. On the grounds that U.S. courts cannot be used to collect the taxes of another country, he struck down the Canadian suit. The Canadian government appealed the judge's ruling, but the appeals court upheld the ruling by a 2–1 vote. When Ottawa appealed yet again, this time to the Supreme Court of the United States, the appeal was again turned down, in November 2002. The U.S. high court took the same view of the matter as the U.S. Justice Department, which had argued that a foreign government cannot bring a civil racketeering claim if its remedy would involve the collection of lost tax revenue.[16]

By the end of the 1990s, despite the spotlight that had been shone on them for their role in the great smuggling explosion in 1993–94, the tobacco companies had won most of what they wanted. The combined effect of the tax rollback, the 1998 settlement in the United States under which tobacco companies agreed to pay out US$206 billion over twenty-five years to settle claims from forty-six U.S. states, and the falling value of the Canadian dollar was that the real price of a pack of cigarettes in Ontario and Quebec was lower than in any U.S. state.[17]

In the five-year period after the tax rollback of 1994, the profits of the tobacco industry in Canada soared by $1.3 billion, while the tax revenues collected on cigarettes by both levels of government plunged by almost $5 billion. As a result of the tax rollback, the long-term downward trend in the smoking rate in Canada was halted, and there was a major increase in youth smoking in Central Canada. Health Canada reported that in 1999 just over forty-five thousand Canadians died as a consequence of the use of tobacco—21 percent of all the deaths in Canada.[18]

For the most part, the myth perpetrated by the tobacco industry—that the smuggling crisis of 1992–94 was generated by a spontaneous tax revolt and by small time smugglers around the Akwesasne reserve—remains the generally accepted view.[19] The winner in the great Canadian tobacco struggle of the 1990s: Big Tobacco, hands down.

––––––

The final instance of what I have chosen to call modern-day rum-running does not involve contraband, but it does involve "border crossings" to subtly subvert public policy in each country. It arises out of the stresses being felt on both sides of the border in the health care sector. In Canada, universal health care has been under assault from provincial governments sympathetic to the cause of private health care, and from a federal government that has made drastic cuts to health care funding in its drive to achieve a balanced budget and debt reduction. South of the border, citizens have fought battles against the limited coverage provided by Health Management Organizations (HMOs) and against the exorbitant price of pharmaceutical products.

In recent years, crises in the health care systems in Canada and the U.S. have led to border crossings in both directions. Canadians go south in search of health care when lineups for treatment at home are too lengthy. Americans come north and use Canadian health cards to fraudulently acquire free health care. Other Americans, usually senior citizens, head north to acquire much cheaper prescription drugs than they can find on their own side of the border.

The Canadian southward migration is of two kinds. First there are individuals who cross the border to bypass lengthy queues at home for specific types of treatment and for access to expensive tools, such as MRIs, that are in short supply in Canada. Television stations in Buffalo, New York, carry advertisements that entice Canadians from Southern Ontario to avail themselves of these services. The second kind of migration involves the sending of Canadians south by provincial health care authorities, at taxpayers' expense, for treatment in U.S. facilities when there is no care available at home. For instance, in the winter of 2002, a number of Ontario women with high-risk pregnancies were being sent to New York State to give birth at the Children's Hospital of Buffalo.[20] The reason for the transfers was that there were no available beds for the expectant moms in Ontario hospitals. An outbreak of chicken pox at one Toronto hospital and an outbreak of the Norwalk virus at another exacerbated the shortage of beds. One interesting consequence of sending Canadian women to the U.S. to give birth is that their "border babies" have a right to U.S. citizenship.

Since 1999, in addition to women with high-risk pregnancies, cancer patients and burn victims have been sent from Ontario to U.S. health care facilities at taxpayers' expense. In 2001, half a dozen burn patients were dispatched to U.S. hospitals by Ontario health authorities. They included Lisa Armstrong, a woman from the small Georgian Bay town of Kincardine, who had suffered second- and third-degree burns to 60 percent of her body. When no burn-unit bed was available for her, she was sent to a facility in Rochester, New York, where she died of her injuries. Between 1999 and 2001, hundreds of Ontario cancer patients, mostly suffering from breast or prostate cancer, were sent for treatment to Buffalo, Cleveland and Detroit as a consequence of unacceptably long waits for radiation treatment in Ontario.[21]

As Canadians go south to seek health care in cases where government cutbacks have opened gaps, Americans head north. Some are dwellers of border towns who have learned of the benefits of free Canadian health care a stone's throw away. Thousands of health cards have been borrowed and stolen to make this illicit traffic possible.

In addition to the illegal use of Canadian health cards by people living south of the border, there is a large-scale northward migration of Americans seeking cheaper pharmaceutical drugs in Canada. For years, American seniors, many of them living on fixed incomes, have had to cope with paying the highest prices in the world for prescription drugs. Comparisons with prices paid in Canada, Mexico and Europe are shocking. For instance, in 2001, Americans could purchase one hundred capsules of Celebrex, used to treat arthritis, at a discounted price of US$128.35. To try to improve on this outrageously high price, the United Health

Alliance, a non-profit, physician-run health system in southwestern Vermont, established MedicineAssist. Through this program, U.S. doctors fax prescription orders to Canadian pharmaceutical outlets, charging the orders to the patients' credit card numbers. This way, their patients were able to purchase one hundred Celebrex capsules for US$45.30.[22] Other comparisons (all prices in U.S. dollars): for Prozac, the price in the U.S. was $254.29, in Canada, it was $123.92; for Lipitor, the price was $156.50 for ninety tablets while in Canada it was $114.04; one hundred tablets of Zocor was $346.00 south of the border, $171.81 north. What made the prices so much lower in Canada was the system of price caps placed on prescription drugs by the Canadian government.

Once, on a car ferry from Port Angeles, Washington, to Victoria, British Columbia, I happened upon a group of revellers who had cheap Canadian pharmaceuticals on their minds. Port Angeles is located on the mountainous northern anvil of Washington State that juts out into the Pacific due south of Vancouver Island. Sitting on the passenger deck as the ferry surged out of the harbour, I found myself in the company of a boisterous group of fifty-somethings, the men attired in cowboy boots and country-style shirts, the women in loose-fitting dresses. About thirty of them were on an outing of some sort. The woman sitting next to me told me that they were a group of square dancers. Coming from small towns and rural areas of Washington State, they went over to Victoria a couple of times a year for a weekend, where they met up with a group of square dancers from Vancouver Island. On other occasions, the Vancouver Island dance enthusiasts would take the ferry to Washington State for more bouts of recreational and competitive square dancing. Due to the low value of the Canadian dollar, when the Americans visited Victoria, they stayed in hotels and availed themselves of such amenities as high tea at the Empress Hotel. On their return visits, though, the Canadians were billeted in the houses of the U.S. square dancers.

I learned from my ebullient new acquaintance that she and her friends travelled to Victoria for more than square dancing. About twice a year, she and a friend would drive to Port Angeles, leave her car there and take the ferry to Victoria as pedestrian passengers. The ferry lands in Victoria right on the edge of the downtown. It was an easy walk from the dock to the office of her Canadian dentist. On these dental pilgrimages, it cost her less than US$100 for care that would cost US$150 in Washington State. She also bought her prescription drugs through a 1–800 number in Toronto.

Americans who make the trip to Victoria can purchase prescription drugs by bringing with them a prescription from a doctor in Washington State. They take it to a doctor in Victoria offering this service, who charges US$45 to write a prescription that can be filled on the Canadian side. As a result, they buy their drugs for a much lower price than they could at home. As long as prescribed drugs are for personal use only, U.S. Customs rarely queries those who import them.

A few minutes later, the woman I had been talking with was telling her friends in the square dance contingent that they could buy over-the-counter drugs, for bargain-basement prices, at the Drug Mart in Victoria.

Part of the U.S. migration to Canada has been undertaken in very public episodes to exert pressure on U.S. lawmakers in favour of cheaper prescription drugs. Busloads of American seniors have crossed the border in recent years in search of cheaper drugs. American activists, who want to publicize the plight of seniors who cannot afford the medications they require, have organized some of these outings. In the summer of 2000, with the U.S. presidential and congressional election campaigns in full swing, citizen groups—Public Citizen, New York Statewide Senior Action Council and Citizen Action of New York—sponsored bus trips for seniors from Albany, Binghamton and Rochester in New York

State to Montreal to purchase prescription drugs. In a press release, the sponsoring groups said the bus riders were risking "their short-term health by embarking on grueling, two-day round trip bus rides . . . to Montreal, Canada to buy the medicines they need to survive at prices up to fifty percent less than in the United States."

One Binghamton resident named Marilyn Gourley was quoted as saying: "I spent most of my adult life as a nurse taking care of people, but now that I'm disabled, the drug companies are price gouging me out of more than half my monthly income for the medicines I need to survive." The sponsors sent copies of their press release to Hillary Rodham Clinton and Rick Lazio, the Democratic and Republican Senate candidates in New York, inviting them to board the bus for one of the trips, and urging them to take up the cause of government-capped prescription drug prices.

Mostly, the migration of Americans in search of pharmaceuticals from Canada is less visible. A large number of Canadian pharmacies catering to the American market now advertise their services on the Internet, inviting Americans to make the trip to their premises in person or, in other cases, to send orders for drugs via the Internet. Many of the pharmacies emphasize the ease of travelling to their stores: "This chain of ten drugstores can be found in south eastern Ontario, a fairly easy drive from upper New York State and New England." "Located in Niagara Falls, very close to the border . . ." "This drugstore in Windsor, Ontario has four locations. They do have an 800 number listed and state they can fill U.S. prescriptions."

Feelbest.com, which advertises itself as "Canada's largest on-line pharmacy" provides on-line advice to non-residents of Canada (read Americans) who wish to purchase prescription and non-prescription drugs. If you require a prescription medication, its Web site states, "the law requires that you must provide us with a prescription written by a licensed Canadian Doctor." To get this prescription, the advice continues, an American may have to visit a doctor in Canada, which usually means making an appointment in advance. Feelbest.com explains how to contact the Canadian Medical Association, and suggests that U.S. residents may well be able to find a Canadian doctor working in their local area, through a local medical association or university medical centre. Finally, there is advice for dealing with U.S. Customs on the way home: keep prescription drugs in the original container, bring along the prescription, carry quantities of a drug that are for personal use only and always be sure to declare prescription drugs to U.S. Customs.

While Feelbest.com suggests that Americans make an appointment with a Canadian doctor, other drugstores advertise that they can now fill prescriptions written by U.S. physicians. A Canadian doctor who then writes a prescription valid in Canada reviews these prescriptions.

The fastest-growing way for Americans to purchase pharmaceuticals in Canada is over the Internet, through a Canadian or U.S.-based company. Medoutletcanada.com, a Manitoba-based operation, advertises itself as a "licensed full service pharmacy" that supplies pharmaceuticals, both prescription and over-the-counter, to residents of Canada and the United States. An American customer can send a prescription from a U.S. doctor that will be reviewed, along with the person's medical history, by a Canadian physician. Medoutletcanada.com charges a flat-rate shipping fee of US$12 for a parcel containing one or more prescription orders as well as any over-the-counter items. Customers are invited to transfer their prescriptions to be refilled by the on-line pharmacy. A lengthy list of prescription drugs and their "discount prices" can be scanned on the Web site.

A U.S. alternative is called We Care Medical Mall. Based in Walnut City, California, this outfit is not a pharmacy. It serves as an on-line middleman between U.S. residents seeking low-cost prescription drugs and licensed Canadian pharmacies. Americans are invited to enrol in the program for either $15 a year per person, with shipping charges to be added, or $35 a year per person, with no shipping charges. A family can enrol for $60 a year. We Care Medical Mall provides a price list on-line. To fend off Canadian on-line competitors, the company warns potential customers:

> Canada is a socialized medicine nation which means the government sets the prices. Therefore, there is little difference in price from one Canadian pharmacy to the next. U.S. customers should be very suspicious of any Canadian pharmacy that advertises lower prices. As more U.S. customers buy from Canadian pharmacies, consumers are finding that some pharmacies are less than reputable. They may short the medications, or more commonly, a Canadian pharmacy will quote one price, and then add multiple charges without informing the U.S. consumer. Then, because the pharmacy is physically located outside the U.S., there is little recourse available to Americans.

Once enrolled, Americans are invited to send in their doctors' prescriptions and We Care Medical Mall takes it from there.

While the sale of prescription drugs in the United States from Canadian outlets is not contraband, it is the subject of growing controversy. The giant pharmaceutical companies stand to lose very sizable revenues if Americans are allowed to do an end run around U.S. pharmacies by directing their purchases to Canada. Lobbyists for the pharmaceutical companies have made the threat that they could cut off shipments of drugs to Canada if the cross-border trade is not stopped.

Chapter 7 | Canadians and Americans Up against the Red River

A s the existence of smuggling suggests, the countries north
    and south of the border differ greatly in many of their
    federal policies. But if I looked at life on a smaller, more
personal scale, would I see the differences? Would communities
react differently, for example, in the face of a natural disaster?
Would shared calamity make the border meaningless? I wondered
how Canadians and Americans, living along the Red River, which
flows north from the U.S. into Canada, faced the great flood of
1997. The catastrophe afflicted people on both sides of the border. Did this flood, and the many that came before, pull people on
the two sides of the border closer together? Or did they face these
catastrophes in different ways?

The little border town of Emerson, Manitoba, was a surreal
place to be in April 1997. Behind the permanent dike that had
been doubled in height with the addition of a temporary structure
of plywood and sandbags, Emerson was a dry island in the vast sea
of the Red River, which had burst its banks. All the inhabitants,
with the exception of a few who had been left behind to fight the

flood, had been evacuated. The electric power still worked, so that at night the island of Emerson was ablaze in a strange white light. Deer and hares and other smaller animals had gravitated to the town to escape the ice-cold waters of the raging river. They stood, frightened sentinels, in the white light of the ghost town.

A remarkable crew made up of town employees, a detachment of troops from the Canadian Forces and local Mounties kept the town of Emerson itself dry and secure. As the river rose to a critical level in late April, with no firm prediction about how high it would get, the struggle to maintain the wall around the town was in deadly earnest. Co-ordinated out of the Emerson Town Hall, the beleaguered warriors filled sandbags and directed them to potential weak points on the perimeter. So close is Emerson to the U.S. border that a portion of the dike actually crossed into the small neighbouring community of Noyes, Minnesota, protecting a U.S. Customs office and several nearby homes on U.S. soil. As residents noted at the time, what they were calling the "Red Sea" did not make distinctions between one side of the border and the other.

Twenty-four hours a day, patrols in Emerson made certain there were no breaks in the wall. During the ordeal, crew members standing on the dike and looking out of town could see water all the way to the horizon. At daily meetings, the team leader made assignments, which were carried out with a high degree of camaraderie. Team members ate together and slept when they could. On a daily basis, military helicopters flew in and out, bringing in supplies and when necessary taking out exhausted soldiers and importing fresh ones. As the flood waters receded in May, the day came when residents were allowed back in to see first-hand what had become of their homes.

I drive into Emerson in mid-April, five years after the town's ordeal. The permanent dike looks innocent enough right across the street from the post office, where I meet Cheryl, who is in her thirties. Like everyone else I encounter in the next few days on both sides of the border, she has vivid memories of the great flood of 1997. She and her husband lived on the outskirts of town. In the frantic digging that went on as the flood approached, the foundation of her house was cracked. When she and her husband were evacuated, a gigantic army of mice—she remembers them as "big" mice—invaded the house through the cracked foundation. She describes it as "being like a Hitchcock movie." She talks breezily enough about what happened five years ago, but it is clear that she doesn't think this is any laughing matter. She and her husband moved back into the stricken house for a time, but after a while they decided they couldn't stand it any more. They've moved to a new dwelling and their old house is unoccupied.

The Hitchcock reference Cheryl made would have been even better suited to the experience of another woman I meet in Emerson, who found a dead duck in her house when she returned to it. "The duck had flown all around the house, crapping every-where," she tells me disgustedly. Another woman, who lived on a farm just outside Emerson, tells me that she and her husband were ordered to leave by the authorities. By the time they left, they had succeeded in building a metre-and-a-half-high wall of sandbags around their house with the aid of people who had come from Winnipeg to help out. But her husband sneaked back to their farmhouse in an old army-style truck.

She is not the only person to tell me that family members or friends made their way back during the flood to try to protect their property even after the authorities had ordered them out. On both sides of the border, I encounter considerable resentment about the evacuation orders. People feel they have the skills to deal with floods, and that with pumps and generators they could have lessened the damage to their homes and farms. Next time the Red River goes on a rampage, a number of people tell me, there is no way they will leave their property.

While people in Emerson are generally full of praise for the firefighters, the police and the Canadian Forces, who did yeoman service during the three weeks of the evacuation, they have nothing but sneers for Prime Minister Jean Chrétien's handling of the crisis. A number will never forgive him for calling a general election when Manitoba was suffering the brunt of the flood. One woman I meet in the post office speaks of Chrétien's visit to Winnipeg during the flood. "He was no help," she says. "He held up the work to have his picture taken. Chrétien threw one sandbag onto the pile and left."

An inexorable feature of spring floods on the Red River is that they migrate from south to north down the river, first hitting the cities and towns south of the border before they move on to southern Manitoba and the city of Winnipeg. The people of Emerson had several weeks to think about the flood and get ready for it as it moved relentlessly first to Fargo, North Dakota, then to Grand Forks, and from there to the border.

In the large new Canada Customs post at the border—built since the flood of '97—I meet two tall, muscular customs officers who have recollections of the mayhem. One of them stayed on his farm, while the other was moved to a customs post farther west. The post leading from Manitoba's Highway 75 to the I-29 in North Dakota was shut down for three weeks. As the stolid officers tell me, there was no way the post could be kept open—the highway was under water.

When asked about the purpose of my trip to North Dakota by a U.S. customs official with grey hair, I tell him I am going to Grand Forks to talk to people on the fifth anniversary of the flood of '97. Not bothering to ask me for ID, he comments sardonically, "Why not go to Pembina? They know at least as much about the flood as anyone in Grand Forks."

I follow his advice and drive into the little town of Pembina, two minutes south of the border. The town had been British territory before it was handed over to the U.S. with the adoption of the forty-ninth parallel as the border across the Prairies in 1818. On the east side of Pembina, there is a high earthen dike to protect the town from the Red River. It is the same on the other side of the river in the tiny hamlet of St. Vincent, Minnesota. This April the Red is tame, but the dike is there for protection against future floods.

On the main street of Pembina, I find an old preacher and his young disciple out trying to win converts. I ask them if they were in town for the great flood of '97. In reply, the old man hands me a pocket-sized pamphlet titled "A Preacher of the Old School." In our conversation, Mr. W. Seed and I are at cross-purposes. He is trying to save my soul from a flood of biblical proportions while I am in search of memories of a mere earthly flood. I manage to get Mr. Seed onto my line of inquiry, and he tells me of the long series of floods that have afflicted this community—in 1897, 1950, 1966 and 1979. In 1997, he says, the dike held and the town was saved.

Later, I take a look at Mr. Seed's booklet, which begins with the rather gloomy thought that "many preachers are giving up the old ideas about the fall and total depravity of man." A page later I learn just who this old-time preacher is: "His name is DEATH."[1]

On the outskirts of town, I stop for a burger at the big truck stop that is right beside the exit from the I-29, my last chance for a bite on this side of the state border. The young waitress who serves me tells me that it was the National Guard who evacuated the townspeople of Pembina in April 1997. She recalls that farmers from the surrounding countryside buttressed the town's dike with a new wooden extension and saved the town. The farmers weren't so lucky on their own properties. The flood deluged fields and farmhouses. Many people took their most valued possessions away with them in their pickup trucks. Others moved their furniture and belongings to the top floor of their house.

Despite the cryptic comment of the customs officer about the people of Pembina knowing as much about the flood as those in

Grand Forks, there is no question that the epicentre of the drama of April 1997 on the Red River was Grand Forks. Like other communities on the Red River, Grand Forks has had plenty of experience with flooding. Indeed, there was a flood in 1996. That year, the National Weather Service predicted that the Red River would crest at Grand Forks at 43.5 feet (13.25 metres).[2] This prediction motivated officials in both Grand Forks, North Dakota, and East Grand Forks, Minnesota, on the other side of the river, to mobilize to stave off damage to the two communities. In 1996, volunteers filled nearly 300,000 sandbags and placed them in low-lying, vulnerable areas. Next to the river, temporary clay dikes were constructed. When the river crested on April 21, people on both sides of the river felt good about having staved off serious damage to their communities.

There are a number of reasons why the Red River is dangerously prone to flooding. First is the fact that this is a north-flowing river, which means that spring breakup downstream, at the northern end of the river, tends to occur late. Spring ice in the north can retard the flow of water from the south. The Red is also a meandering river, which flows 875 kilometres to cover the 505-kilometre distance from its source to the point where it empties into Lake Winnipeg. Linked to its circuitous path is that the Red River's slope decreases along its course, from about 0.3 metres per kilometre at its source to about 0.1 metres when it reaches the Canadian border. In addition, it drains a huge basin and is fed by numerous tributaries. While these factors make the river highly susceptible to floods, they do not guarantee them. Many springs pass without one. There have been long stretches, such as the 1920s and 1930s, when the threat of floods was relatively low. During the 1930s, grasshoppers and dust storms were more feared in the Red River Valley than floods.

A severe flood on the Red River occurs only when a number of cumulative factors are in place. Without the presence of even one of these elements, a serious flood is avoided. Add them all together, though, and a flood is a sure thing. First, the autumn before must be unusually wet. This saturates the ground, reducing the amount of water it can absorb during spring runoff. Next, there must be an unusually cold winter, which has the effect of penetrating the ground with deep frost, further lessening the ability of the earth to absorb the spring runoff. A very cold winter also makes for thicker ice, which takes longer to melt in the spring, thus contributing to ice jams that can narrow the course through which the river must flow. On top of this, in years with severe floods, there is usually a heavier than average snowfall during the winter. The *coup de grâce* to this unholy mixture is a cold spring followed by rapid warming.[3]

Ominously, in the leadup to the spring of 1997, all of these contributing conditions were in place. From late autumn to early spring, the Red River Valley was hit with unusually heavy snowfalls. In February and March 1997, the U.S. National Weather Service predicted the Red River would crest at Grand Forks at between 47.5 and 49 feet (14.5 and 15 metres), a level that would be on par with the worst flood of the century, that of 1979.[4] Despite the warning, the success against the rising Red River in the spring of 1996 had lulled the public into a false sense of security.

Phrases like "storm of the century" are thrown around loosely, but there is no doubt that by the end of April 1997 that is exactly what was hitting the city of Grand Forks.

Grand Forks is a pleasant, largely middle-class city, population fifty thousand, whose character is shaped by the campus of the University of North Dakota in its midst. Five years after the flood, I still find its after-effects everywhere I go. On the western bank of the Red River are some of the loveliest homes in the city. Many such houses have been expropriated and torn down since the flood to make way for a huge extension of the dike that runs along the shore of the river. Five years after the flood, much of the

CHILDREN·OF·A·COMMON·MOTHER

The famed Peace Arch Park straddles the border between B.C. and Washington State south of Vancouver. After September 11, it was the scene of frequent border crossing delays.

Port Angeles, Washington, where the ferry from Victoria, B.C., lands. In December 1999, U.S. Customs arrested Ahmed Ressam at the wharf here when an officer found explosives in his car.

The car ferry from Campobello, New Brunswick, to Deer Island, New Brunswick. In the background is the coast of Maine.

A remote corner of southern Alberta on the road to Montana.

St. Nicholas Orthodox Church, built in Juneau, Alaska in 1894.
A symbol of Alaska's Russian legacy.

The border between Alaska and British Columbia at the summit of the White Pass,
one of the two routes taken by the miners of 1898 to the Yukon gold fields.

On Saturday morning, the Finnish Hoito Restaurant in Thunder Bay is a happening place.

Wolfe Island General Store. The island was a key to Britain's defence of Upper Canada against American invasion during the War of 1812.

A retro lover's dream. Motels in Niagara Falls, New York, and Niagara Falls, Ontario.

PHOTO: Sandy Price

*In April 2001, the author is at the Akwesasne Reserve south of Cornwall, Ontario.
En route to Quebec City, U.S. protestors who oppose the Free Trade Area of the Americas
are about to cross the border here.*

PHOTO: Reproduced with permission of the Minister of Public
Works and Government Services Canada, 2003.

Rum seized at Pictou, Nova Scotia, 1928.

Line ups at the Peace Bridge, Fort Erie, 1931.

The Ambassador Bridge, linking Windsor, Ontario, to Detroit, Michigan, is the lifeline of Canada's most important manufacturing sector, the auto industry.

Demonstrations in Toronto, against (March 2003) and for (April 2003) the U.S. invasion of Iraq.

February 2003. Demonstrators in New York City say no to the Iraq War.

work on the dike remains uncompleted. Sadly, the demolition of houses in this attractive quarter of Grand Forks is continuing. Streets that once ran through to the old earthen dike now come to an abrupt end against barriers. A woman in her fifties, who works at the Museum of Art on the university campus, tells me that her house, once on a lovely long street, is now smack up against a dead end, next to where extensive dike construction is to take place. She and her husband had expected only about ten centimetres of water in their house; instead they got 1.25 metres, their furniture floating in the living room. In their laundry room, the washing machine was also floating, and they had to replace it. Like many other families in Grand Forks, they had to buy a new furnace after an official investigation determined that the old waterlogged furnaces were unsafe.

I drive into Grand Forks on the first really warm day of spring. Down the long boulevard that runs through the university campus, the boys are sitting out on the lawns of their fraternity houses. They have brought out sofas and are lounging on them in shorts and T-shirts. A few of them toss footballs lazily back and forth. It is the same in front of the sorority houses, where the girls sit in circles on the fresh green lawns.

Five years ago this week, all of this was under water. I am driving toward the downtown, where the greatest devastation was wreaked in the flood of '97. Grand Forks is an old city by the standards of the upper Midwest, and it boasted a substantial number of fine old office buildings. At the height of the flood, when the frigid waters of the Red were overwhelming the city, the downtown was turned into a vast lake, with buildings standing as sentinels in the water. The earlier forecasts of a crest of 47.5 to 49 feet, dramatic though they were, did not come close to foretelling what was to come——a catastrophic crest of 54.33 feet (16.60 metres).[5]

Thousands of people—city crews, National Guardsmen and volunteers—made a superhuman effort to save Grand Forks and

East Grand Forks. Clay and earthen dikes were stretched to their limit. Thirty times as much water as usual hurtled down the river between the two cities. In the raging water were trees, debris and huge blocks of ice, which could strike a dike and breach it at any time. From the air, the perilous situation could be seen at a glance. Dikes, with the surging river straining at their rims, curled around communities whose homes lay below. If the dike gave way, the homes would soon be inundated.

Saturday, April 19, was the terrible day when despite the efforts—all the shifts taken by residents to reinforce the dikes with sandbags—the cities were lost to the torrent. Water burst through the dikes at weak points on both sides of the river and whole neighbourhoods, where the struggle had been long and heroic, were flooded. The major bridges connecting the two cities succumbed to the water and were closed. The majority of streets in Grand Forks and East Grand Forks were inundated. People who had stayed in their homes, many of them working day and night to save their neighbourhoods, were now told they had to leave. The loud and unwelcome wail of sirens signalled the residents that it was now the turn of their district to be evacuated. By noon on the 19th, at least 50 percent of Grand Forks had been hit by flood damage and three-quarters of the city's population had been ordered to leave their homes. Across the river in East Grand Forks, all of the residents had been evacuated.[6]

With water in the streets of most of the city, including the commercial downtown, and most of the residents evacuated, the officials running the effort to counter the disaster could be forgiven for believing that the worst must now be over. But the situation deteriorated. At about 4:15 in the afternoon, members of the National Guard and the coast guard who were patrolling the downtown in boats saw smoke coming from the Security Building in the heart of the commercial district. It quickly became apparent that the fire department would have a terrible job on its hands. The ranking officer in the nearest fire station set out for the scene of the blaze in a Humvee, but it soon started to sink in the frigid water and its engine was drowned. The officer had to continue to the fire in a coast guard air boat.

To make matters still worse, as the firefighters closed in on the scene of the blaze, they discovered that a number of apartment dwellers had ignored the order to evacuate, remaining in their apartments on second, third and fourth floors. Outfitted with food and drinking water, they had figured they would be safe and could wait out the flood. But now, with fire spreading through nearby commercial buildings, panicked residents came out on their fire escapes and begged to be evacuated. The firefighters had to put the saving of human lives ahead of the fight to extinguish the blaze. In some cases, apartment dwellers still refused to leave their quarters, and firefighters had to search nearby buildings, sometimes chasing people down the halls to force them out.[7]

As the blaze spread to other buildings, the firefighters closed in to do battle. Most fire trucks could not make it to the scene in water that was 1.2 to 1.5 metres deep and was surging through the streets with a current of about forty kilometres an hour. When one pumper truck did get to the location of the fire, those on board decided to try to pump the raging flood waters onto the flames. But after sucking water into its engine for a couple of minutes, the truck's engine blew. If they couldn't use the flood water to fight the fire, they could try the city's hydrants. Tragically, the previous day the city's water treatment plant had failed, and there was not enough water pressure in the hydrants to direct any kind of stream at the burning buildings. With all of these problems, the situation in the commercial district was like a bizarre nightmare. Above the heads of the firefighters, military and media helicopters churned, making a terrific din.[8]

Americans watched the horrific scene unfolding on live television, and many people around the country phoned in their ideas on what to do about the fire. Some of the ideas were completely fanciful, but others made sense. A firefighter in Fargo, up the Red River from Grand Forks, suggested that the fire department mount fire trucks on flatbed trailers that would be able to drive to the scene. The idea was tried—and it worked beautifully. Then a second truck was sent in by the same technique. Using this method, and with the aid of trucks from the Grand Forks Air Force Base and the Grand Forks International Airport, the firefighters managed to contain the fire by midnight on the 19th.[9]

Eleven commercial buildings were destroyed in the conflagration. When the fires were finally quenched, the ruined buildings were skeletons, gaping lifeless above the water. Fortunately, much of the city's treasured downtown core survived the flood, as I saw when I visited a coffee house on the main floor of a beautiful old office building. The Urban Stampede features comfortable chairs and stools, and a wide array of coffees and teas, served under a high ceiling with a green pressed-tin surface. The building, flooded in April 1997, shows no ravages from that time.

The flood and the conflagration have left their mark on both sides of the Red River, in Grand Forks as well as in its smaller sibling. In conversations in both towns, it is natural for people to order events as either before or after the flood. East Grand Forks, population 7,200, with its much smaller centre, has seen a major spate of rebuilding since the flood. The city's population has fallen by over a thousand since 1997. Restaurants and bars, some of which existed before the disaster, are housed in log-style prefab buildings that are designed to evoke a cheerful hint of bygone frontier days. But the "fake old" structures seem genuinely inviting.

In one of them, there is an outlet for Cabela's, the Minnesota chain that sells hunting and fishing gear on a lavish scale. The sign inside the front door reads: "All firearms, bows and arrows must be checked at Information Desk." Inside, I find a veritable wooden cathedral with a vaulted ceiling. In this vast space, there is an idealized outdoor world to whet the appetite of the would-be angler or hunter. Against the far wall is a waterfall, surrounded by fake rocks, brush and trees, with the odd toothy stuffed beaver standing by. On the walls are the heads of big game animals—deer, bears and bison—displayed as trophies. The heads seem happy in these surroundings, as do the fake fish, suspended artfully in mid-air, as though they are struggling with an ardent fisherman in hip waders. Cabela's sells a wide array of camouflage hunting wear, attire for those who are purchasing air rifles and bows and arrows here. You can dress as a virtual forest, with leafy shirts, jackets, trousers and hats. I picture myself sliding silently toward my prey with a vague fear that another hunter could mistake me for a tree. I pay for a camouflage shirt at a cash register. Beside me stands a stuffed bear and atop the counter are bearskins and stuffed ducks.

———

The conclusion I reached after talking to Americans and Canadians about the Red River flood of 1997 is that people on both sides of the border were acutely aware of what was happening to their neighbours on the other side. There was institutional co-operation across the frontier, much of it based on procedures that had been put into place years earlier. What was most important to Manitoba authorities as they prepared to meet the 1997 flood was receiving accurate information from U.S. forecasters on expected flood levels. In turn, when an ice storm struck both sides of the border weeks before the flood, Manitoba Hydro dispatched one hundred workers to the U.S. side to help Minnkota Power when 100,000 American residents were left without power. As the crest of the flood moved north up the river, communities on both sides offered excess sandbags to their neighbours on the other side.

As neighbours, Canadians and Americans have long recognized the value of helping each other grapple with common catastrophes as well as with catastrophes unique to one side of the border or the other. Firefighting teams have regularly been sent both south and north to aid in battles against forest fires. Snow-clearing equipment has often been dispatched across the border to help communities dig out in the aftermath of major blizzards. The largest area of co-operation, as well as of periodic conflict, has been in the management of waterways that cross the border, both rivers and lakes. In 1909, under the Boundary Waters Treaty signed by Britain and the U.S., Canada and the United States established the International Joint Commission (IJC) for the management of boundary waters. The IJC's six members, three appointed by Washington, three by Ottawa, are responsible for dealing with any use, diversion or obstruction of boundary waters, or with any activities on one side that may affect the level and flow of these waters in the other country.

While there was co-operation across the border during the flood, Americans and Canadians largely faced the catastrophe on their own turf, calling on their own military and emergency insti-tutions to see them through. The focus was local. No one I spoke to mentioned what was happening on the other side of the border unless I prompted them to do so. But despite this, and despite the fact that Canadian political leaders are not much known south of the border, there is one whose memory shines along the Red River in North Dakota: Duff Roblin, the premier of Manitoba who undertook the construction of the Red River floodway, designed to protect the city of Winnipeg from the periodic rav-ages of the river. The young man who worked at the motel where I stayed in Grand Forks mentioned "Duff's Ditch" to me. He wasn't quite sure when it was built, but he knew that Duff Roblin had pushed through the project that protects the biggest city on the Red River from the threat of floods. The woman I spoke to at the Art Museum on the university campus also knew about Duff Roblin and his famous "Ditch," and said she believed something like that should have been constructed at Grand Forks a long time ago.

Duff's Ditch was built as a consequence of the terrible flood of 1950, the worst ever to savage the city of Winnipeg. In 1950 as in 1997, the catastrophic swelling of the Red River was the result of a winter of heavy snowfalls that continued right into April. Again as in 1997, the drama began in the south and moved inexorably up the river toward Winnipeg. The city of half a million people is located at the forks of two rivers. From the west the Assiniboine River empties into the north-flowing Red in the heart of Winnipeg. This is a city whose highest hill is a landfill site, and whose flat terrain is dangerously low in the event of a surge of the Red River. Winnipeg, like the rest of the Red River Valley, experienced many floods over the course of the last century. The flood of 1950 forced the evacuation of eighty thousand people from the metropolis. For two months, as the high water approached and crested, and then as the flood waters receded, the disaster consumed the life and energy of the city. Cleanup and restoration went on for months and even years afterwards.

In June 1958, Duff Roblin led his Progressive Conservative Party to a minority victory in the provincial election. Roblin had been very critical of the previous Manitoba government for having dithered for years about what to do to avert another flood on the scale of that of 1950. In March 1959, when the Roblin government suffered a procedural defeat in the legislature, the second election in less than a year resulted in a majority victory for the new premier. Manitobans endorsed Duff Roblin's platform, which included the building of a floodway to protect Winnipeg.

The immense project involved moving more earth—100 million cubic metres in all—than was displaced to construct either the St. Lawrence Seaway or the Panama Canal. The projected price tag was $63 million. The idea was to dig an enormous ditch from the south in an eastward curve around Winnipeg. In the event of a flood, the floodway would be opened and the water routed into the ditch and away from the city.

Construction could not begin before 1962, to allow time for the rerouting of infrastructure that serviced Winnipeg. It took six years to create the 47.3 kilometre ditch. The channel ranged in width from 116 to 165 metres. Its average depth was 9 metres, although in places it was 20 metres deep. The federal government joined Manitoba in funding the project, sharing initial costs on an approximately equal basis. In the end, the federal government picked up 58 percent of the total tab. With great good fortune, Duff's Ditch was completed in time for the flood of 1969. That spring, it handled water on the scale of the 1950 flood. In dramatic contrast to that earlier disaster, no basements in the metropolitan area of Winnipeg were flooded. Similarly, in 1997, while Grand Forks faced disaster, Winnipeg, through the use of the floodway, stayed high and dry. There were, however, complaints from farmers and townspeople south of the city that had Duff's Ditch been opened sooner, their properties would have suffered less damage.

North of the border, voices were heard both for and against Duff's Ditch in the late 1950s and early 1960s. Those calling for the building of a great public work to prevent future flooding prevailed. South of the border, while the Winnipeg floodway is widely known, its example has not yet inspired similar action in cities like Fargo and Grand Forks. In part, that is because Winnipeg is by far the largest of the three cities. But the outcome is not surprising, given the stronger Canadian tradition of undertaking public sector projects to achieve goals seen as being for the public good.

In April 2003, Prime Minister Chrétien was in Winnipeg to meet Manitoba premier Gary Doer. The two leaders announced that their governments would each contribute $80 million to undertake a major expansion of the floodway over the next five years. Coming on top of an earlier $130 million federal-provincial investment to protect rural Manitoba against flooding, the expansion of Duff's Ditch was intended to protect Winnipeg against a super flood that experts believed would occur only once in seven hundred years.

Chapter 8 | Other Borders

F or those on both sides of the border who struggle to stop smuggling, or who regard refuge seekers as a problem, there is one obvious potential solution: remove the border. I am reminded of this whenever I drive across the border from France to Germany, or from France to Italy. Considering that France and Germany went to war three times between 1870 and 1939, it fills me with guarded optimism about the human future to drive past a customs post in Strasbourg, across the Rhine River and into Germany, where I again pass a customs post without stopping. When I lived in Menton, France, a pleasant little city on the Mediterranean that is snug up against the Italian border, it was literally one hundred metres from my apartment to the border. In 1940, when Mussolini played the jackal and declared war on France when the French were reeling toward defeat under the German attack in the north, the Italian army shelled this area in a brief period of fighting and then occupied the town. Now, when you drive past French and then Italian customs, you are not even required to stop.

For nearly two decades, Western European countries have been moving toward a radical change in the management of their borders. It all began in Schengen, Luxembourg, in 1985. Five of the six countries that were the founders of what had by 1985 grown into the twelve-member European Community sent representatives to the meeting in Schengen. The governments of France, West Germany, the Netherlands, Belgium and Luxembourg were determined to speed up the opening of borders within the EC. Opening the borders to allow the free passage of goods and people was already an EC goal. Standing in the way of progress on the issue were a number of governments, the most important of which was Margaret Thatcher's Tory government in Britain. A stubborn nationalist, Thatcher felt much closer to the Reagan administration in Washington than to the governments across the Channel in continental Europe. Despite the fact that Thatcher had signed on to the Single European Act in 1985, an act that was crucial to the further integration of the EC, she had no intention of carrying out one of its provisions—the elimination of customs checks for people entering the U.K. from other EC countries.

The meeting in Schengen reflected the frustration of the governments in attendance at the slow advance toward the opening of frontiers, brought on in large measure by Thatcher. The solution reached by the so-called Schengen countries was to make their own way forward, hoping the rest of the EC would be won over to their initiative. The Schengen countries decided that they would work out the arrangements necessary to open their frontiers to the free passage of people and goods. To take this large step, they had to devise practical solutions to a whole range of problems that would arise when frontiers were opened. With open frontiers, would they have to harmonize their immigration and refugee policies? How would they prevent people from taking national treasures out of the country? How would they block the importation of banned substances, including drugs, weapons and explosives? How would they regulate the passage of transport trucks through their territories? Dealing with these matters forced the partners to cope with some very ticklish issues. For example, there was the question of co-operation among police forces across borders. With an open border between, let's say, France and Germany, would the two countries permit high-speed police chases of fugitives across the border and into the neighbouring country?

The Schengen process continued among participating states through a number of stages. The 1985 agreement was followed by an accord signed in 1990. When the accord came into effect in 1995, it abolished the internal borders of the participating states to establish a single external border for the Schengen area. Common rules regarding visas, refugee rights and checks at the common external border were adopted so that free movement inside Schengenland could proceed without threats to law and order. To combat organized crime and terrorism within Schengen borders, a Schengen Information System (SIS) was established to exchange data on such matters as people's identities and stolen goods. By 1996, all European Union member states, with the exception of the U.K. and Ireland, had joined the Schengen group. In May 1999, the Schengen process was incorporated into the structure of the EU with the signing of the Treaty of Amsterdam. Today, in Schengenland, people travelling through airports and ports are separated into two streams, those travelling within the area and those arriving from outside it. Within the Schengen area, in addition to rules about visas, refugees and information sharing, there is an agreement about rights of surveillance and hot pursuit on the part of authorities.

Now, when people drive across the frontier from Menton to the nearby town of Ventimiglia in Italy, they are not required to stop at customs. On top of that, both the French and the Italians use the euro, the common European currency. When the French visit the huge outdoor market in Ventimiglia on Friday mornings, as thousands do, they don't have to worry about exchange rates. (Even before the euro, but after Schengen, it was pretty simple: all prices were posted in lire and francs.) They buy their goods and frequent the local restaurants using euros, and then head back home, driving across the border without having to stop or declare a thing.

The opening of frontiers and the adoption of the euro have had dramatic consequences for Europe's border regions. Particularly in areas where there are no sharp cultural divisions marked off by the boundaries between states, the change has been significant. One such case is the Basque country in northern Spain and southern France where the border runs along the Pyrenees mountains. The Basques, who speak their own language, which is remote from Spanish and French, live on both sides of the border, with the majority on the Spanish side. In the decades that followed the Spanish Civil War in the late 1930s, the dictatorship of Francisco Franco kept the border with France tightly shuttered. Basque small towns and villages on the two sides of the frontier were largely isolated from one another.

The emergence of Schengenland altered this situation. France and Spain, both Schengen countries, opened the border, allowing people to move back and forth without stopping at customs posts. Villages and towns were reunited, commerce across the border grew quickly, and people on one side of the border were able to seek employment on the other side. In some cases, they even sent their children to schools across the border. The same kind of development has occurred along many of Europe's frontiers, with an effect on regional economies as well as on the lives of communities.

With thirteen nations now included in the effort and a combined population of about 300 million, Schengenland is the most significant attempt in the contemporary world to open frontiers between nations. You can now drive all the way from Spain through France, the Benelux countries and Germany without having to stop at a customs post.

The major reason for the emergence of open frontiers in Europe, and indeed for the rise of the European Union, was the history of warfare that tore the continent asunder between 1870 and 1945. The EU, the European single market, the euro and open frontiers are all aspects of a European agenda, dating from the early 1950s, designed to put Europe's fratricidal past behind it.

The EU is the world's greatest experiment in the voluntary pooling of sovereignty by nation-states to a common supranational authority. The experiment, which began with a common market in coal and steel for six countries, has burgeoned through a series of stages and a growth in the number of member countries. First came the common market, launched in 1958. Then, after a long period in the doldrums, the single market followed, implemented in the 1980s and completed in 1992. The Maastricht Treaty of 1991 transformed the European Community into the European Union, creating a common European citizenship for the citizens of member countries. At the beginning of 2002, the euro became the common currency for the people of twelve of the fifteen EU states, with euro banknotes and coins replacing national currencies.

Could Canada and the United States follow the course of Schengenland and remove border controls between them? On occasion, politicians such as former prime minister Brian Mulroney and former Ontario premier Mike Harris have suggested this idea. It is natural enough for Canadians to observe the Schengen experiment to see if it might work for them. On close examination, though, it is highly improbable that North

America will follow the European route on this crucial question. The reason is that in the decisive country, the United States, there is simply no appetite in any part of the political spectrum for an experiment in supranationalism. *No one* in American politics is interested in ceding sovereignty to a North American federal state, or to common continental institutions, that would embrace Mexico and Canada.

An additional reason the United States is unlikely to show any interest in opening its northern frontier is the explosive condition of America's 3,200-kilometre-long southern boundary with Mexico. Most of the illegal immigrants living in the United States—estimates indicate there are between 9 and 11 million of them—are Hispanics from Mexico, Central America and South America. Each year, about 340,000 Mexican labourers immigrate to the United States. About half of them enter illegally.

American attitudes toward illegal Hispanic migrants are deeply contradictory. In the Southwest, many employers are heavily dependent on Mexican migrants as a source of labour that costs them an average of sixty dollars a day. And these labourers receive no benefits and have no right to severance payments when they are laid off. What drives the migrants north is the fact that in Mexico they are often paid five dollars a day for their labour. Over the course of the 1990s, the proportion of California agricultural workers made up of illegals from Mexico increased from 10 percent to 40 percent. Alan Greenspan, president of the U.S. Federal Reserve and America's leading economic guru, has described these illegal immigrants as playing an increasingly essential "anti-inflationary" role in the U.S. economy. That is a polite way of saying that cheap labour keeps costs down.

Mexicans have been crossing the border to look for work in the United States for well over a century. Indeed, in the late nineteenth century, the U.S.–Mexico border was essentially wide open. It was easy for migrants to cross into the U.S., and most of them returned south to their families following a period of labour for American bosses. In recent decades, however, the movement of Hispanics into the United States has become a major migration that is rapidly altering the demographics of America.

Today, there are more than 30 million Hispanics living in the United States, 9 million of them born in Mexico. (At present, by contrast, about 300,000 Canadians reside in the United States.) The U.S. Bureau of the Census has produced three levels of projections for the growth of the American population over the next half century: a lowest series, a middle series and a highest series. By 2010, according to the middle projection, the Hispanic population in the United States, at 41.1 million, will exceed the African-American population, projected to be 40.1 million. The Bureau of the Census projects that by 2050 there will be 96.5 million Hispanics in the United States, which would give them just over a 24 percent share of the American population, projected then to be 393.9 million.[1] California recently became the first state in modern times to have a population in which non-Hispanic whites constitute a minority of the population. A similar trend exists in the great crescent of territory that includes Texas, Arizona and New Mexico.

The rise of the Hispanic population in the United States, in part caused by the desire of American employers to have access to this enormous labour pool, has also provoked a negative, nativist reaction among many Americans. Over the past decade the U.S. government has spent billions of dollars beefing up its defences on the Mexican border to keep out illegal migrants. For instance, on the southern edge of Nogales, Arizona, there is a 4.6-metre-high metal wall that was built, beginning in 1994, to keep out illegals. Immediately across the wall is the city of Nogales, Mexico. A single urban area, intersected by the border, has been divided by a wall that has been compared to the Berlin Wall. Unlike the Berlin Wall, though, this one was built not to keep inhabitants in but to keep migrants out. Surrounded by a trench and a no-man's land, the wall is manned by armed soldiers who have floodlights and high-tech tracking devices such as infrared night-vision scopes, low-light TV cameras and ground sensors. Helicopters and all-terrain vehicles patrol the area at night. Residents of the divided city call the wall the "iron curtain." It would be easy to imagine that this wall separated two deadly military enemies rather than the United States and its southern free trade partner.

In the mid-1990s, while the Clinton administration was in office, the U.S. Immigration and Naturalization Service launched Operations Gatekeeper and Safeguard, efforts to staunch the flow of illegal migrants through the areas of San Diego, California, and Nogales. In the five years prior to the September 11 terror attacks, Washington doubled the number of border patrol agents posted on the Mexican border to about 8,200. The budget of the border patrol on the Mexican frontier trebled over that half decade, from $374 million to $952 million. In addition, Washington assigned about ten thousand soldiers to the job of building fences and roads along the border. While the soldiers are not authorized to arrest illegal migrants, they stand guard along the border and operate the high-tech surveillance gear.

Despite the massive mobilization, the northward stream of migrants across the frontier has barely been slowed. But militarization has driven many illegal migrants away from the most heavily guarded sections of the border, mostly in California and Texas, to seek passage across the desolate desert regions of the Southwest. Between 1996 and 2000, 1,185 illegal migrants died— from drowning, dehydration and being run down by vehicles—in attempts to make it into the U.S. across the desert. In 1999 alone, the U.S. border patrol rescued more than 800 migrants in the area around Tucson, Arizona.

In the debate in America on the issue, the point is often made that the illegal migrants are simply people looking for work from employers eager to hire them. Why, then, should they have to risk their lives to make it to where they can earn a living? The response from those who oppose the migration is that the United States cannot tolerate flagrant disregard for its laws. Besides, it is argued, along with those seeking work come the drug dealers and smugglers, for whom this is the most popular route into the U.S. It is estimated that 400 tonnes of cocaine, 150 tonnes of methamphetamines and 15 tonnes of heroin are smuggled from Mexico into the U.S. every year. A sign of the contradictory attitude of the United States toward the migration is the fact that among the advanced industrialized countries, the United States has the toughest penalties against smuggling and the most lenient rules about employing illegal labour.

Given the politics of the Bush administration, there is virtually no prospect for a move to open the frontier with Canada in the absence of a similar move on the U.S. border with Mexico. That is because to prevail in the presidential election in 2004, Bush strategists are counting on winning the support of a higher proportion of the rapidly rising Hispanic vote in the U.S. At a meeting in Washington with Mexican president Vicente Fox just before the terror attacks of September 11, 2001, George W. Bush proclaimed that no relationship is more important to the United States than that with Mexico.

Even before September 11, it was going to be a very tough sell to convince American policy-makers to open their frontier with Mexico. Opening the frontier to allow completely free access for Mexicans to the U.S. would encourage a still higher movement of people northward in search of better jobs. While such a step has support from some Republicans, it is bitterly opposed by other members of the president's party. The terror attacks have hardened the positions of those opposed to opening the border with Mexico. Opening the border with Canada without a similar arrangement with Mexico would be seen as a slap in the face to Hispanics. The present calculus of American politics rules that out.

———

In Europe, it has been possible to construct a unique supranational community because of the lessons learned from a history of terrible wars and because no single power dominates the whole. In North America, Mexico and Canada have the option of ceding sovereignty to the United States, but any thought of a community along the lines of the European Union is no better than a pipe dream.

Chapter 9 | **Down the Dark Road**

Social and political paroxysms in the United States have wreaked havoc with the relationship between the United States and Canada in the past. The American Revolution ended with the northward flight of the Loyalists that completely transformed the colonies remaining under the British flag. The American Civil War goaded Washington into tearing up the first free trade deal between the U.S. and British North America. That great American conflict was one of the major causes of Canadian Confederation in the 1860s. Today, a new convulsion in the United States is transforming the relationship between Canada and its superpower neighbour.

The shock struck on a tranquil, late summer morning—September 11, 2001. Since that day, American politics has entered a new age whose consequences have changed the world. At home, under the leadership of an administration that has seized on fear in order to pursue its extreme global and domestic agendas, the United States has taken a very dark road. The patriotism of critics has been questioned, and democracy and civil liberties have been cast into a shadow.

The new road taken by the United States has forced a re-examination of basic assumptions about Canada's most crucial external relationship. Analyzing where the U.S. is headed is of immense importance to Canadians. That is because what the United States does globally and in its own immediate neighbour-hood has a very real impact on Canada and Canadians. And for an important segment of the Canadian political and economic elite, the United States serves as a highly admired role model. For the decade prior to September 11, the prevailing view in Canada was that we were living in the age of globalization, an era in which the state was receding in importance while commercial ties between nations were growing ever stronger. Canadians and Americans, it seemed, were on a certain course toward greater economic and societal convergence. That assumption was one of the casualties of September 11.

Canadians were deeply shocked by the events of September 11. Many, this author included, spent that terrible day absorbing the tragedy and its meaning in front of a television set. Only those old enough to remember the assassination of John F. Kennedy on November 22, 1963, had anything to which they could compare the day.

Two acts of the Bush administration directly affected Canadians on September 11. The U.S. closed the Canada–U.S. border, and Washington asked Ottawa to allow all overseas flights incoming to U.S. destinations to land at Canadian airports. Huge lineups developed at the border. For Finance Minister Paul Martin, the great anxiety of the day was to get those border crossings opened again as quickly as possible. The longer they remained closed or were subject to severe bottlenecks, the greater could be the damage to Canada's economy.

Canadian air traffic controllers were suddenly faced with the unprecedented challenge of rerouting and landing hundreds of aircraft in a very short period of time. On the afternoon of

September 11, a Korean Airlines jet en route to Alaska was transmitting a signal that warned authorities that the plane had been hijacked. The North American Aerospace Defence (NORAD) headquarters in Colorado went on high alert. Two U.S. fighter planes trailed the south Korean aircraft. The decision was made that the plane would not be allowed to land anywhere in Alaska. Instead, it would be required to put down in Whitehorse, in the Yukon, a relatively remote airport, not close to a large population centre or a major military installation. At home at 24 Sussex Drive in Ottawa, Prime Minister Jean Chrétien was consulted about the incoming jet. When it became clear that Canadian jet fighters would not be able to reach the aircraft in time, Chrétien authorized the U.S. fighters to follow the south Korean airliner into Canadian airspace. The prime minister also gave permission to the U.S. fighters to shoot the suspect aircraft down, despite its three hundred passengers, if it failed to land in Whitehorse and headed south toward a major population centre such as Vancouver. The anxiety passed when the plane touched down without incident at Whitehorse, where the RCMP was on full alert, and where local children had been sent home early from their schools. The transmission from the plane, it turned out, had been a false alarm.

When the border was reopened to personal and commercial traffic, a Code Red Alert was in effect on the U.S. side. This meant long lines, especially at key border points such as the Windsor–Detroit Ambassador Bridge and tunnel, the Peace Bridge between Fort Erie, Ontario, and Buffalo, New York, and south of Vancouver at the border point just north of Blaine, Washington. Businesses fumed that they would be harmed in the U.S. market. The passes that allowed low-risk travellers to drive across the border with a minimum of fuss were suspended.

In the days and months following the attacks, the Bush administration made much of America's friendship with the

British Prime Minister, Tony Blair, while Canada's prime minister enjoyed no such celebrity. On hand for George W. Bush's speech to Congress after the terror attacks, Blair was toasted by the president as America's most reliable ally. Chrétien, under assault from the Opposition in Ottawa for his lack of fervour on the American side, was slow to pay a personal visit to Ground Zero in New York. Despite Canada's hospitality to many thousands of U.S. travellers who were briefly stranded north of the border after September 11, there was no thank-you to Canada in a presidential speech that praised a long list of countries for their friendship and support.

As the United States geared up to make security the top priority of government, some Canadians felt the effects much more than others. Those who travelled to the United States on a frequent basis, for business, education or tourism, encountered a changed border.

Most negatively affected were Canadian citizens of Middle Eastern origin. In the aftermath of the September 11 attacks, the U.S. government decided to carry out intensive interrogations of people entering the United States from a number of countries. The new rules, embodied in the Patriot Act, passed in the autumn of 2001, authorized the U.S. Immigration and Naturalization Service (INS) to track the arrival and departure of non-immigrants travelling to the U.S. On the first anniversary of the terror attacks, the U.S. National Security Entry-Exit Registration System (NSEERS) went into effect. Under NSEERS, it is the long-term goal of the Bush administration to closely monitor all visitors to the United States. By 2005, under the legislation, all foreigners, including all Canadians, will be subject to the program. On September 11, 2002, American authorities began registering, photographing and fingerprinting all persons entering the U.S. from Iraq, Iran, Syria, Libya and Sudan. The policy extended beyond persons holding the citizenship of these countries to people who had been born in them. Canadian citizens born in one of the five countries were initially subjected to this regimen on entering the United States. In addition, they had to inform U.S. authorities of their travel plans inside the country. They were also required to check in with U.S. authorities as they left. The "special" attention meted out to these Canadians—lengthy interrogations—could be expected to recur each time they returned to the United States.

Amal Kaitash, a computer-chip engineer, was a victim of "special" treatment when he flew to San Francisco in September 2002. When U.S. authorities noticed that Kaitash, a citizen of Canada for the previous seven years, was born in Tehran, Iran, they took him aside and interrogated him. "They did fingerprints, they did an interview on tape, and I had to sign an affidavit," the thirty-five-year-old Ottawa resident told a reporter. U.S. authorities asked Kaitash about his family, and whether he had come to Canada as a refugee. He was asked why he had come to the United States and where he was staying. He was instructed to inform American authorities before travelling anywhere else in the U.S. As a result of the hour-long questioning, Kaitash missed his flight.[1]

A highly alarming case was that of Maher Arar, a Syrian-born man who had been a Canadian citizen for fifteen years. Arar, married with two young children, worked in the field of communication engineering. For four years he had been travelling on business to the United States with no problems at the border. Returning from Zurich en route to Montreal two weeks after the new U.S. entry rules went into effect, Arar was taken aside by U.S. authorities at New York's JFK airport. He had not been aware that the new rules required all persons born in Syria to be registered when entering the United States. Photographed and fingerprinted, the Canadian citizen was interrogated by INS agents for nine hours without a lawyer present.

Held overnight in an airport jail cell, Arar was transferred the next day to the Metropolitan Detention Center in Brooklyn, where he was placed in solitary confinement. A few days later, Arar was allowed to place a phone call to relatives in Ottawa. Until then, his family had no idea where he was. While his family was getting in touch with Canadian officials, Arar was charged with three counts of immigration violations and one count of belonging to a terrorist organization—the latter a charge he stoutly denied.

When Canadian officials visited Arar the following day, they found him to be in a fragile emotional condition. The Canadian consulate in New York filed a formal protest with the American government for having failed to inform Canadian officials as soon as Arar was taken into custody. On October 9, the Syrian-born Canadian citizen was moved to an undisclosed location, and the following day he was deported to Syria for his alleged immigration violation. Under the circumstances, one would have expected the U.S. government to deport Arar to Canada or to Zurich, the point of origin of his trip. Although Canadian officials have pressed the Syrians for his release, the consequence of his stopover in New York is that he now sits in a jail cell in Syria.[2]

In response to the new U.S. border regime, Canada's Department of Foreign Affairs issued a travel advisory that warned Canadians born in the listed countries to "consider carefully" whether they should travel to the United States "for any reason, including transit to or from third countries." The advisory also warned that Canadians born in Pakistan, Saudi Arabia or Yemen "could also attract special attention from American immigration and security authorities."

Foreign Affairs Minister Bill Graham told the House of Commons that in a conversation with U.S. Secretary of State Colin Powell, he protested the invidious treatment of Canadians born in the listed countries. "We can't tell the Americans what to do on their own territory," Graham declared. "What we're telling them is that we don't accept this and we find it very troubling . . . I am certain that in due course common sense will prevail."[3] Much less diplomatic than the foreign minister, Natural Resources Minister Herb Dhaliwal, who moved to Canada from India at age six, told a reporter that the U.S. policy was essentially racist. "We are seeing the ugly face of America and it is simply unacceptable," he said.[4]

Issuing the travel advisory turned out to be a highly effective way of embarrassing the U.S. government. The American media noticed that their usually placid northern neighbour was accusing the U.S. of racial profiling, a hot issue south of the border. In response to strong remonstrations from the Canadian government and a wave of hostile media stories in Canada, the U.S. changed course—but only slightly. On October 31, 2002, Paul Cellucci, the U.S. ambassador to Canada, informed Bill Graham that the United States would not apply the stringent new measures to people carrying Canadian passports. Canada had won on the issue that our neighbour must not divide Canadian citizens into two groups, one that would be subject to heavy interrogation at the border and another that would not.

The formal U.S. concession on the issue did not mean, of course, that Canadians of Middle Eastern descent would not be singled out for special treatment at the border on a case-by-case basis. Having made a concession to Canada, U.S. authorities moved quickly to minimize its extent. Jorge Martinez, a spokesman for the U.S. Justice Department, which oversees the INS, told a reporter that the U.S. move was more of a clarification of border policy than a reversal by Washington. He indicated that while place of birth wouldn't automatically trigger a requirement that a Canadian be registered at the border by U.S. authorities, other factors, such as intelligence about an individual, could lead to registration. He said that the extra scrutiny meted out to people born in the targeted countries applied as well to U.S. citizens. "All nationals of all countries may be subject to stricter scrutiny," Martinez commented.

For Canadians of Middle Eastern descent, the fog at the border remained. If anything, it thickened a week later when U.S. Attorney General John Ashcroft, one of the toughest of the tough guys in the Bush administration, appeared at Niagara Falls, New York, to reassure Americans about the new security measures that were in place at entry points into the United States. Ashcroft spoke on a cold morning, with his back to the Niagara River and Canada. He reminded his listeners that two centuries ago Americans had stood fast to defend this frontier against British troops, and that what he was now doing was a part of that long and honourable tradition. His Canadian audience—the large contingent of Canadian media on hand and those watching live on CBC Newsworld—may have found these remarks rather divisive. Just across the river behind the U.S. Attorney General was the statue of General Isaac Brock, who died at Queenston Heights defending Canada against American invaders in 1813.

In his prepared remarks, Ashcroft extolled the new U.S. National Security Entry-Exit Registration System. Under the system, he explained, non-residents entering the United States were subject to the possibility of being registered and fingerprinted. Ashcroft said that he himself had just gone through the process, and that it was highly efficient, taking only three minutes to complete the digital fingerprinting. Those entering the U.S. who were carrying passports from countries that were state sponsors of terrorism—Iran, Iraq, Syria, Sudan and Libya— would be automatically registered, Ashcroft said. Those bearing passports from other countries could also be registered on the basis of intelligence information concerning them or if the U.S. border agent made an on-the-spot judgment that someone should be registered. Anyone registered was required to provide information to

U.S. authorities on the details of their travel plans in the United States, including addresses where they would be staying. No country's citizens were exempt from the program, Ashcroft underlined. The attorney general later reiterated this point in answer to Canadian reporters who asked for details about the American ambassador's undertaking that Canadians born in the listed countries would not automatically require registration. Birthplace alone would not trigger registration, Ashcroft agreed. It was clear, though, that a Canadian passport was no guarantee against registration.

In the eight weeks since the program had gone into place, Ashcroft revealed, INS agents had registered 14,000 people from 112 countries. Moreover, he said, the program had resulted in the arrest of 179 aliens for whom warrants were already outstanding.[5]

In the days following Cellucci's undertaking to Graham, and Ashcroft's Niagara Falls appearance, more Canadian citizens of Middle Eastern origin complained to the media that they had been singled out for interrogation and registration on entering the United States.

Early in November 2002, while the issue of how Canadian citizens of Middle Eastern origin would be treated at the border was in full swing, U.S. officials revealed that Washington was considering requiring landed immigrants to Canada to acquire visitor visas to travel to the United States. Despite objections to the plan from Immigration Minister Denis Coderre,[6] on March 17, 2003, the United States initiated the scheme. From that day on landed immigrants from most Commonwealth countries have needed a visa to cross the border for even a few hours or a day. Included on the list were landed immigrants from the Bahamas, Jamaica, Kenya, South Africa, India and Pakistan.

The problem of harassment at the border was not limited to landed immigrants. Complaining that he had repeatedly been subjected to "unbearable" humiliation at U.S. airports, Rohinton Mistry, one of Canada's most distinguished authors, cancelled the remainder of a U.S. book tour. The Indian-born Canadian author, who was nominated for the Man Booker Prize, explained that he had decided to stay at home to avoid any further degradation. A spokesperson for Mistry's U.S. publisher wrote in a memo, sent to those affected by the decision, that the author "has been extremely unhappy about the way he has been treated in airports around the U.S. in the first half of the tour. As a person of colour he was stopped repeatedly and rudely at each airport along the way—to the point where the humiliation for both he and his wife has become unbearable."[7]

If many foreigners crossing into the United States were shocked by the changes at the border, what was happening to citizens and non-citizens alike within the U.S. could be no less distressing. Both American public sentiment and the U.S. government were undergoing remarkable changes.

During the dizzying, sickening day of the terror attacks, Americans went from stunned disbelief to bewildered horror. From there it was a short journey to anger laced with fear. In a few hours, the outlook of Americans was transformed as surely as if brain surgery had been performed on everyone in the nation simultaneously. Within hours, Rudolph Giuliani, the mayor of New York City, near the end of his term of office, had begun his odyssey from impotent philanderer to Horatio at the bridge, to national hero, to demigod. George W. Bush, widely regarded in the early months of his presidency as not up to the job, got off to a shaky start on September 11, when he flew in Air Force One from Florida to Colorado before returning to Washington, DC, and the White House. While Giuliani was at his post, Bush appeared to be hiding from his. Within ten days, however, after his strong speech to a joint session of the U.S. Congress, Bush was being lionized as a man of granite resolve who was building a global coalition to strike back at the terrorists. Even his short-comings were now virtues. His simple masculine firmness, his ability to see the world in black and white, seemed to fit him for the job in preference to some deep thinker who might worry about complexity.

Instantly the Stars and Stripes became the symbol of American resolve. The flag was everywhere—on cars, trucks and homes, on lapels and T-shirts, and woven into the logos of television networks. Flag sets, featuring a flag for every occasion, vehicle and item of clothing, were advertised on TV as "God Bless America" played in the background. Friends of members of Congress could get very special flags that had been run up the flagstaff on Capitol Hill for a day.

A tidal wave of patriotism swept across the United States. The outlook of political leaders and of the mass media became fused in implacable unity. While the frenetic flag-waving of the American people would soon subside, and many Americans would begin to contemplate some of the political issues raised by the attacks, the U.S. administration began instead a race to change the American political landscape. If the U.S. and Canada had been following separate paths before, they were now moving further apart as each day passed. In the months following September 11, liberalism in the U.S. would be dealt a crippling blow as dissent was suppressed, civil rights were curtailed and the surveillance capabilities of the state were strengthened.

Dissent against the new oneness was allowed, of course, in principle. In practice, there was very little of what could be called true dissent. Disagreements about the details of American policy were aired in the mainstream media, but very few voices were heard taking issue with the basic direction of that policy. After he wrote a column in which he accused George W. Bush of having "skedaddled" on the day of the attacks, Dan Guthrie, a writer for the *Daily Courier* in Oregon, was fired by the paper's publisher. In a similar case, Tom Gutting, a columnist for the *Texas City Sun*, lost his job after he wrote that the president was "flying around the country like a scared child, seeking refuge in his mother's bed after having a nightmare." In a well-publicized case, Bill Maher, the host of the television show *Politically Incorrect*, made the mistake of thinking he was still free to fire off his wicked one-liners in the aftermath of the attacks. Some of his show's main sponsors pulled their advertising from the program after Maher commented that the terrorists who flew to their deaths in hijacked aircraft were not cowards, but that the United States was cowardly to fire cruise missiles at faraway targets. A repentant Maher apologized for his remarks.[8]

Dissidents on university campuses soon felt the wrath of the determined majority. A couple of months after the terror attacks, a conservative group called the American Council of Trustees and Alumni (ACTA), founded by Lynne Cheney, wife of Vice President Dick Cheney, published a report titled "Defending Civilization: How Our Universities Are Failing America and What Can Be Done about It." The report pointed a finger at academe as "the only sector of American society that is distinctly divided in its response [to the terror attacks]." The report stated that "in the wake of the September 11 terrorist attacks, Americans across the country responded with anger, patriotism, and support of military intervention . . . Not so in academe. Even as many institutions enhanced security and many students exhibited American flags, professors across the country sponsored teach-ins that typically ranged from moral equivocation to explicit condemnations of America." The report published 117 statements made by faculty and students that ACTA thought were flagrant examples of absence of patriotic commitment on campuses. Some of the cited statements were amazingly innocuous. Here, in its entirety, is a statement by Todd Gitlin, professor of communications at New York University: "There is a lot of scepticism about the administration's policy of going to war." Also causing offence to ACTA was this statement by the dean of the Woodrow Wilson

School at Princeton: "There is a terrible and understandable desire to find and punish whoever was responsible for this. But as we think about it, it's very important for Americans to think about our own history, what we did in World War II to Japanese citizens by interning them." Another statement by a speaker at the Harvard Law School read: "[We should] build bridges and relationships, not simply bombs and walls." A professor of religious studies at Pomona College was cited for saying: "We have to learn to use courage for peace instead of war." A sign raised at a Harvard student rally, was quoted in the report as having said: "An eye for an eye leaves the world blind." (The sign was clearly modelled on Martin Luther King's maxim: "An eye for an eye leaves everyone blind." A professor emeritus at Boston University gave offence when he said: "[O]ur security can only come by using our national wealth, not for guns, planes, and bombs, but for the health and welfare of our people, and for people suffering in other countries."[9]

In addition to ACTA's high-toned effort to clamp down on dissent in the name of American unity, there were demagogic outpourings on talk radio against campus dissenters. Sometimes the line taken was that those universities that are publicly funded should not allow meetings or protests in opposition to the Bush administration's war on terrorism. In some cases, talk-radio hosts came very close to inciting listeners to physically assault anti-war academics.[10]

Remembering September 11, and using its memory in pursuit of a political agenda, became the touchstone of the Bush administration. In answer to criticisms of the administration's policies, from abroad or from Americans, the conversation returned inexorably to September 11.

In the first days following the attacks, the numbers given for those who had perished in the twin towers of the World Trade Center were enormously higher than turned out to be the truth. In some cases the first estimates ran as high as six or seven thousand killed in New York City. As the weeks passed, the numbers kept falling. When the final reckoning of those who died in New York came in at under three thousand, there was a palpable response— something close to disappointment, a concern that the final number would make September 11 appear less historically consequential, that somehow the event would not live up to its original billing as one of the major turning points of history, on a par with Pearl Harbor, although of course no one had wanted more people to die.

There was a point to all the remembering that was nakedly political. The point of departure was one on which virtually everyone in the United States and around the world was in agreement, that the perpetrators of the terror attacks should be hunted down and punished. On that foundation, however, the Bush administration was to erect a foreign policy that would become so controversial over the next year and a half that it came to eclipse concerns about terrorism in many parts of the world. "Americans will never forget the murderous events of September 11, 2001," began the last paragraph of *The National Strategy for Homeland Security*, published by the White House in the summer of 2002. "Our Nation suffered great harm on that terrible morning. The American people have responded magnificently with courage and compassion, strength and resolve. There should be no doubt that we will succeed in weaving an effective and permanent level of security into the fabric of a better, safer, stronger America."[11] The U.S. would prevail against its foes as it had in the past; that was the message. "Our enemy is smart and resolute. We are smarter and more resolute," George W. Bush declared as he released the strategy for homeland security.

After September 11, the Bush administration reeled in shock and then mobilized for military action. In his address to Congress on September 18, nine days after the terror attacks, Bush put the nations of the world on notice that the U.S. would prosecute this new, if unconventional, war to victory and that all countries must line up with Washington. Otherwise, they would be assumed to be on the side of the terrorists. The war against terrorism became the defining issue of George W. Bush's presidency. The president's response to the attacks of September 11 came to be known as the "Bush doctrine," the rather grand claim being that it would serve as the cornerstone of U.S. global policy for many years to come.

He made it the top priority of his administration to search out and destroy terrorist networks with a global reach. The Bush doctrine equated the states that harboured terrorists with the terrorists themselves. States that continued to harbour terrorists could expect to be attacked by the U.S., the president declared. "Every nation in every region," Bush announced, "now has a decision to make. Either you are with us, or you are with the terrorists." There could be no neutral ground. The president and his administration framed the issue as an epic struggle between civilization and its foes—ultimate good versus ultimate evil. (On more than one occasion, he wondered aloud why there were people in the world who hated the United States. How could such a good nation be so misunderstood by so many? The answer inevitably came back to the "evildoers" who had spread calumnies about America that now needed to be refuted.) This take on the issue made it seem unpatriotic to analyze the "root causes" of the attacks of September 11. Since the contest was between good and evil, those who attempted to analyze the causes of the evil could be denounced as providing excuses for it.

As it built its anti-terrorist coalition and mobilized its military to punish the Al Qaeda terrorist network of Osama Bin Laden and the Taliban regime in Afghanistan, the Bush administration showed the world exactly how special was the role of the United States in the global system. The administration rested its case for military action on the right of the United States to self-defence— the right of a country that has been violated to strike out at the perpetrators even if they are half a world away. In theory, the same rationale could be used by any nation that has been brutally assaulted. In practice, however, the United States is the only nation that has the means to mount a military campaign in any region of the world. The power to do this rests on the fact that the U.S. spends almost as much on its military as all the other nations combined.

In 1982, Britain sent its navy to the South Atlantic to repel the invasion of the Falkland Islands by Argentina. But that mission could only be carried out with the tacit permission of the U.S. Without such American sanction, no country could mount any military operation in a region remote from its home territory. And even with such sanction, only a handful of countries could consider undertaking such an operation. In reality, the doctrine of self-defence, proclaimed by American leaders as though it were universal, was a right that belonged to the U.S. alone. The Bush administration was actually proclaiming the right of the global hegemonic power to intervene under its own flag anywhere in the world when it deemed its interests were threatened.

As a consequence of September 11, relationships between the United States and the entire international community were transformed. The people of Afghanistan felt the transformation first. A short but extraordinarily violent U.S. air assault, supported by allies on the ground in the local Northern Alliance, drove the Taliban regime from power and made the Al Qaeda forces harboured by the Taliban international fugitives.

Because the September 11 attacks were mounted in the name of a radical Islamic rejection of the United States and its ally Israel, the whole Muslim world was pushed into crisis by the terror attacks and the Bush administration's response. For the European allies of the United States, the transformation was less dire, but it was substantial nonetheless. Europeans rallied to the side of America in the aftermath of the attacks, their citizens and elites deeply appalled by what had happened. For the first time in its history, the North Atlantic Treaty Organization (NATO) invoked Article Five of its charter, to assert that the attack on New York and Washington was an attack on the entire NATO alliance.

Indeed, multilateralism seemed to be the order of the day in the first weeks after September 11. That proved to be an illusion. The Bush administration chose to prosecute the war in Afghanistan largely on its own. Under the leadership of its staunchly pro-American prime minister, Tony Blair, Britain dispatched forces. Less dramatically but just as surely, so did Canada. And Russia provided the most valuable assistance by lending support for U.S. operations in the highly sensitive region on its southern perimeter. The war, however, was Washington's to win in its own way. Since the Bush administration did not much value foreign military contributions and did not want its hands tied by entangling alliances, while the U.S. made a show of having allies, the war was prosecuted under firm American direction. That way, Washington could dictate the course of events once victory was achieved.

In the winter of 2002, the Bush administration shifted its focus from hardening the U.S. against further terrorist attacks and overturning the Taliban regime in Afghanistan to a much broader agenda. The change came with the State of the Union address delivered by President George W. Bush on January 29, 2002. The highlight of the speech was Bush's labelling of North Korea, Iran and Iraq as an "Axis of Evil." With the label came the clear warning that Washington was prepared to deal as it saw fit with so-called rogue regimes. The Axis of Evil speech signalled a widening of the Bush doctrine from that first conveyed in his speech to Congress the week after the terror attacks on September 11, 2001. Initially, the doctrine pointed to a lengthy struggle against globally significant terrorist movements and the states that supposedly harboured them. With the Axis of Evil thesis, it became clear that states hostile to the United States that possessed or aspired to possess weapons of mass destruction could also be legitimate targets of the United States. If necessary, it would be legitimate for the United States to launch pre-emptive military assaults against such states.

Although Bush mentioned Iraq last as a member of the Axis of Evil, he gave it the most attention, stressing that "Iraq continues to flaunt its hostility toward America and to support terror." The president issued an ominous warning: "The United States of America will not permit the world's most dangerous regimes to threaten us with the world's most destructive weapons."[12] Iraq was to be the first test of the Bush doctrine. Indeed, it was to test the ability of the United States to manage the global order over which it presided.

In mid-February 2002, *The New York Times* reported that the Bush administration had reached a consensus that the Iraqi regime of Saddam Hussein had to be overthrown. The *Times* story said that military plans were being drawn up to carry out the mission and that a political strategy was being developed to win the support or at least the acquiescence of other powers. "At some point," one unnamed administration official told *The New York Times*, "the Europeans with butterflies in their stomachs—many of whom didn't want us to go into Afghanistan—will see that they have a bipolar choice: They can get with the plan or get off."[13]

That outburst came in response to mounting European criticism of the Axis of Evil line being taken by the Bush administration. French foreign minister Hubert Vedrine called Bush's denunciations of Iraq, Iran and North Korea "simplistic." Joschka Fischer, Germany's foreign minister, warned Washington that "an alliance partnership among free democrats can't be reduced to submission. Alliance partners are not satellites . . . European foreign ministers see it that way. That is why the phrase 'Axis of Evil' leads nowhere."[14]

President Bush, who seemed happiest when he was pursuing a unilateralist agenda, was reported to be welcoming, even egging on, the differences between U.S. and European attitudes toward his concept of the Axis of Evil. He was said to be fuming in private about weak-kneed "European elites" and Arab leaders who, he believed, lacked the courage to stand up to regimes that could someday provide terrorists with nuclear or biological weapons.[15]

The dismissive tone toward the Europeans was based on the administration's calculation that the U.S. could deal with its foes in the world with or without the support of its allies. The thinking behind the tone was revealed in a luncheon speech delivered by Vice President Dick Cheney to the Council on Foreign Relations in February 2002. Cheney, who had been out of public view much of the time after September 11, told the Council: "America has friends and allies in this cause, but only we can lead it. Only we can rally the world in a task of this complexity against an enemy so elusive and so resourceful. The United States and only the United States can see this effort through to victory."[16]

The administration's stance reflected a muscular triumphalism that was widespread in American thinking in the aftermath of the military assault on Afghanistan. Writing in *The Washington Post* during the 2002 Winter Olympics, columnist Charles Krauthammer basked in the glow of American power. But he suggested that the United States should not rub its supremacy in the faces of foreigners.

> America won the Cold War, pocketed Poland and Hungary and the Czech Republic as door prizes, then proceeded to pulverize Serbia and Afghanistan and, en passant, highlight Europe's irrelevance with a display of vast military superiority. We rule the world culturally, economically, diplomatically and militarily as no one has since the Roman Empire. So tell me this: Can we not live without winning the two-man bobsled? . . . We control

everything else in the world. Can't we let somebody else have a bit of sporting glory?"[17]

Signs of contempt for the opinions of foreigners were followed by a story of substance that the Pentagon did not want to become public. In March 2002, the details of a secret Pentagon report were revealed on the front page of *The New York Times*. In its *Nuclear Posture Review*, the Pentagon pointed to the need to produce new nuclear weapons with a lower yield than strategic nuclear weapons, in other words weapons that would produce less radioactive fallout.[18] The *Review* expanded the list of potential nuclear targets for the U.S. to include states that were now high on Washington's hate list. Explicitly on the list were Iraq, Iran, North Korea, Syria and Libya. What made this so shocking is that these five countries were signatories to the nuclear non-proliferation treaty, a treaty signed by 182 countries, including Canada. In 1978, to give nations an incentive to sign it, the United States, the Soviet Union and Britain formally pledged never to launch a nuclear attack on signatories to the treaty, except in a case where a non-nuclear state attacked a nuclear state in tandem with another nuclear state. In 1995, France and China joined these three states (with Russia in place of the Soviet Union) in reiterating this pledge. As former U.S. defence secretary Robert McNamara and Thomas Graham Jr. wrote in a newspaper column, "the Pentagon plan undermines the credibility of that pledge, which underpins the Nonproliferation Treaty. To strike directly at this pledge of nonuse is to strike at the treaty itself."[19] "If another country were planning to develop a new nuclear weapon," said *The New York Times* in an editorial, "and contemplating preemptive strikes against a list of non-nuclear powers, Washington would rightly label that nation a dangerous rogue state."[20]

(In the autumn of 2002, the regime of Kim Jong II in North Korea claimed it possessed nuclear weapons. Placed on the Bush administration's hit list, North Korea chose to highlight, or even exaggerate, its possession of weapons of mass destruction, in the hope that this would allow it to drive a bargain with Washington for aid and a non-aggression pact.)

The Bush doctrine places great emphasis on pre-emptive action as the key to American defence in a radically altered world. This is a crucially important shift in doctrine away from the pillars of U.S. strategy during the Cold War, when the stress was on containment and deterrence. The Cold War was a chess match in which moves were taken with great care to signal to the other side, as well as to take countermoves against it. Containment against the expansion of the Soviet bloc became a pillar of U.S. strategy in the late 1940s, as Washington took up the burdens of a faltering Britain's role in the global system. Deterrence was the key to U.S. strategy in the nuclear standoff against the Soviet Union. Bipolar nuclear security was based on the doctrine of Mutual Assured Destruction (MAD), the notion that neither side had any hope of prevailing through a sudden pre-emptive strike. Both sides strove mightily to ensure that an overwhelming nuclear capability would survive a first strike. The U.S. system was the so-called Triad, a strategic nuclear strike force consisting of Strategic Air Command (SAC) bombers, land-based ICBMs housed in dispersed silos and nuclear submarines armed with nuclear missiles.

The Bush doctrine jettisoned this careful Cold War choreography. The new strategic situation involves a struggle against an enemy that is vastly different from the Soviet Union. The United States is in a much more powerful position in the world than it was during the days of its struggle with an adversary that represented an alternative international system, and that possessed the military means to devastate the United States. But the new adversary has capabilities, even some advantages that the Soviet Union did not have. This was dramatically demonstrated on September 11.

The United States has entered a new era of what strategists call "asymmetrical warfare." While the U.S. holds the military high ground, from conventional through nuclear weapons, from outer space to tactical communications, terrorist opponents have a huge range of potential targets to consider. First, they can hurt the U.S. itself. More important, they can sow widespread fear among Americans, while offering few attractive targets against which the Pentagon can retaliate. Unlike a conventional state, which has a population, cities, industries and resources to be attacked, a terrorist organization can strike with lethal force and then melt back into a myriad of locations. Against this, the strategic military forces of the United States can be rendered practically impotent.

Some analyze the onset of an age of asymmetrical warfare as though it were an entirely new development. It is no such thing. While new nuclear, biological and chemical weapons give asymmetrical warfare novel features in our age, it is a very old form. It rests on the differences in might between a great imperial power and satellite peoples and states. Asymmetrical warfare has always been practised by great imperial powers against smaller powers, and against restless peoples within their own sphere of power.

The best available evidence suggests that at least as early as April 2002, at a meeting between George W. Bush and Tony Blair in Crawford, Texas, the U.S. administration had decided to launch a military assault against Iraq. Prior to taking that decision, the Bush administration had been embroiled in an internal debate about how best to secure America's strategic interests in the Persian Gulf, while preventing the Israeli-Palestinian conflict from undermining America's position throughout the region. There were two basic options under consideration, one traditional, the other radical.

Pursuing the traditional option would have involved a U.S. effort to shore up its alliance with Saudi Arabia, while trying to keep the lid on excessive Israeli military intervention in the West Bank and Gaza. That option rested on the American conviction that with its massive reserves of cheap conventional oil, Saudi Arabia holds the key to a stable global supply of petroleum. To keep Saudi Arabia securely in the U.S. orbit, the approach of important members of George Bush Sr.'s administration, such as Secretary of State Lawrence Eagleberger and National Security Adviser Brent Scowcroft, was to avoid a posture that was so pro-Israel that it shut out the Arabs. The mantra of these Republicans was that settling the Palestinian question had to precede the strengthening of the U.S. position throughout the Middle East.

The fact that most of the September 11 terrorist hijackers were Saudis, and the increasing evidence of the role of Saudis in financing Al Qaeda, had undermined U.S. faith in the soundness of the Saudi link. Concern about Saudi Arabia opened the door to the radical option favoured by most of the key players in the Bush administration.

The centrepiece of the radical option was a U.S. invasion of Iraq. With Saddam's regime overthrown and the U.S. military installed in its place, Washington stood to gain multiple benefits. The Americans could establish a military base in Iraq from which to keep a wary eye on Saudi Arabia, as well as on both Iran and Syria, two countries that also border on Iraq. From a secure base in Iraq, which has its own ample oil reserves, the United States would be much more able to sustain its strategic position in the region than it could ever hope to do by depending on the unreliable Saudis.

The proponents of the radical option, key among them Deputy Defense Secretary Paul Wolfowitz, contended that Iraq was the ideal Arab country in which to establish a new democratic Islamic regime. Wolfowitz is a believer in the proposition that a moderate strain of Islam that is in harmony with democracy could develop. "There can be a separation of religion from the state that is completely compatible with personal piety," he said in an important address on U.S. foreign policy. Under American tutelage that is sometimes compared to the U.S. role in post-war

Japan, people like Wolfowitz think that a democratic Iraq stands a chance of becoming a governing model that could be exported to other Arab countries. According to this highly Utopian theory, the Iraqis are the equivalent of a tabula rasa, a blank slate, on which the Jeffersonian Americans will etch a new political culture.

The Iraq adventure is propelling U.S. global policy in a radical new direction. Never before in its history, outside of the Western Hemisphere, has the United States carried out a preemptive attack on another state without being able to make a valid, or at least plausibly manufactured, case that it was acting in self-defence or in the defence of a state that that had invited the U.S. to help it out. That is why the U.S. attack on Iraq infuriated so many governments around the world and their populations. As Prime Minister Chrétien wondered aloud, if great powers are allowed to engineer changes of regime in other countries when they feel it necessary, how can any nation be secure? Indeed, who might be next?

In the months following his meeting with Tony Blair at his ranch in Crawford, Texas, in April 2002, George W. Bush repeatedly said that his goal in Iraq was regime change. Under pressure from Secretary of State Colin Powell, Bush backed off this line in the autumn of 2002 to win the support of the United Nations Security Council for a new round of inspections to ferret out Saddam's much-touted weapons of mass destruction. This was a change of tactics, not of strategy. Stipulating that a false declaration by Iraq on its weapons programs would constitute a "material breach," the UN resolution gave Bush the opening he required to launch a war. War, when it came, would not be about eliminating Saddam's weapons of mass destruction but to open the door to a grand American scheme to remake the Middle East in its own image.

For obvious reasons, the U.S. could not own up to such geopolitical motives for invading Iraq. Instead, the Bush administration, in the absence of any evidence of Iraqi involvement in the

September 11 attacks, developed the case that Saddam Hussein was a threat to the United States and its friends because it was developing weapons of mass destruction. A pre-emptive strike would thus excise this tumour from the international body politic.

On September 20, 2002, came a development that is sure to be marked as a seminal moment in the new century. For the previous decade, analysts had been debating the question of whether the United States would follow the course of former powerful states, such as Britain and Rome, and proclaim itself an empire. In *The National Security Strategy of the United States*, submitted to the U.S. Congress by President George W. Bush on September 20, 2002, the White House espoused a doctrine that is explicitly imperialist. The document envisions a world in which the United States will enjoy permanent military dominance over all countries, allies and potential foes alike. Indeed, in its sweeping declaration that the U.S. "has no intention of allowing any foreign power to catch up with the huge lead the United States has opened since the fall of the Soviet Union," the distinction between friends and foes has become much less important than it was in the past. According to the Bush document, the U.S. military will "be strong enough" to dissuade any potential challenger from "pursuing a military buildup in hopes of surpassing, or equaling, the power of the United States."

The meaning of the doctrine is clear. It dashes the aspirations of those who hoped that the world was moving toward a system of international law that would allow for the peaceful resolution of conflicts, through covenants and courts. In place of this, a single power that shuns covenants and courts has proclaimed that it intends to dominate the world militarily, intervening pre-emptively where necessary to exorcise threats.

Through the decades of the Cold War, the United States portrayed itself as first among equals, the leader of the free world. Its doctrine rested on the proposition that through containment and deterrence the U.S. and its allies could prevent aggression by hostile states. The new doctrine consigns containment and deterrence to the dustbin, and with them the notion of the United States as first among equals. Instead, for the first time in a formal statement of U.S. policy, the United States is portrayed as standing above all other states. Its role as guardian of a global system with itself at the centre is conceptualized as being of a higher order than the roles played by all other states. This feature of the doctrine makes it explicitly imperialist.

Throughout its history, the United States has sought to influence others through its values, its culture and the way of life of its people. Americans have never seen themselves as militaristic. Now, though, the U.S. government is resting its claim to global power on military might, and that puts the Americans in the company of the Roman emperors and their legions. To be sure, the Bush document displayed a fine Orwellian touch when it proclaimed that the United States would not use its power to seek "unilateral advantage." The 95 percent of humanity that was non-American was to be lulled into accepting the benefits of "a distinctly American internationalism." Those who were not pacified would have to contend with the American legions, which would strike pre-emptively, long before a threat to American interests was allowed to develop.

Today, it may very well be true that there is not much the rest of the world can do about America's military might. But former imperial powers who have proclaimed their right to dominate others have ended up creating adversaries who multiply faster than the means to control them. However comfortable the yoke that is offered, people won't accept it over the long term. Those who want a world in which no power is supreme, and in which laws and covenants are used to settle conflicts, will begin a new debate—about how to contend with imperial America.

Americans might live to rue September 20, 2002—the day they turned in the old republic for a new global empire.

However the long-term debate about America and its empire turns out, the tone of life inside the United States changed dramatically after September 11. The terror attacks instantly made national security and homeland defence the only issues that counted in the drastically revised U.S. political agenda. September 11 brought down the curtain on the gilded age that coincided almost exactly with the Clinton presidency. It had been an age of booming stock markets and the exploding "new economy" built around the Internet and distinguished from the disdainfully labelled "old economy" of manufactured goods, construction and primary products. It was the age of globalization, and of a new world in which investments could be moved instantaneously from country to country at the flick of a cursor. The nation-state, the well-informed insisted, was a thing of the past.

All that ended on September 11.

Repression at home soon became a hallmark of the new era. Within a few weeks, American authorities rounded up over a thousand potential suspects and material witnesses, all of them non-citizens. Most if not all of them were males from Middle Eastern countries. Those in detention were held without the usual processes of American law. The government would neither reveal exactly how many people were being held nor release the names or the suspected violations of those being detained. The conversations of the detainees were taped, including those with their lawyers. In the hour of crisis, the lawyer–client privilege that was so prized in America vanished with scarcely a whisper of dissent.

As some of those held were released, stories circulated about detainees being held in prison in shackles. On top of that, there was very little expression of public concern about what in other circumstances would have seemed enormous violations of human rights. The American public dialogue turned very dark as some commentators discussed whether torture should be used to force those suspected of being members of terrorist networks to divulge information. About six weeks after the attacks, *Newsweek* columnist Jonathan Alter, considered a liberal, wrote an article entitled "Time to Think about Torture." In it, he declared that in "this autumn of anger, even a liberal can find his thoughts turning to . . . torture." He went on to say that while he was not necessarily advocating the use of "cattle prods or rubber hoses," he was trying to find "something to jump-start the stalled investigation of the greatest crime in American history." Later, in an interview, he said: "I'm in favour of court-sanctioned sodium pentothal. I'm against court-sanctioned physical torture." The Fox News Channel raised the torture issue in the form of a question, asking, "Should law enforcement be allowed to do anything, even terrible things, to make suspects spill the beans?" Journalists reported that the issue of torture to make suspects talk was out there in the public, in bars, on commuter trains and at dinner tables.[21] In this eerie climate, Alan Dershowitz, the liberal lawyer, who attained national fame as a member of the O.J. Simpson defence team, mused about what he called a "torture warrant." His idea was that judges would decide whether torture was warranted to force an individual to talk in cases where hundreds of lives could thereby be saved. Dershowitz said that the use of torture could be constitutional, provided that the information gleaned from it could be used for information only and not to convict the detainee. (Used to obtain convictions, it would violate the individual's Fifth Amendment right against self-incrimination, he reasoned.) Dershowitz concluded: "I'm not in favour of torture, but if you're going to have it, it should damn well have court approval."[22]

While the torture discussion did not involve the Bush administration, the White House took steps to deal with a crisis that ranged far outside the long-established norms of American justice. On November 13, 2001, President George W. Bush signed an order to allow special military tribunals to conduct the trials of foreigners charged with terrorism. According to the administration's plan, such trials could be held in secret. Following the military defeat of the Taliban in Afghanistan, the administration was preparing to hold such tribunals in Pakistan and Afghanistan. Not since World War II has the U.S. held such trials. It would be George W. Bush himself, according to the order, who would have the power to determine who is an accused terrorist and therefore liable to trial before a military tribunal. The tribunals would have the authority to sentence a defendant to death on the basis of a two-thirds vote of a tribunal's judges, and this sentence would be subject to no appeal. In criminal cases in civilian courts, guilty verdicts must be unanimous, and death sentences are subject to appeal. Laura W. Murphy, the director of the Washington national office of the American Civil Liberties Union, described the order to set up the tribunals as "deeply disturbing and further evidence that the administration is totally unwilling to abide by the checks and balances that are so central to our democracy."[23]

What made the president's order particularly alarming was that it was so broadly worded that it could apply to anyone who was not a U.S. citizen. In theory, tribunals could be set up to try anyone among the 20 million aliens in the United States whom the Bush administration suspected of contributing to terrorism. From a Canadian standpoint, the prospect of the tribunals posed a direct, if shadowy, threat. Three hundred thousand Canadians reside in the U.S. Those expatriate Canadians, along with Canadians who were visiting the U.S. or were doing business there, no longer had the guarantee that if they were charged with a serious offence, they would appear in a civilian court, at a public trial, with the right to consult Canadian consular officials. So unwilling was the Chrétien government to say anything critical of the U.S. in the weeks after September 11 that Ottawa did not complain to Washington about this threat to Canadian citizens. In an extraordinary irony, the supposed North American community that was emerging through NAFTA now consisted of two sets of people: American citizens, who were guaranteed a trial before a civilian court, with the right of appeal in the case of conviction, and Canadians and Mexicans, who could be condemned before a U.S. military tribunal, with no right of appeal.

In March 2002, smarting under criticism both foreign and domestic, the Bush administration issued rules for military tribunals that went partway toward meeting the concerns. Under the new rules, persons who were not citizens of the United States, including non-combatants and persons who were not members of Al Qaeda, could still be subject to trial by a military tribunal. The rules denied any right of appeal from a tribunal to a civilian court. A non-American being held in military detention would have no right to apply to a civilian court for a ruling on whether the detention was lawful or whether the government's resort to a military tribunal was lawful. The new rules did, however, provide a number of fair-trial guarantees that had not been included in the president's original order. The standard for a conviction was changed to proof beyond a reasonable doubt, which established the presumption of innocence. Trials were to be held in public, with the accused having access to a defence attorney. And the accused would be allowed to see the prosecution's evidence and to cross-examine witnesses. In another significant change, the rules stipulated that a tribunal could impose the death penalty only with the unanimous agreement of the judges.

At the same time as the administration issued the new rules in an effort to meet some of the criticisms of human rights proponents, it took a giant step in precisely the opposite direction. *The New York Times* reported that Pentagon sources were insisting that being acquitted by a military tribunal would not necessarily be the end of the incarceration of someone who had been detained. "If we had a trial right this minute," said Pentagon lawyer William J. Haynes II, "it is conceivable that somebody could be tried and acquitted of that charge but may not necessarily automatically be released."[24] The administration's rationale for this astonishing position was that it could be necessary to detain people who posed a threat to America for the duration of the conflict. The problem, of course, was that the "conflict"—an open-ended worldwide struggle against terrorism—could go on for years, even decades.

In mid-November 2001, in tandem with Bush's original executive order to authorize military tribunals, the U.S. Justice Department asked police forces across the United States to round up and interrogate five thousand men, most of whom were from Middle Eastern countries. Those to be questioned, whose names were compiled from immigration and State Department records, were males aged eighteen to thirty-three who had entered the U.S. on tourist, student or business visas since January 1, 2000. While the list of countries from which the men came was not made public, it included mostly Middle Eastern nations associated with the activities of Al Qaeda.[25] On November 9, 2001, Attorney General John Ashcroft asked federal prosecutors and anti-terrorism task forces to complete the interviews within thirty days.[26]

Ashcroft, whose nomination to the post of attorney general had been vociferously opposed by liberals, also pushed for the FBI to be allowed much more latitude to spy on religious and political organizations in the United States. The restrictions on domestic spying by the FBI had been established in the 1970s following the death of the Bureau's founding director, J. Edgar Hoover. During the latter years of Hoover's regime, the FBI had run a massive surveillance program, called Cointelpro. Monitored under the program, among others, were anti-war militants, the Ku Klux Klan, the Black Panthers and Dr. Martin Luther King. *The New York Times* reported that many long-time FBI and Justice Department officials were opposed to the proposed changes and were negative about other steps announced by Ashcroft. They feared that if the FBI became involved again in spying on domestic groups, it could involve the Bureau in dirty politics as an arm of the administration. These doubters were also disturbed by the prospect of military tribunals being set up to try foreigners suspected of involvement in terrorism. In part, their concern was that the tribunals would remove these suspects from the realm of the Bureau and place them in the ambit of the military. And the doubters were also concerned about the arrest and detention of hundreds of people after September 11 under the direction of John Ashcroft. They noted that there had been no consultation with the FBI in undertaking the roundup and that very few Al Qaeda suspects were among those detained.[27]

Bush's executive order authorizing military tribunals and Ashcroft's moves to return the FBI to domestic spying were soon followed by another development that led to widespread accusations of human rights abuse by the United States. In the autumn of 2001, the swift and deadly airborne assault of the U.S. military on the Taliban regime in Afghanistan quickly turned the tide of the ground war in favour of the Northern Alliance and other anti-Taliban forces. After holding out for a period of weeks, the Taliban forces fled from the major cities and quickly disintegrated. Inevitably, military victory placed thousands of captives in the hands of the victors. While the Northern Alliance and other Afghan forces held most of those captured, by January 2002 the U.S. military was holding over four hundred prisoners. What focused the world's spotlight on the prisoners was the decision of the Bush administration to move many of them nearly halfway around the world, to the U.S. base in Guantánamo Bay, Cuba.

The debates about torture, military tribunals and the treatment of foreign prisoners could be said to concern matters that are peripheral to the mainstream of American life—-however unpleasant they might be for those on the receiving end. That could not be said, however, about the powers the Bush administration sought for itself after the September 11 attacks. A few weeks after the attacks,

Attorney General John Ashcroft unveiled the Anti-Terrorism Act of 2001, an act that would enormously widen the powers of the federal government to track the communications of those suspected of terrorism. Some of the powers would broaden existing laws to encompass new technologies such as cellphones. Others would give the attorney general the power to declare immigrants to be terrorists, and to detain them indefinitely without laying criminal charges or holding a trial. They could be released only when the attorney general decided that they no longer posed a threat. In addition, the legislation would allow U.S. authorities to expel legal immigrants without offering any proof of wrongdoing. Without hearings, and in an atmosphere bordering on hysteria, the act was rushed through Congress and signed by President Bush on October 26, 2001, in a compromise form known as the USA-Patriot Act.[28]

The Patriot Act, as enacted, significantly broadens the surveillance and investigative powers of American law enforcement agencies. Under the act, law enforcement agencies received enhanced authority to install devices that collect the numbers called from a specific telephone line as well as the incoming numbers of those calling that line. The Patriot Act allows the U.S. government access to an individual's financial information and student data, even in cases where no suspicion of wrongdoing exists. All the government must do in such cases is certify that the information to be collected is germane to a criminal investigation.

While the Patriot Act broadened the authority of law enforcement agencies to intercept voice and data communications, this was subject to a tougher standard to convince a judge that such interception was necessary. The act allows the government to undertake electronic surveillance on foreigners or American citizens in the United States when a judge issues a judicial order based on a probable cause that the target is a foreign power or is working for a foreign power. Under the act, the government has gained additional power to carry out secret searches of the premises of individuals in cases where the court is convinced that immediately informing the target of the search would adversely affect an investigation.

An important power contained in the Patriot Act was the granting of authority to government to request an order "requiring the production of any tangible things (including books, records, papers, documents, and other items)." This power applies to investigations of international terrorism and clandestine intelligence activities. Under this section of the law, the FBI can override state library confidentiality laws that shelter library records. Without being required to demonstrate probable cause in support of the assertion that a crime has been committed, the FBI can compel production of business records, medical records, educational records, library records, as well as stored electronic data and communications. The standard for the FBI in such cases under the act is merely that the desired records may be related to an investigation having to do with terrorism or intelligence activities.[29]

A year after the Patriot Act was signed into law, a number of U.S. lawmakers expressed alarm at how it was being used. Russ Feingold, a Democrat from Wisconsin and the lone senator to vote against the act, said that "we now know that bookstores and libraries have received . . . subpoenas asking for the purchase or lending records of their patrons. It is a truly frightening day in America when bookstores are considering destroying their records so when the government comes knocking at the door to find out what their customers have been reading they will have nothing to turn over."[30]

The Patriot Act added enormously to the power of the U.S. government to hold foreigners in indefinite detention. Under the act, the U.S. Department of Justice must file criminal or immigration charges against a non-citizen within seven days of detention, and these charges need not relate to terrorism. While this sounds quite fair, under two circumstances the person being held can be detained indefinitely. First, if the removal of the non-American is unlikely because the country from which he or she comes declines repatriation, the person can be held indefinitely. Second, if the attorney general of the United States decides every six months— and it is solely up to his discretion—that the release of the non- citizen poses a threat to national security "or the safety of the community or any person," the alien can be held indefinitely.

Another early step taken by the administration in the weeks following September 11 was the creation of the new Office of Homeland Security, with Tom Ridge, then governor of Pennsylvania, as director. This was to serve as a stepping stone toward the cre- ation of a massive new government department. In a televised statement to the American people from the Oval Office on July 16, 2002, President George W. Bush trumpeted the release of *The National Strategy for Homeland Security*, whose central proposal was the creation of the new federal department. The job of the new department would be to oversee all of the diverse efforts that were to go into the achievement of homeland security. The doc- ument stated:

> Our structure of overlapping federal, state and local gover- nance—our country has more than 87,000 jurisdictions—pro- vides unique opportunity and challenges for our homeland security efforts. The opportunity comes from the expertise and commitment of local agencies and organizations involved in homeland security. The challenge is to develop inter-connected and complementary systems that are reinforcing rather than duplicative and ensure essential requirements are met. A national strategy requires a national effort.[31]

Under Bush's proposal, the new department would have con- trol of the principal border and transportation security agencies:

the Immigration and Naturalization Service, the U.S. Customs Service, the U.S. Coast Guard, the Animal and Plant Health Inspection Service and the Transportation Security Agency.[32] It would work in tandem with the Department of the Attorney General, where control over the FBI was vested.

The new department would have its fingers in so many pies that it was bound to engender major turf wars inside the U.S. government. For those White House operatives who resented the high profile of the attorney general, the prospect of the new department cutting John Ashcroft down to size was a welcome one. But the new department would threaten many other fiefdoms as well, including those of state and local governments. Indeed, the idea of a new department with such wide-ranging authority was bound to be perceived in many quarters as a gigantic power grab. Despite the careful language in the document outlining the strategy for Homeland Security about co-ordination with other levels of government, the Bush administration's vision of the Department of Homeland Security was clearly a centralizing one. Under the cover of September 11, the Bush administration was aiming to shift the balance within American federalism to the advantage of the federal government. In the process, it was creating nothing less than a new kind of American polity.

Again despite careful language about acting within the law and defending the liberties of Americans, this is a very spooky document. *The National Strategy for Homeland Security* is a blueprint for the creation of what we can call the Surveillance State. In the Surveillance State, the U.S. government will keep a very close eye on the comings and goings of people, both Americans and foreigners, and on the networks of which they are a part. Personal communication, particularly over the Internet, will be heavily monitored. The Department of Homeland Security will vet the ideas people have to make a determination about whether these ideas could lead to actions that would constitute a threat to the United States. Spying on Americans and on foreigners, especially those engaged in political or intellectual activities not to the liking of the Bush administration, will be the order of the day.

The impact of the U.S. Surveillance State will by no means be limited to citizens of the United States. As America's nearest neighbours, and those most involved in commerce and cross-border travel with the U.S., Canadians will be intimately affected.

The U.S. envisions the creation of "smart borders," a term already used in border agreements with Canada over the past several years. Here is how the Homeland Security blueprint sees "smart borders":

> Our future border management system will be radically different from today's which focuses on linear borders. It will create a "border of the future" that will be a continuum framed by land, sea and air dimensions, where a layered management system enables greater visibility of vehicles, people, and goods coming to and departing from our country. This border of the future will provide better security through better intelligence, coordinated national efforts, and unprecedented international cooperation . . .

A goal of this Surveillance State will be no less than to keep track of all the people entering and leaving the United States. "The Department [of Homeland Security] would develop and deploy the statutorily required entry-exit system to record the arrival and departure of foreign visitors and guests," the blueprint states. "The United States will require visitors to present travel documentation that includes biometric identifiers." The blueprint specifically mentions the need to "work closely with Canada and Mexico to increase the security of our shared borders . . ."[33]

Following months of sometimes fierce debate, the U.S. Senate approved the bill to create the new Department of Homeland Security on November 19, 2002, by a vote of 90–9.

Having been passed by the House the previous week, the bill proceeded to the White House for the president's signature. At a ceremony on November 25, George W. Bush signed the bill into law and announced that he was nominating Tom Ridge to become the first secretary of Homeland Security. The new department, with nearly 170,000 employees stationed in the United States and around the world, is the most massive transformation of the U.S. federal government in many decades. It will be years before the twenty-two major entities being absorbed by Homeland Security will overcome their separate cultures and learn to function as one. While the FBI and the CIA, the two key anti-terrorism agencies, are not being subsumed within the new department, Homeland Security will manage immigration, border protection, emergency management, intelligence analysis and the protection of the president.[34] Given the long history of fierce rivalry between the FBI and the CIA, it is reasonable to forecast that with a third major security agency on the terrain, rivalries are likely to become even more pronounced in the Byzantine world of Washington.

Particularly in the aftermath of September 11, the U.S. stress on improved security may sound innocent enough. But let us not forget that the need to provide security—as Hobbes recognized so clearly—has always been the rationale the state has used to prod the citizenry into giving up its liberty. The acts of terrorists have often been used by rulers to increase the power of the state at the expense of privacy and liberty. The list includes Stalin's campaign against so-called wreckers and saboteurs during the 1930s; Hitler's ferocious assault on political opponents after the Reichstag fire in the winter of 1933; de Gaulle's development of the means of repression in the wake of terrorist acts by right-wing opponents who wanted to maintain French rule in Algeria; the British use of widespread detention in Northern Ireland during the violent campaigns of the IRA; and in Canada the invocation of the War Measures Act and the detaining of hundreds of people without charges being laid in the October Crisis of 1970.

It used to be the pride of the western democracies that only Communist countries monitored the departure from as well as the entry into their territory. Now the U.S., making use of a technology that earlier states could only dream about, intends to keep a watchful eye on everyone, American and foreign, who crosses the U.S. border in either direction. The U.S. government is intending to carry out surveillance on its own people and on foreigners on a scale unprecedented in history. The system it envisions will carry the law enforcement agents of the United States government, responsible to the new Department of Homeland Security, to the far corners of the earth. The blueprint states:

> Internationally, the United States will seek to screen and verify the security of goods and identities of people before they can harm the international transportation system and well before they reach our shores or land borders. The Department of Homeland Security would improve information provided to consular officers so that individual applicants can be checked in comprehensive databases and would require visa-issuance procedures to reflect threat assessments . . . The Department, in cooperation with colleges and universities, would track and monitor international students and exchange visitors.

FBI agents and operatives of the Department of Homeland Security will be based in U.S. diplomatic offices abroad to assist in the accumulation of information about potentially dangerous foreigners. In addition, as already agreed with Canada, "the United States will place inspectors at foreign seaports to screen U.S.-bound sea containers before they are shipped to America . . ."[35]

All this is being done ostensibly to counter terrorism. But the United States is casting a very wide net, and many millions of people will end up in the databases and monitoring systems of this surveillance. Anyone who believes that the U.S. Surveillance State will be scrupulous in the use of all this information in upholding the rights of political opponents, domestic and foreign, has learned little about the way states use the power they accumulate.

In early December 2002, Canadian Deputy Prime Minister John Manley travelled to Washington to meet with Homeland Security secretary-designate Tom Ridge. In two days of meetings, they reached a number of agreements—and encountered one major stumbling block. The meetings involved work on the agenda established one year earlier, when Manley and Ridge signed the Smart Border Declaration in Ottawa in December 2001. In Washington, they agreed on procedures to speed up truck traffic across the border and on enhanced security measures to deal with ships landing in North American harbours. They also noted in their first-anniversary report on the progress of the Smart Border Declaration that Canada and the United States had signed the Safe Third Country Agreement (on August 30, 2002), an under-taking that refugee claimants to either country would be required to make their refugee claim in the first of the two countries they entered. The import of this agreement was that refugee claimants to Canada who entered the country from the U.S. would be sent back to the United States to make their claim in that country. The details of implementing this agreement were to be worked out in succeeding months. On a long range of issues—biometric identifiers, permanent-resident cards, visa policy, the provision of information about high-risk travellers, immigration databases, integrated border and marine enforcement teams, integrated intelligence, sharing of fingerprint data—the two countries were at work on a common agenda.

John Manley, reported to have developed a strong friendship with Tom Ridge and to be the Bush administration's favourite minister in the Chrétien cabinet, was, however, unable to make any headway on the issue of the tough new border regimen being put into place by the Americans to handle the entry and exit of individual travellers.

A friendly dinner hosted by Manley in Ridge's honour at the Canadian embassy did nothing to soften the U.S. position. For his part, Manley stressed the massive problems for cross-border travel and commerce that the new system—requiring visitors from Canada to be photographed, fingerprinted and registered—would bring when it was fully implemented in 2005. Putting the most neighbourly possible spin on it, Ridge told the media that the U.S. was taking the position not because of any hostility toward Canadians but to prevent those with evil designs on America who might have gained entry to Canada from making it into the United States. Regardless of the Canadian government's objections, crossing the border promised to become a more difficult proposition in the future.

Chapter 10 | **Fortress North America**

The September 11 attacks dramatically altered the American view of the outside world. Prior to that date, as the Bush administration's blueprint for the creation of a Department of Homeland Security stated, the United States had "relied heavily on two vast oceans and two friendly neighbours for border security." The uniquely favoured geographical location of the United States had been one of the factors that had allowed the nation to rise to unprecedented global power. Safe behind the oceans and blessed with weak neighbours, Americans had always been subject to the tug of isolationism. Let other nations quarrel and fight—that was not the concern of America. Right up until September 11, 2001, George Washington's famous farewell presidential address delivered in 1797, calling on the United States to avoid "outside entanglements," had resonated with the citizens of the country he had led to independence.

Even though the United States was inexorably drawn into global power struggles over the course of the twentieth century, isolationism remained strong. The U.S. entered World War I in

1917, close to three years after it began, because it felt threatened by the reach of German sea power in its unrestricted submarine warfare campaign. The U.S. was also deeply alarmed by Germany's ill-advised overtures to Mexico to consider joining in alliance with the Central Powers in return for the prospect of taking back territory it had lost to the United States in the Mexican-American war of 1846. When the U.S. dispatched vast armies across the Atlantic, victory for the western allies against Germany and Austria-Hungary was ensured. Under the leadership of President Woodrow Wilson, the U.S. remade the world through the Treaty of Versailles and the creation of the League of Nations. But the U.S. Senate rejected Wilson's handiwork, and the United States lapsed back into isolation from European security matters for two decades.

By the time Japan attacked Pearl Harbor on December 7, 1941, President Franklin Roosevelt was already looking for ways to increase U.S. involvement in World War II on the side of Britain. It was Pearl Harbor, the event that would be most often compared to September 11 in the days following the attacks on New York and Washington, that propelled the United States back into global power struggles. And this time there was no relapse into isolationism.

Nevertheless, the geographical location of the United States continued to be seen as uniquely favourable throughout World War II and through the decades of the Cold War. On September 11, 2001, terrorists did what no foreign power had ever been able to do to the United States in the nearly two centuries since the War of 1812. An enemy had reached into the greatest of American cities, destroyed a potent symbol of American commerce and inflicted massive casualties.

After September 11, Americans would never look at the oceans and their neighbours as they had before. The United States has a 3,200-kilometre border with Mexico and an 8,890-kilometre border with Canada. Each year, more than 500 million people legally enter the United States, through an air, land or sea point of entry. Of these, 330 million are non-citizens. Eighty-five percent of those who enter the U.S. legally do so across a land border, many of these as daily commuters. A gigantic volume of goods is imported into the United States and exported from it. In 2001, $1.35 trillion worth of goods were imported across U.S. borders, and $1 trillion worth of goods were exported from the United States.[1] In each of these categories, Canada is at the top of the list: longest border, largest number of people crossing and biggest trading partner.

In the aftermath of the attacks, these previously benign-seeming statistics appeared to depict potential threats aimed at the heart of America. As the blueprint for Homeland Security put it:

> The increasing mobility and destructive potential of modern terrorism has required the United States to rethink and rearrange fundamentally its systems for border and transportation security. Indeed, we must now begin to conceive of border security and transportation security as fully integrated requirements because our domestic transportation systems are intertwined inexorably with the global transport infrastructure. Virtually every community in America is connected to the global transportation network by the seaports, airports, highways, pipelines, railroads, and waterways that move people and goods into, within, and out of the Nation.[2]

In a world that was suddenly polarized between good and evil in the minds of many Americans, the top priority of the U.S. government was to plug the holes to make sure the atrocities of September 11 could never be repeated. Security became the watchword no matter what the topic under discussion. Through these altered optics, the U.S. border with Canada flashed onto the radar screen. The northern neighbour, so genial, so pliant, so easily taken for granted, now seemed to pose a threat.

For several years prior to the terror attacks, Canada had been subjected to harsh criticism both at home and from the United States as a haven for groups intent on mounting attacks on American targets. David Harris, a former Canadian Security and Intelligence Service (CSIS) officer, was fond of describing Canada as a "jihad aircraft carrier" aimed at the United States. Congressional committees and U.S. security agencies in Washington warned that Canada was an easy entry point for terrorists whose real target was the United States. In Ottawa, members of the Opposition parties made the same critique.

One event was overwhelmingly responsible for giving Canada its reputation as a haven for terrorists. On December 14, 1999, a U.S. Customs officer at Port Angeles, Washington, stopped Ahmed Ressam when he drove his car off the ferry from Victoria, British Columbia. The customs officer later said she noticed that Ressam was sweating heavily and was behaving suspiciously. An inspection revealed that the ingredients for a home-made bomb were stuffed in the back of Ressam's car. During his subsequent trial and in his testimony in the trial of Mokhtar Haouari, an accused co-conspirator, Ressam divulged the details of his scheme to plant a bomb in Los Angeles International Airport. What was truly chilling about the Ressam case was how he was able to train as a terrorist and plan his scheme for a year prior to being stopped at U.S. Customs. After being admitted to Canada, Ressam lived in Montreal, where for a time he was on welfare. He then travelled to Afghanistan, where he spent time in a terrorist training camp. Returning to Montreal, he bought guns, made contact with collaborators in the U.S. and stole fertilizer from a store in Vancouver. The Ressam case revealed just how easy it was for someone to falsify the documents needed to obtain a Canadian passport.

Ahmed Ressam became the poster boy both for those in the U.S. who were worried about the security of the northern frontier and for members of the Opposition parties in Canada who wanted to accuse the Chrétien government of being asleep at the switch. The busting of Ressam made big news across the continent just prior to New Year's 2000, when people were already spooked by the predictions that the Y2K computer glitch would trigger meltdowns of computer systems and massive electric power failures.

Twenty-four hours after the September 11 terror attacks, the Canadian border was fingered as the hole in the perimeter through which the terrorist hijackers entered the United States. ABC News broadcast a story that cited unidentified U.S. authorities as saying that most of the hijackers had entered the U.S. through Canada. The officials, who spoke on condition of anonymity, said they were investigating the possibility that some of the terrorists crossed the Canadian border and proceeded to Boston, where they could have been involved in hijacking the American Airlines aircraft that was flown into the World Trade Center. ABC reported that U.S. authorities were checking on whether a group of the hijackers had crossed the border from Quebec en route to Jackman, Maine. A hamlet about twenty-five kilometres inside Maine, Jackman is located in remote, lightly populated mountainous country.[3] Canadian media outlets picked up the story that some of the hijackers had entered the United States from Canada. Writing in *The Toronto Sun*, columnist Matthew Fisher declared:

> [It] has not gone unnoticed in Washington that several of those believed to have been involved in Tuesday's outrages passed through Canada on their way south. Colin Powell, the decorated general and U.S. Secretary of State, alluded to this on Wednesday when he said that border and immigration issues were being looked at. He did not mention any country by name, but he said: "They are going to know what we mean."[4]

Not many days passed before it became clear that the hijackers had not entered the U.S. from Canada. The trail of the nineteen terrorists who carried out the suicide attacks led to various places, but there was no evidence of a Canadian link. Some of the perpetrators were students in Hamburg, Germany, before they came to the U.S. As the investigation proceeded, the theory grew that it was the Hamburg terrorist cell that hatched the plan for the attacks of September 11. Eleven of the nineteen hijackers travelled to the United States from Britain, where they had operated and trained for some time before the attack, and still others came from the United Arab Emirates. Some had trained for nearly two years in Florida to become pilots.

The fact that none of the hijackers crossed the border from Canada to the U.S. was repeated frequently by Prime Minister Jean Chrétien and members of his cabinet. But the damage of those first incorrect news stories lingered. The impression of Canada as a weak link in the defences of the United States, established by coverage of the Ressam case in 1999, had been dramatically reinforced.

In the weeks following September 11, many stories in the U.S. media continued to depict Canada as a terrorist haven. An article in *The Christian Science Monitor* said that "Canadian and U.S. terrorism experts alike say the giant, genial nation—known for its crimson-clad Mounties and great comedians—has also become an entry point and staging ground for Osama bin Laden's terrorist 'sleeper cells,' as well as for other terrorist groups."[5] A story in *The Seattle Times* declared: "While thousands of U.S. soldiers are being shipped halfway across the globe to fight terrorism, little manpower has been focused on a problem much closer to home: Canada. Experts on both sides of the 4,000-mile border say the nation to the north is a haven for terrorists, and that the U.S.–Canada line is little more barrier than ink on a map."[6] New

York senator Hillary Clinton said that the U.S. should lobby Canada to tighten border security: "We need to look to our friends in the north to crack down on some of these false documents and illegals getting in."[7]

Perhaps the most damaging of all the U.S. sources in reinforcing the image of Canada as a safe haven for terrorists was the highly popular television show *The West Wing*. After September 11, the writers and cast of the show quickly put together a new season opener in which a Middle Eastern terrorist crosses the border from Canada to the U.S. The writers showed themselves to be geographically challenged when they had their suspect cross the border from Ontario to Vermont.

In Canada, members of the two right-wing Opposition parties in Parliament, the Canadian Alliance and the Progressive Conservatives, far from speaking up to offset the American impression that Canada was a haven for terrorists, launched an assault on the Chrétien government that reinforced the American impression. Stockwell Day, then the Alliance leader, adopted a stance that was relentlessly negative toward the Chrétien government and endlessly forgiving toward Washington. It is no exaggeration to say that he and his party acted like a fifth column in Ottawa, a virtual U.S. lobby in the House of Commons. Despite the fact that there was no evidence of a Canadian link with the attacks on September 11, Day repeatedly implied the existence of such a link in his assaults on the government during Question Period. On September 20, 2001, he asked a question about Nabil Al-Marabh, who had been arrested by U.S. authorities as a suspect in terrorist activities. Al-Marabh, who had been a refugee in Canada since 1994, had been living in Toronto until several weeks before the attacks. "Does the Prime Minister still maintain there is no Canadian connection in the U.S. investigation of this terrible activity?" asked Day. A week later, he again raised the Al-Marabh matter. Day's question: "Two weeks ago the Prime Minister was quick to say there was no Canadian connection to the attacks. Will the Prime Minister now admit that there may well be some Canadian connection?" In answer to a further question from Day, Foreign Affairs Minister John Manley replied that "over the past two weeks, we have repeatedly asked the question [of American authorities] whether there was any evidence that any of those suspected in the events of September 11 entered the United States through Canada or had substantial connections with Canada. They have repeatedly assured us that they have no such information. If the Alliance Party has different information, it should make it public."[8]

On the issue of refugees, Day talked of "thousands of these claimants roaming around Canada who should have been detained and some possibly deported . . . We know that there have been terrorists living among us. We know that they get here illegally through our refugee system." Elinor Caplan, the minister of citizenship and immigration, replied that "not all refugee claimants are criminal and it is wrong for the Leader of the Opposition to suggest it. That is just fear mongering." Again, on October 22, the leader of the Opposition rose in Question Period and declared that "we hear reports continually about suspect terrorists hiding in Toronto, or in Fort McMurray or simply roaming the countryside."[9] He presented no evidence to support these alarming claims, based as they were on highly speculative newspaper stories. Day's purpose seemed to be to reinforce the American impression that Canada was indeed a haven for terrorists. In the U.S. after September 11, virtually the whole of the American political class rallied around the Bush administration, with criticisms of the White House muted. North of the border, there was no such patriotic effect. Right-wing Opposition parties tore into the Chrétien government's handling of the crisis from day one.

The terror attacks instantly made the notion of establishing a North American security perimeter a hot political issue. The idea, which had been around for some time prior to September 11, was that the United States and Canada, and possibly Mexico, would adopt a continental rather than a national approach to territorial security. One of the first things Paul Cellucci, the U.S. ambassador to Canada, did when he took up his new post in Ottawa in the spring of 2001 was to make the issue of the security perimeter, or Fortress America, his personal hobby horse. Canadian business lobbyists loved the idea, seeing it as a step toward further economic integration with the United States. In the autumn of 2000, former prime minister Brian Mulroney declared himself in favour of removing customs posts along the Canada–U.S. border to allow for unfettered travel between the two countries. For the influential segments of the business community who approved of further integration with the United States, the next two steps they wanted to take were to open the border and then to adopt a single currency with the United States.

In its pre–September 11 version, the idea of Fortress North America featured the quest for common immigration and refugee policies and common visa requirements for visitors to the continent. Canadians would forgo their own customs and immigration authorities to create a new continental authority. With a hardened continental perimeter in place, it would be possible to eliminate the borders within the continent and to allow full mobility of persons in North America. Crossing the border from Canada to the U.S. would be like crossing an interprovincial border. It would be the same between Mexico and the U.S.

September 11 significantly altered what had been a business agenda, making it both a business and a security agenda. The terror attacks put the issue squarely on the front burner, not as something to be approached over time, like the signing of a free trade deal, but as a critical matter of national security. Precisely because of the vastly heightened U.S. concern for national security, the business agenda became both more urgent and more difficult to achieve. As soon as the attacks occurred, as a customs official in Washington, DC, explained to me in a telephone interview, the U.S. went on a "level-one, code-red alert" and cancelled programs for the rapid entry of low-risk travellers from Canada to the U.S. Prior to September 11, programs such as Autopass and Nexus had allowed frequent travellers entering the U.S. from Canada to undergo a security check so that they could be issued with an ID and a car window decal, which allowed them to use designated rapid passage lanes. Now these programs were indefinitely suspended. A few days later, Washington announced that the number of customs officials on the northern border would be trebled, to about five thousand, a step in exactly the direction the business lobbyists did not want to go.

But business spokespersons also saw the crisis as one they could turn to their advantage. Within days of the attacks, with the support of Opposition politicians, a major business lobby was pressuring the Chrétien government on behalf of the perimeter concept. On November 1, 2001, the Coalition for Secure and Trade-Efficient Borders, a coalition of forty business groups that was formed on October 3, 2001, released a report entitled *Rethinking Our Borders*. Perrin Beatty, the former Conservative cabinet minister who was now president and CEO of Canadian Manufacturers and Exporters, described the coalition's approach as "addressing both security and border management." The coalition foresaw the development, in concert with the United States, of three lines of security: offshore interception; first point of entry into North America; and the Canada–U.S. border.

The idea was a simple one. To persuade the Americans to expedite the flow of traffic from Canada to the U.S., Canada would agree to set up a harmonized regime with the United States to handle the entry of people into North America. A perimeter thus would be drawn around Canada and the United States, lessening the importance of the border itself. To entice the United

States into such an arrangement, the supporters of the perimeter scheme conceded that Canada would have to agree to dovetail its immigration, refugee and visa policies with those of the U.S. A *Toronto Sun* columnist put the matter bluntly: "Canada must finally cut the crap and agree to longstanding U.S. demands for stringent common visa procedures."[10]

In addition to his relentless insistence on the presence of terrorists in Canada, Alliance leader Stockwell Day took up the cause of the North American security perimeter. Endorsing the ideas of the U.S. ambassador and other U.S. officials, Day impressed upon the prime minister the virtue of a Canada–U.S. security perimeter. "In that way both countries would enforce security and screening standards and the entire continent would be better protected . . . Will the Prime Minister abandon his go-slow approach and move quickly to protect Canadians and to protect the billion dollars' worth of trade a day that moves back and forth?"[11] Conservative leader Joe Clark launched the idea of a border management agency that would be run by the U.S., Canada and Mexico. While this was clearly a version of the Fortress America idea, Clark dressed it up to make it appear to be a way to maintain Canadian sovereignty. Without his initiative, Clark said, Canada ran the risk of allowing Washington to impose a "made-in-America" border policy. "It's much easier if you want to maintain a sovereign identity in Canada for Canada to do the proposing than simply sit back and let the Americans roll over you," Clark told a news conference.[12]

It was not just the Conservative and Alliance parties and business lobbyists who were promoting the Fortress North America idea. The American response to the terror attacks immediately subjected Canada to immense pressures to alter the management of the border and to harden its immigration and refugee policies to meet American security concerns. The U.S. government moved quickly on two fronts to grapple with the perceived

Canadian security problem. First came the announcement that Washington would station more customs officers on the northern border. At the time of the announcement there were more than 9,000 American officers patrolling the border with Mexico, compared with only 334 border patrol agents and 498 inspectors on duty on the border with Canada.[13] Second, Washington began a campaign to pressure Canada to harmonize immigration, refugee and visa policies with those of the U.S., and even to accept the creation of a binational customs authority that would oversee the arrival of outsiders at entry points into North America.

Under pressure from the media and U.S. and Canadian critics, the federal government stiffened refugee, immigration and anti-terrorism regulations. Citizenship and Immigration Minister Elinor Caplan announced in the House of Commons on September 25, 2001, that the government would fast-track the production of new high-tech photo ID cards for new immigrants. Ottawa had been urged to replace the IM 1000 document, the letter-sized paper document carried by new immigrants, because it had been subject to widespread counterfeiting. Caplan's ministry also expedited the passage of Bill C-11, the Immigration and Refugee Protection Act, which enhanced the powers of the federal government to deal expeditiously, some would say harshly, with newcomers to Canada suspected of having links to terrorism.

Considering the widespread criticism of Canada as a soft touch for terrorists, it is something of a shock to see just how broad had been the powers of the government to deal with suspected terrorists, and how much broader they were to become under the new Immigration Act. Bill C-11, which was drafted well before the terrorist attacks on the United States, gave the federal government the power to deport those who were not citizens or landed immigrants without a hearing. It allowed the government to detain non-citizens without a warrant. And it permitted the deportation of refugees and other non-citizens to countries where they could face torture, with no oral hearing before an independent decision maker. Critics of the bill who were concerned about the rights of refugees in Canada pointed out that a major problem with both existing Canadian immigration law and the new bill was that they provided no clear definition of "terrorism" or "terrorist group." Lack of clear definitions left the authorities with considerable discretion in dealing with individual cases.

Bill C-11, which received royal assent in November 2001, came into force on June 28, 2002.

The federal government also moved to freeze the assets of the individuals and organizations named by President Bush as terrorist groups, their leaders and their supporters, or so-called non-profit groups believed to be willing or unwitting fronts for the movement of money to suspected terrorists.

In addition to Bill C-11, the Chrétien government swiftly introduced Bill C-36, a sweeping anti-terrorism act that handed law enforcement authorities ominous new powers to deal with suspects. The bill amended the Criminal Code to create what was called a "preventive arrest" power, under which a suspected terrorist could be arrested without being charged with an offence on the grounds that the person was suspected of being about to commit a terrorist act. It was clear as the debate on Bill C-36 took place in parliamentary committees and in the Commons and Senate that a major motive for the bill was to impress the Americans with how serious Canada was on the subject of anti-terrorism. The Chrétien government hoped its anti-terrorism bill would persuade the Bush administration to ease up on the Canada–U.S. border. Civil liberties were being traded away, in large measure, in the hope that Canada–U.S. trade would not suffer. The Chrétien government was making a Faustian bargain.

The initial wording of Bill C-36 alarmed civil libertarians, political activists and trade unionists, who worried that the bill could be used to target persons involved in mass demonstrations or in strikes. In November 2001, the government announced a series of amendments to the bill in response to criticisms, including an amendment to delete the word *lawful* from the definition of "terrorist activity." This was to ensure that protest activity, whether lawful or unlawful, would not be considered a terrorist act unless it was intended to cause death, serious bodily harm or serious risk to the health or safety of the public.[14] Despite the amendments, Bill C-36 continued to concern many groups, who feared that it could be used to strike out at them. A coalition of community groups and religious and ethnic advocacy groups wrote an open letter to Prime Minister Jean Chrétien in which they warned that "the anti-terrorism Act is itself a threat to the legal and civil rights that Canadians now enjoy."[15] The amended bill received royal assent on December 18, 2001.

The anti-terrorism act was soon followed by Bill C-42, the Public Safety Act, an omnibus bill whose public rationale was that it would give the government a wide range of new powers to deal with terrorist threats. One such power was the right to establish temporary "military security zones," not only to protect Canadian Forces and visiting Forces personnel but also to protect property, places and things the Canadian Forces have been directed by the government to protect. The unveiling of this concept in the bill struck political activists as a threat aimed directly at them. Even though the Public Safety Act was first introduced in the weeks following September 11, it came only a few months after the massive demonstrations in Quebec City in opposition to the proposed Free Trade Agreement of the Americas. Suppose the act had been in place at the time of the demonstration, and Ottawa had designated the area around the summit a temporary military security zone. Demonstrators could then have been threatened with lengthy jail terms for protesting inside the zone. In the summer of 2002, the leaders of the G8 were to meet near Calgary, at Kananaskis, Alberta. Could Ottawa set up a zone around the summit and use it as a weapon against demonstrations? In the future, would demonstrators be faced with a system of martial law that could be used against them whenever and wherever the government chose?

As it turned out, this did not come to pass. Unlike the Anti-Terrorism Act, Bill C-42 did not sail through Parliament. Following considerable public criticism, the bill was reintroduced as Bill C-55 in April 2002, and then was withdrawn again to be introduced a third time in October 2002 as Bill C-17. The consequence of pressure and rethinking was a new draft of the bill that removed the provision for the creation of temporary military security zones. The proposal for the zones was not abandoned entirely, however. While it was removed from the bill, the government decided through Order-in-Council to set up what it called controlled access zones in Halifax, Esquimalt and Nanoose Bay harbours. These naval ports, the first on the East Coast and the two others on the West Coast, would be subject to controlled access, although in a much more limited way than would have been the case with the original zone proposal. The government also left the door open for the creation of further such zones on a case-by-case basis should an altered security situation make this expedient.

With one eye on the Bush administration, the Chrétien government charted its course in the tumultuous weeks following the attacks of September 11. On Monday, December 3, 2001, with a Christmas tree, Canadian and U.S. flags and uniformed Mounties for a backdrop, the Canadian and U.S. governments signed a Joint Statement of Cooperation on Border Security and Regional Migration Issues, as well as an RCMP–FBI agreement to improve the exchange of fingerprint data. U.S. Attorney General John Ashcroft, who had done more than anyone else to sweep away civil liberties in the United States since the attacks, was in Ottawa for the signing ceremony.

Solicitor General Lawrence MacAulay and Citizenship and Immigration Minister Elinor Caplan represented Canada at the signing. In his fumbling way, MacAulay welcomed Ashcroft to Ottawa, describing him rather pathetically as a personal friend, an intimacy Ashcroft did not return. On the eve of the visit, Ashcroft had spoken publicly about the U.S. plan to station troops and helicopters on the border. The appearance of the border being militarized was not the optics the government of Canada would have chosen for the signing ceremony. But clients can't be choosers.

The Ottawa border deal included measures to increase the integration of the policing of the border by the RCMP, the U.S. border patrol, and other Canadian and U.S. police forces. Experimental Integrated Border Enforcement Teams, already in existence, were to be expanded. As part of the deal, Canada and the U.S. agreed to adopt similar lists of countries whose citizens require visitors' visas, as well as co-ordinated immigration measures. Joint networks of immigration control officers were to be set up overseas. The accord contained the agreement that would require refugee claimants to apply for status in the first of the two countries they passed through, either Canada or the U.S.

Prior to the deal, in only two countries, Argentina and Uruguay, did citizens require a visa to visit Canada but not the United States. On the other hand, in twenty-eight countries citizens required a visa to visit the U.S. but not Canada. Many of those were Commonwealth countries, located in the Caribbean, Africa, Asia and the South Pacific. The only Middle Eastern countries whose citizens did not require a visa to visit Canada were Saudi Arabia and Israel. In theory, Saudi Arabia was a leading ally of the United States, but it was also the country of origin of many of the September 11 suicide attackers. Canada did not require a visitor's visa for Israelis who held national passports (which excluded Palestinians in the territory of the Palestinian Authority).

Since the deal went into effect, changes have been made to visa requirements in both countries. The United States now requires visas for visitors from Argentina. Meanwhile Canada has moved toward harmonization with the United States, reducing to eighteen the number of countries whose citizens require a visa to visit the U.S. but not Canada. For instance, citizens from Saudi Arabia, Hungary, Grenada, Malaysia, and Zimbabwe now require visas to visit Canada.

The accord on refugees was likely to have palpable consequences, particularly for those claiming status in Canada from Western Hemisphere countries. Prior to the agreement, between 40 and 50 percent of those claiming refugee status in Canada entered from the United States. A large number of these were people from Latin America and Central America who were fleeing countries where militias were regularly killing their foes or those who just happened to be in the way. Historically, Canada had always been much more welcoming than the U.S. to people seeking refuge from these countries. Thousands of Chileans had fled the Pinochet regime after a U.S.-backed coup toppled the democratically elected government of President Salvador Allende in 1973. Under the new rules, those who had made their way to Canada after crossing the United States would be turned down as refugee claimants in Canada.

Soon the pressure shifted from border arrangements to continental defence. Following the attacks on September 11, the Bush administration had persuaded Tom Ridge to take up the post of director of Homeland Security. While Ridge had little direct authority, he had the ear of the president and would be an important player in working out the details of future border arrangements with Canada. Along with this new post, the Bush administration decided to create a new military structure for the defence of the American homeland. The idea was that an "America's Command" would be established, with naval, land and air units at its disposal, for the defence of the United States. The operational area to be covered by the new command was still being considered. In principle, it could be expanded beyond the U.S. to deal with the whole of North America. The new command would inevitably downgrade the importance of NORAD, which was established in 1958 through a treaty between the United States and Canada. Under NORAD, a U.S. four-star general is in command, with a Canadian air force general as deputy commander. While NORAD involves a nod in the direction of Canadian sovereignty, the new structure could well function with an American general in sole command.

For the Chrétien government, the question was how to respond to the proposed command structure. Since the end of the Cold War, the Canadian military has set as a high objective the seamless integration of its forces with those of the United States. For instance, in the American military buildup for the assault on the Taliban and Al Qaeda in Afghanistan in the autumn of 2001, Canadian naval vessels served as pickets for American naval forces. After being turned down for participation in the peace-keeping mission, Canada dispatched 750 soldiers to Kandahar to serve in a combat role under direct U.S. command. It was the first time since World War II, when a joint Canadian-American unit served in Italy, that Canadian troops at the unit level served under direct U.S. command.

The proposed U.S. structure for homeland defence could, in theory, involve the formal expansion of NORAD to add land and sea operations to its air operations. But such an extension of NORAD's role would mean that Canada's naval, land and air forces would be directed from a single point in the United States, with the commanding officer an American. It would mean a U.S. commander for Canadian ships patrolling Canadian coasts, as well as the High Arctic, where there is a serious dispute with the U.S. over whether the waters in the Northwest Passage are Canadian or international.

If the bulk of the Canadian forces end up in a continental command structure with a U.S. general at the helm, what are the implications for Canada's ability to decide on a case-by-case basis whether to participate in U.S. military operations?

Chapter 11 | Deep Integration

T he smoke had barely cleared from the site of Ground Zero in New York after September 11 before the new debate about the future of Canada commenced. While the policy of the ever wily Canadian prime minister, Jean Chrétien, was to proceed with caution and muddle through, one powerful wing of Canadian opinion was quick off the mark making the argument that the world had changed and that Canada needed to press for a wide-ranging deal with the United States to promote much closer North American integration. As was the case with the free trade debate of the 1980s, the new debate was kicked off by those on the political right, who admire American economic and social values and want Canada to emulate them.

When Stephen Harper was elected leader of the Canadian Alliance in the spring of 2002, he took up where his predecessor, Stockwell Day, had left off on the issue of Canadian-American relations. In his maiden speech in the House as leader of the Opposition on May 28, 2002, Harper made the case for an Alliance motion that charged the Liberal government with failure in its management of relations with the United States. Harper's thesis was that the Chrétien government had been insufficiently staunch in its support for the positions adopted by the U.S. administration.

Harper accused Chrétien of "open meddling in U.S. domestic politics prior to the 2000 presidential election when the Prime Minister stated his preference with regard to the outcome of that election." He quoted the comments of the former political counsellor at the U.S. embassy, David Jones, who said in January 2001 that Chrétien exhibits "a tin ear for foreign affairs, especially those involving the United States." Harper's conclusion: "It is no secret that this poisoned the relationship between the government and the new American administration." Quoting an unnamed source in the *National Post* to the effect that the prime minister is not a player with the Bush administration, Harper said that "the Americans could not care less about the views of the current Prime Minister. This is particularly evident in President Bush's passivity in dealing with the softwood lumber dispute."

Not a word of criticism in Harper's speech was directed at Washington for its failure to seek a solution on the softwood lumber issue; all the blame was laid at the door of the prime minister. Apparently it did not occur to Harper that taking the side of the government in its tough negotiations with Washington on the issue could make it clear to the Bush administration that Canadians were united on the question. Instead, Harper made it appear that Canadians were hopelessly divided and that the Official Opposition was delighted with the anti-Canadian position of the U.S. on softwood lumber.

Harper then broadened his attack on the Chrétien government, beyond trade issues, to lambaste it for its entire foreign policy stance vis-à-vis the United States. "Downright hostility to the United States, anti-Americanism, has come to characterize other dimensions of Canadian policy," he declared. "In 1996–97 Canada aggressively pushed forward with the treaty to ban land mines without giving due consideration to U.S. concerns about the potential implications for its security forces in South Korea. What did we end up with? We ended up with a ban on land mines that few major land mine producers or users have signed," Harper charged. Having dismissed an anti–land mines treaty signed in Ottawa by most of the nations of the world, Harper went on to toe the Bush administration's line on the development of an anti-ballistic missile defence system. "Most recently we have been inclined to offer knee-jerk resistance to the United States on national missile defence despite the fact that Canada is confront-ed by the same threats from rogue nations equipped with ballistic missiles and weapons of mass destruction as is the United States." Harper's litany of complaints against the Chrétien government ended with this nod to those who allege that Canada's refugee sys-tem makes it vulnerable to terrorists: "The government has not adequately addressed the matter of security in the context of conti-nental security. Because of the unreformed nature of our refugee determination system, we continue to be subject to unique internal security and continental security dangers."

Having dismissed Jean Chrétien as a leader who was always anti-free trade, Harper commended Brian Mulroney for having "understood a fundamental truth. He understood that mature and intelligent Canadian leaders must share the following perspective: the United States is our closest neighbour, our best ally, our biggest customer and our most consistent friend." Harper concluded with his own set of principles for dealing with the United States. "Not only does the United States have this special relationship to us, it is the world leader when it comes to freedom and democracy . . . If the United States prospers, we prosper. If the United States hurts or is angry, we will be hurt. If it is ever broadly attacked, we will surely be destroyed."[1]

Here was a theory of Canadian-American relations that allowed for no differentiation between the interests of the United

States and those of Canada. If there were problems in the relationship, it was because Canadian leaders have been insufficiently devoted to supporting the United States on all essential matters of continental and global policy.

Those like Harper who were pressing for Canada to opt for Fortress America showed themselves to be unconcerned by the threats this posed not only to Canadian sovereignty but to Canadian security as well. They began from the presumption that the United States had been doing a better job than Canada in screening out potential terrorists, and from the notion that Canada posed more of a security threat to the U.S. than vice versa. It never occurred to them that the prospect of an open border with the U.S. would raise serious security concerns for Canada. For instance, the Bush administration has opposed an international accord to limit the world's trade in small arms on the grounds that this violates the Second Amendment to the U.S. Constitution, which guarantees the right of Americans to bear arms. An open border would inevitably import the American gun culture into Canada, something most Canadians strongly oppose. I've seen weapons that are illegal in Canada removed from U.S. vehicles stopped at the border. The weapons are held by customs until the visitors leave the country.

Guns would not be the only problem for Canada. As the Europeans discovered when they set out to open frontiers, Canadians would have concerns about the movement of banned drugs, explosives, pornography, toxic waste and certain categories of animals, plants and food. In addition, what would be the Canadian attitude to the idea of high-speed police chases across the border, something the Europeans had to consider?

The problem, of course, is that unlike the European case, where there was a balance in size and power among the states involved in opening frontiers, there is no such balance between Canada and the United States. It would be the American way or the highway on this list of important matters that bear heavily on the kind of society Canadians want.

In addition, there is the matter of illegal immigrants. Estimates of the number of illegal immigrants in Canada run at about 200,000, with about half of them thought to be living in the Greater Toronto Area. But in the United States, the number of illegal immigrants is estimated to be between 9 and 11 million people, most of them of Hispanic origin and living in California and the Southwest. On a per capita basis, that means the number of illegal immigrants in the United States is about five times as high as in Canada.

As the debate about Canada's attitude to American global policy intensified, the insistent voice of those favouring the deep integration of Canada with the United States was increasingly heard. For decades, the C.D. Howe Institute has been a think-tank devoted to fostering an ever closer relationship between Canada and the United States. The Institute was publishing papers advocating a free trade deal between Ottawa and Washington more than a decade before the Mulroney government made this a live political issue in the mid-1980s. Following the September 11 terror attacks, the Institute began publishing "The Border Papers," described as "a project on Canada's choices regarding North American Integration." "The Border Papers" were published with the financial backing of the Donner Canadian Foundation, also a well-known supporter of continentalist causes.

In April 2002, Wendy Dobson, director of the Institute of International Business and professor at the Joseph L. Rotman School of Management, University of Toronto, authored the first "Border Paper," which argued that Canada ought to take the radical step of initiating a scheme of deep North American integration. Dobson proposed what she called a Big Idea, "one that addresses U.S. objectives while creating new economic opportunities for Canada." She argued that given the way power is dispersed in the

U.S. system and the Bush administration's "exclusive focus on homeland security and defence," only such a Big Idea could succeed in attracting attention south of the border. The thesis of her paper was simple enough. It is in Canada's interest to achieve a level of economic integration that goes well beyond that which exists through NAFTA. To interest the Americans in such a proposition, Canada would be required to propose steps that Washington would find attractive in the following areas: border security, immigration, defence and energy security. Among other things, deeper integration would involve the creation of a Canada–U.S. code of conduct for subsidies and other government programs so that Canada could finally be done with trade disputes with the U.S., such as the softwood lumber dispute. Such a code has always been a cherished goal of Canadian continentalists, but from the days of Mulroney's free trade deal to the present, it has been an elusive goal. The United States has never been willing to give up its right to promulgate its own trade law. A common Canada–U.S. code of conduct, even if its content was virtually dictated in Washington, as it certainly would be, would involve a theoretical loss of sovereignty for the U.S. Congress. To date, there is no sign this is somewhere Washington is willing to go. But Dobson's hope is that if Canada is highly compliant on a list of other security- and border-related issues, Washington's interest could be piqued.

(One American analyst published a book on the eve of the terrorist attacks that did express interest in closer continental integration. In his book *Toward a North American Community*, Robert Pastor, a professor of international relations in Atlanta, made the case for full continental integration, including the creation of a continental currency, which he would call the amero.)[2]

Dobson's critique of Canada's situation was that while the country had benefited historically from steps toward international economic openness, it had fallen significantly behind the U.S. in productivity and standard of living during the 1990s, following the implementation of NAFTA. One might have thought the fact that Canada has suffered during the new age of free trade would be reason to rethink whether continentalism is the way to go for the future. Dobson reaches exactly the opposite conclusion: only deeper integration with the U.S. can solve the problems created by the current level of integration. This paradoxical reasoning shows up in virtually all continentalist writings in Canada. So sure are the proponents of integration with the U.S. about the soundness of their position that any difficulties that have arisen already are written off as evidence that the process has not gone far enough. If the patient seems to be suffering from the medicine being taken, the solution is to increase the dose.

Well aware that Canadians are highly sensitive about the preservation of their national sovereignty, Dobson tried to square the circle by dressing up her proposal for deep integration as an example of the creative exercise of sovereignty. To do this, she first had to dispense with traditional notions of sovereignty by labelling them outdated. As Dobson states, "The traditional definition of sovereignty refers to a country's determination of key policies and national control of decisions affecting its governance." From this unobjectionable statement, she proceeds to the brave new world of the twenty-first century.

> Thus, a common theme in the international debate about economic integration—that it erodes national sovereignty and causes the nation-state to wither away—needs to be put in a different perspective. States are the architects of their own constraints through the decisions they make, such as supporting international regimes that make them more accountable to other public and private sector participants, and through the decisions they avoid by failing to exercise their sovereignty."

In this wonderland, when a country like Canada bargains away its sovereignty in binding arrangements with a superpower, this can be redefined as a brilliant exercise of sovereignty.

Dobson wants to be able to claim that at the end of the deep integration she proposes, Canada would still enjoy what she calls "political independence," although exactly what Canadians would be allowed to do with it she doesn't say. Beyond issuing stamps and flying the Maple Leaf flag, it's not clear what this politically independent Canada would do.

A couple of months after Dobson's Big Idea paper, historian Jack Granatstein continued in the same vein with a "Border Paper" on Canada's military options for the future. Giving voice to ideas espoused by an influential body of opinion on the political right and among strategic studies analysts, Granatstein, a Distinguished Research Professor of History Emeritus at York University and chair of the Council for Canadian Security in the 21st Century, made the argument for a new and deeper military alliance with the United States. The case he makes is much like Dobson's. Canadians must make a virtue of necessity—and call it an exercise in the use of sovereignty—by going along with the U.S. on all key security and defence questions, in return for a seat at the table with the Americans. Granatstein begins with a rehearsal of Canada's defence history, particularly since 1940, when Canada and the United States established a military alliance and a permanent Joint Board of Defence. His brief history lesson is designed to illustrate the central truth he wishes to impart: continental integration, in defence and other matters, despite detours from time to time, is the main thoroughfare of Canadian history.

Granatstein's argument is that in the wake of September 11, the United States is determined to defend itself, with or without the co-operation of Canada. Therefore, "there is no choice at all: Canada must cooperate with the United States in its own interest." Dismissive of what he calls the Canadian penchant for "poking the

Americans with the sharp stick of supposedly superior Canadian morality," he is sympathetic to the U.S. view of things. "The superpower neighbour," Granatstein writes, "has global responsibilities and burdens, and it often tires of Canadian caution, endless remonstrances, and prickly independence when what it wants and needs is support."

Having upbraided Canadians, Granatstein paints a picture of the new world in which we live. "Fueled by militant Islam, terrorism has suddenly become the major threat to secular, democratic, and pluralist states," he writes. While the United States has been gearing up to face this threat, and to develop a ballistic missile defence system as well, Canada has been allowing its armed forces to wither, Granatstein argues. "Canada's defence spending of U.S.$265 per capita is less than half the NATO average of U.S.$589, and its 1.1 percent of gross national product (GNP) devoted to defence is precisely half the NATO average," he writes. The consequence, he states, is that "the Canadian Forces have all but lost the capacity to undertake operations for a sustained period." Granatstein's conclusion: " . . . Canada is now all but undefended at a time of danger. Although terrorism poses a real threat, it is not the most serious crisis. The danger lies in wearing blinkers about the United States at a time when it is in a vengeful, anxious mood."

Granatstein insists that only one course of action is open to Canadians: Canada must align itself with the Bush administration on crucial defence and security issues. A key strategic question is Canada's position on the Bush administration's highly controversial plan to develop a National Missile Defence (NMD) system, despite very widespread opposition in many parts of the world to the destabilization such a course may entail. For Granatstein, once again, it is a choice between "high morality" and "great practicality"—really no choice at all. Since the U.S. would likely want to put a workable NMD system——should one ever be developed—under

NORAD, Canada's opposition to the system could dismantle NORAD as an effective integrated command system. "On the other hand," Granatstein writes, "if Canada accepted NMD and missile defence went to NORAD, Canada's influence might actually increase."

This advice means that even if the Canadian government believes, along with many Europeans, the Russians and the Chinese, that Bush's NMD plan could push the world into a dangerous new arms race that would have negative consequences for Canadians, Ottawa ought to forget about this. Granatstein believes that signing on to NMD might give Canadians increased influence. But what sort of influence? Granatstein immediately qualifies his answer: "No one suggests that Canada would acquire 'go/no go' authority over NMD if NORAD runs the show. But Canada would have the right to consultation, the right to participation, and the right to a place at the table when decisions are made."

Here Granatstein comes close to admitting what ought to be obvious. In a real crisis, the decision to act or not would be taken in Washington. Canadians would be bystanders, the only difference being that they would be at the table. Indeed, Granatstein's own history recital reveals the truth in this. During the 1962 Cuban Missile Crisis, U.S. commanders put Canadian forces on full alert without the government of John Diefenbaker signing off on this. On this grave breach of Canadian sovereignty, Granatstein is frank: "Without waiting for Cabinet approval, belatedly and grudgingly granted, the RCN put to sea to shadow Soviet submarines in the Atlantic, and the Royal Canadian Air Force (RCAF) went on alert, ready to counter any attack by Soviet bombers." Granatstein calls this "the single greatest breach of proper civil–military relations in Canadian history." Nevertheless, he proposes that we set ourselves up for just such a situation at a moment of international crisis in the future. Being at the table with a superpower is no guarantee of influence. Indeed, as a practical matter, Canada is more likely to influence the outcome of events by taking a stand along with other countries against the Bush administration's plan to proceed with NMD. Many influential Americans oppose NMD, and they value the support of countries such as Canada.

Not surprisingly, Granatstein wants Canada to attempt to expand the responsibilities of NORAD to cover much of the ground for which the Bush administration has established the new "America's Command." He says, quite rightly, that it is "very unlikely that Canada will be invited to participate" in the planning or command structure of NORTHCOM, the new United States integrated command for homeland defence. NORTHCOM will operate next door to NORAD at Cheyenne Mountain, Colorado, and will be led by the same U.S. four-star general who heads NORAD.

The problem with an expanded NORAD is that Canadians could end up with most of their armed forces—army, navy and air force—under the command of a U.S. general. Former Canadian foreign minister Lloyd Axworthy has raised concerns about the implications of putting Canadians under U.S. command. "What does a Canadian soldier do," he queries, "if asked to handle land mines on Canadian soil, in contravention of our treaty undertakings? What if we apprehend someone considered a war criminal . . . ? U.S. law would prevent them being turned over to the [International Criminal Court], while our obligations require it." Axworthy has also pointed to another problem with putting our armed forces under U.S. command: it would mean that Canada could not exercise authority in the Arctic, where Canada has serious sovereignty disagreements with the U.S. over Arctic waters. While not dismissing these questions as unimportant, Granatstein ultimately sweeps them aside by suggesting that Axworthy's concerns "seem to be motivated by deep-seated anti-Americanism." Like it or not, Granatstein concludes, Canada has no real choice but to bargain for an expanded NORAD in which we will place our forces under U.S. command.

Then, for good measure, Granatstein raises the question of the then possible U.S. invasion of Iraq. Here again he brushes aside potential Canadian objections to an invasion.

> Canadian officials tend to argue that, if Iraq is clearly linked to September 11, then war is defensible, but otherwise, it is not . . . We know that Iraq supports terrorists, though possibly not including Al Qaeda . . . So what should Canada say when the United States asks for Ottawa's support . . . ? Anti-Americans have their answer ready: U.S. wars of aggression are no more moral than Iraqi ones, and we have no proof that Iraq was involved in the events of September 11.
>
> Nevertheless, an attack against Saddam and his replacement by a leadership that is not so ruthlessly megalomaniacal would be a major gain for the war on terrorism, Iraqis, the region, and the world community. [For Canada] the price of opposition . . . would likely be severe . . . If Canada hangs back, reinforcing the perception that Canadian anti-Americanism and high falutin' morality too often verge on the unbearable, the costs to Ottawa might be very high indeed. To participate militarily in a war on Iraq would be a Canadian choice. To support the United States in such a war would be a Canadian requirement.

Having advised Canada to support the U.S. on National Missile Defence and on an invasion of Iraq, in addition to offering to place Canadian forces under U.S. command, Granatstein regards it as essential that Ottawa increase Canada's military spending.

> Does it matter if we are freeloaders? It does, to the military, of course, but also to the nation and to the rest of the world because it indicates our lack of seriousness . . . Perhaps the

reflexive anti-Americanism that characterizes so much of public debate in Canada springs from our guilty conscience. Canada is a defence freeloader, and like spongers everywhere, we dislike those who carry the burden for us.

Granatstein's analysis leads him to the view that the best course for Canada is to do what the Americans want us to do before they insist. This idea of "sovereignty" is highly reminiscent of what U.S. analysts called "Finlandization" in the 1970s. The term referred to the tendency of the government of Finland to kowtow to the wishes of the Soviet Union on key issues. The sorry plight of Finland was portrayed as a warning to the West as a whole of what would happen if it failed to stand up to the Soviets. Today, it is Canada that risks Finlandization; and we are being pushed down that road by the continentalists at the C.D. Howe Institute, and the likes of Wendy Dobson and Jack Granatstein.

———

In December 2002, a new defence accord was reached between Canada and the United States. Under the agreement, announced by Defence Minister John McCallum, U.S. troops could be deployed in Canada in an emergency, such as a terrorist attack on North America, and conversely, Canadian troops could be deployed in the United States. Ottawa insisted that the arrangement did not threaten Canadian sovereignty because the Canadian government would have to approve the use of American troops on Canadian territory. The federal government presented the accord as an alternative to formal adherence by Canada to the U.S. military's new Northern Command or the expansion of NORAD to place Canadian army and navy units under U.S. command.[3]

Under the accord, U.S. troops in Canada would serve under Canadian command and Canadian troops in the U.S. would serve under American command. The U.S. State Department announced that U.S. and Canadian officials had concluded that cross-border military co-operation was essential. In a release, the department stated that since September 11, 2001, "the overall threat to the North American continent from the air, land and sea has greatly increased, including the potential for the use of weapons of mass destruction delivered by unconventional means, by terrorists or others."[4]

Despite the Chrétien government's insistence that Canada was not ceding sovereignty to the U.S., the new arrangement was a functional step in the direction of meshing Canadian army and navy units into a continental defence system. A Canada–U.S. planning group is to be established to work out how to jointly deploy military forces in an emergency. Joint army and navy exercises will be initiated and co-ordinated by the planning group, which will be headed by Canadian Lieutenant General Ken Pennie. Pennie, the deputy commander of NORAD, reports to the American commander of NORAD.

As was the case with the general notion of adopting a Fortress North America approach to border management, the Chrétien government was refusing the hot-button label, but it was clearly pursuing the functional implementation of deeper integration of Canadian with U.S. military forces. Without Canadians being fully aware of what is happening, Canada and the United States are proceeding toward Fortress North America, but on the instalment plan.

Despite the road toward closer integration with the United States that his government was taking, there was clear evidence that Jean Chrétien was annoyed with the muscular stance and the unilateralism of the Bush administration. In an interview taped for CBC television in July 2002, which was broadcast in September on the first anniversary of the terror attacks, the prime minister made the case that the global disparity in power and wealth was the root cause of the attacks. "It's always the problem when you read history—everybody doesn't know when to stop, there's a moment when you are very powerful," Chrétien said. "I do think that the Western world is getting too rich in relation to the poor world," he continued. "And necessarily, we're looked upon as being arrogant, self-satisfied, greedy and with no limits. And the eleventh of September is an occasion for me to realize it even more."

Prior to the terror attacks, Chrétien told the CBC, he remembered hearing complaints from Wall Street capitalists about Canadian economic links to Cuba and other foreign policy disagreements between Ottawa and Washington. "I told them: When you are powerful like you are, you guys, it's the time to be nice," Chrétien said in the interview. "And it is one of the problems—you cannot exercise your powers to the point of humiliation of the others. And that is what the Western world—not only the Americans but the Western world—has to realize."[5]

U.S. right-wing media outlets savaged the prime minister for his remarks. Fox News commentator Bill O'Reilly commented that Chrétien "is a socialist who believes the West owes something to radical Muslims and to the rest of the world . . . [H]is government allows nearly everyone into Canada even if they have false documentation. Of course, this puts all of us at risk. Chrétien doesn't care." Opposition leader Stephen Harper appeared on another Fox show and said he agreed with the charges about Canada's "porous borders and immigration system."[6]

In the interview, Chrétien was walking a path that had been trodden by his predecessors. In the twilight of a career in which he had encouraged tighter ties between Canada and the United States, he was seeing the dangers. John Diefenbaker had seen them when the Kennedy administration tried to stop him from selling wheat to China, and when it tried to force Ottawa to accept nuclear warheads for Canada's Bomarc missiles. Lester Pearson, previously Canada's great friend of America, had seen the risks when Lyndon Johnson savaged him in a meeting at Camp David for proposing a pause in the U.S. bombing of North Vietnam. Pierre Trudeau, who had come to power as an anti-nationalist, spoke in his last years in office of the threat U.S. power posed to Canada from an economic, cultural and even military point of view.

The job of a Canadian prime minister is always difficult where relations with the United States are concerned. No one wants to antagonize such a powerful neighbour, ally and trading partner. During their years in office, Canadian prime ministers have to represent Canadians in Washington, where Canadian concerns are very low on the list of priorities. They do it as best they can. And in the last years of their careers, it is characteristic of them to warn their fellow citizens of the difficulties of sustaining a sovereign Canada next door to the United States. As Chrétien said almost wistfully, in his CBC interview reflecting on his responses to September 11, "Canadians don't want me to act like we're the fifty-first state."

———

For Canadians, today's border debate is the successor to the free trade debate of the 1980s. When the government of Brian Mulroney put the idea of a free trade deal with the U.S. on the table, it buttressed its case with the written guarantees of the finest classical economic thinkers in Canada. The Macdonald Royal Commission on the economy, headed by former Liberal cabinet minister Donald S. Macdonald, reported in 1985 that free trade with the United States would result in a one-time significant increase in the well-being of Canadians. The commissioners predicted that " . . . on the basis of analyses made for this Commission by competent professionals, we are prepared to say [the increase in Canada's Gross National Product] would be in the order of a three to eight percent increase of our national income."[7]

With the imprimatur of distinguished economists standing behind the prediction, voiced through a Royal Commission, the business community united behind the Mulroney government to forecast great benefits for Canada under free trade. The predictions were very clear. Failure to opt for free trade meant Canadians would be poorer and therefore less able to sustain their social programs, especially medicare. Choosing free trade, on the other hand, would mean higher living standards and a stronger Canadian economy.

For generations prior to that seminal debate, it was assumed that for Canada to be a nation with its own values and way of life, capable of governing itself, it required its own economy. Of course, that economy would not be self-contained. Established as an extension of European mercantilism, Canada had always existed as part of a wider international economy, and it always would. But that did not deny the potential for the development of a national economy, in which the regions grew interdependent. Over time, Canada would emerge as a stronger nation.

From the late nineteenth century until the onset of free trade with the United States in 1989, that idea prevailed. Prior to free trade, Canadians shared a broad, if often inchoate, belief that theirs was a young country whose great days lay in the future. Since Confederation, particularly in English-speaking Canada, nation building had always been an essential ingredient of politics. Whatever were the ideological divisions among political parties, nation building was a common cement. Conservatives, Liberals and social democrats could conduct heated debates, but they were grounded in a usually unspoken, but nonetheless very real, loyalty to the idea of Canada as a nation.

From the perspective of the early years of the twenty-first century, it is now clear that Canada crossed a watershed when it entered the FTA and later NAFTA. Free trade has robbed Canadians of their sense that the future involves doing great things together as they have in the past. Revisiting the free trade debate helps us understand the wider and even more sweeping debate of our time—the debate about the border.

If railways have held one of the keys to the Canadian identity, so too have passionate debates about tariffs, trade and capital investment. In what other country have scholars so intensely probed musty tariff schedules in a quest for the soul of their nation?

Prior to free trade, economic integration was rooted principally in the activities of U.S.-based multinational corporations on both sides of the border, in American head offices and Canadian subsidiaries. In the branch-plant economy of the post-war decades, the subsidiaries of U.S. corporations did the greater share of manufacturing in Canada, and U.S. corporations were heavily involved in the extraction and processing of primary products in Canada. Even though Canadian tariffs were levied on imported U.S. manufactured goods, Canada–U.S. trade was extensive. Canada exported minerals, pulp and paper, and other semi-fabricated products to the U.S. From the U.S., Canadians imported finished products, as well as machinery and parts and components to be used in the manufacturing process in Canada. Over half of all the trade between the two countries was conducted by U.S. multinationals sending products both north and south across the border.

The onset of free trade, first through the Canada–U.S. Auto Pact in 1965 and later through the Canada–U.S. Free Trade Agreement in 1989 and NAFTA in 1994, changed the pattern of trade in some ways but left its institutional framework largely unaltered. The major new development came with the continental integration of production in the automotive industry. Following the Auto Pact, the Canadian auto plants of the major U.S. auto producers retooled to produce for segments of the entire North American market. While there had previously been only a small-scale trans-border trade in finished automobiles, this trade now became gigantic. Within a few years, most of the assembled auto-mobiles produced in Canada were exported to the United States. And most of the Big Three's vehicles purchased in Canada were assembled south of the border. The trade in auto parts also grew exponentially. Today, auto exports to the U.S. are Canada's largest single export, crucial to this country's large trade surplus with the United States. Once the Auto Pact was fully in place, the value of the automotive trade between Canada and the United States for a time exceeded the value of the total trade between any other two countries in the world.

Following the onset of the FTA and NAFTA, Canada–U.S. trade was reshaped less fundamentally. The volume of trade expanded, but U.S.-based multinationals remained the conduit for half the trade. What did change, and dramatically, was the pattern of investment. In the early years of free trade, fresh flows of U.S investment into Canada slowed to a trickle. On the other hand, Canadian investments in the United States increased by leaps and bounds.

Before considering this money trail in greater detail, we need to be clear about our focus when we contrast the Canadian and American economies. Comparisons of the economic performances of Canada and the United States usually contrast Canada with the United States as a whole. A more meaningful look at Canada and its neighbour comes into view when we measure Canada against the U.S. states that border on Canada, the states that are most similar to Canada in climate, terrain and economic activity.

Thirteen U.S. states have borders with Canada. Let's call them the Border States of America (BSA). (I am defining a border state as any state that has a land or water frontier with Canada.) From east to west, the border states are Maine, New Hampshire, Vermont, New York, Pennsylvania, Ohio, Michigan, Minnesota, North Dakota, Montana, Idaho, Washington and Alaska. (Wisconsin, a close call, is not a border state since its borders in Lake

Superior touch on Michigan and Minnesota but not on Ontario.)

As is the case with Canadian provinces, the border states vary enormously in population, terrain, resources and economic activity. The BSA has major metropolitan states that are financial and manufacturing hubs—New York, Pennsylvania, Ohio and Michigan—which are comparable in many ways to Ontario and Quebec. The border states have New England members—Maine, New Hampshire and Vermont—that have features in common with the Atlantic provinces and parts of Quebec. The plains and mountain states in the BSA—Minnesota, North Dakota, Montana and Idaho—overlap in types of terrain and economic activity with the Prairie provinces. And Washington and British Columbia have much in common, as do Alaska and the Yukon.

In 1999, the BSA had a population of just over 68 million people, making it a little more than twice as populous as Canada, with a population of just over 31 million in 2000. During the nineties, the Canadian population appreciated by 12.5 percent, while that of the BSA grew by only 5.2 percent. The population of the United States as a whole increased by 9.4 percent over the course of the decade, totalling 271.6 million in 1999. The trend of more rapid population growth in Canada than in the United States as a whole, and much more rapid growth than in the border states, has been under way for decades. The BSA has been a slow-growth region of the U.S. The population centre of the United States has been moving south and west for a considerable period of time.

Prior to the 1990s, Canada substantially outpaced the BSA not only in population growth but in economic growth as well. During the 1990s, however, Canada's rate of economic growth slowed markedly in comparison with overall U.S. economic growth and in comparison with economic growth in the border states. Measuring the growth in Gross National Product in the BSA, the U.S. and Canada in billions of current U.S. dollars, the results were as follows in the 1980s: growth in the BSA from 1980 to 1989 was 88 percent, in the U.S.A. it was 90 percent, and in Canada, from 1980 to 1990, it was 96.5 percent. During the 1990s, the results were as follows: in the BSA, growth was 48 percent, in the U.S.A. it was 51 percent, and in Canada it was a mere 9.6 percent. (The lower rate of growth is exaggerated in the Canadian case as a consequence of the falling value of the Canadian dollar against the U.S. currency during the 1990s. When Purchasing Power Parities are used to make the comparison with Canada in the 1990s, the rate of growth is 43 percent, still below rates in both the BSA and the U.S. When considering what happened to Canadian growth in the 1990s compared with that south of the border, both the 9.6 percent and the 43 percent results need to be considered. That is because the falling dollar in Canada was also a measure of Canadian economic weakness.)

As it turned out, the bounties of free trade, so confidently forecast by the pro-free trade forces, did not materialize. Indeed, in the way the conditions faced by the average Canadian deteriorated, the 1990s was the second-worst decade of the twentieth century, exceeded only by the 1930s. Until late in the decade, the real incomes of the average man and woman in the workforce actually fell. When real incomes began to climb near decade's end, they made it back only to where they had been at the beginning of the nineties.

An underlying reason for the poor performance of the Canadian economy was the major shift in capital flows that occurred in the decade following the onset of free trade. With free trade, Canadian investment flowed south to the United States at a record rate, while U.S. investment in Canada grew much more slowly. During the first decade of free trade, Canadian investment in the manufacturing sector in the United States nearly trebled from US$9.8 billion in 1989 to US$26.3 billion in 1999. Direct Canadian investment in the United States in total shot up by more than 250 percent from US$30.4 billion in 1989 to US$79.7 billion in 1999. Over the decade, U.S. direct investment in Canada did not quite double, rising from US$63.9 billion in 1989 to US$111.7 billion in 1999.[8]

With free trade, Canadian investors were in a position to shift investments and productive operations south to the United States while fully retaining their markets in Canada. For U.S. investors, it was a similar story: access to the Canadian market was no longer tied to investment in Canada, as had been the case since protective tariffs were mounted in the late nineteenth century. In 1989, Canadian direct investments in the United States were 47 percent as large as American direct investments in Canada. By 1999, after a decade of free trade, Canadian direct investments in the United States were 71 percent as large as American direct investments in Canada. For many decades, on a per capita basis, Canadian investments south of the border had been much larger than American investment north of the border. By the end of the 1990s, however, the absolute level of Canadian investment in the U.S. was rising very rapidly in relation to the absolute level of American investment in Canada. The real effect of free trade was not to lessen the dependence of Canadians on American multinationals for their jobs; what it did was allow Canadian investors to run away from their own economy.

Integration of global capital markets and the rise of commodity flows between nations have altered the reality of life within nation-states. As a continental nation with a narrow band of population next to the U.S. border that does the overwhelming bulk of its trade with the United States, Canada has been particularly affected. The integration of the Canadian with the U.S. economy, and adherence to the rules established in the Canada–U.S. Free Trade Agreement (FTA) and NAFTA has significantly weakened the role of Ottawa in the management of the Canadian economy. Free trade rules prohibit Canada from pursuing a robust industrial strategy and from operating an independent strategy in the petroleum sector. A cardinal feature of the free trade regimen is the concept of "national treatment" for the firms of the three participating countries— Canada, the United States and Mexico. With national treatment, Canada is prevented from establishing tax and subsidy policies for Canadian firms that differ from those offered to U.S. and Mexican firms. Canada is no longer allowed to pick "national champions" to favour key sectors the way Europeans support Airbus and the Americans, through defence spending, subsidize Boeing.

The curious outcome of the FTA and NAFTA for Canada has been that the country remains far from achieving security of access to the U.S. market, supposedly the original goal of the exercise. Whenever the Americans feel that Canadian producers are besting them in an important sector, they slap on punitive tariffs, as in the case of softwood lumber. If the trade deals were never really about free trade, they have proven very effective as a self-limiting ordinance for Canada that denies the country the right to pursue its own national economic strategy.

The political and business leaders who promoted free trade during the federal election campaign of 1988 claimed that all they wanted was for Canada to do a little more trade with the U.S. Moreover, they wanted to do it secure in the knowledge that American protectionism would never again threaten Canadian exports. They adamantly denied that their agenda for continentalism went even a single step further than the Canada–U.S. FTA. Canadian culture, they said, was strong and would stand up to more trade with the U.S. Those who feared that Canada was on the slippery slope to dissolution, they insisted, were selling Canada short. At the climax of the free trade election in 1988, with John Turner, the Liberal leader, rising in the polls with his anti-free trade message, Brian Mulroney's Conservatives fired back. The Liberals had run a television commercial in which they said the effect of free trade would be to wipe out the Canada–U.S. border. In the Liberal ad, the border itself was graphically removed from the map. The Conservatives replied with a television ad of their own in which they staunchly put the line of the border back in place. Their goal was to strengthen Canada, not wipe it out, they insisted.

The victory for the forces of free trade in 1988 was a consequence of Canada's antiquated first-past-the-post electoral system. In the 1988 campaign, Brian Mulroney's Conservatives, with the almost total backing of the business community, featured the free trade deal with the United States as the central plank in their platform. John Turner's Liberals and Ed Broadbent's New Democrats were both committed to tearing up the trade deal that Mulroney had negotiated with the Reagan administration. On election day, 53 percent of those voting cast ballots for either the Liberals or the NDP, while 43 percent chose the Tories. The outcome, however, was a majority Conservative government. On January 1, 1989, the Free Trade Agreement came into effect.

In comparison with the U.S. and even its slow-growth border states, Canada's economy was hit over the head by a two-by-four during the 1990s. Under the circumstances, one might have expected an intense re-examination of the nation's economic policies, including free trade, to get to the bottom of the poor performance. What did take place was a useful debate about the way Canada's high interest rate policies in comparison with those in the U.S. slowed economic growth north of the border. But there was virtually no debate about free trade and the capital flows it provoked.

During the wretched 1990s, the same pressure groups that had fought for free trade moved on to promote yet more initiatives to increase still further the economic integration between Canada and the United States—this despite their solemn protestations that free trade was all they ever wanted. The new items on the continentalist agenda were Canada's adoption of a common currency with the U.S.; a Canada–U.S. customs union; and the opening of the Canada–U.S. border along the lines of the arrangement of the Schengen countries in the European Union. Ironically, in the face of worsening economic conditions after the FTA went into effect, those who had advocated free trade argued that yet more integration with the U.S. was the solution. With the benefits of the FTA nowhere to be seen, the continentalists showed no sign of caution. They offered not the slightest hint that they could have been wrong in the first place.

The ground on which the border debate is taking place is crucially different from that on which the free trade debate was waged. That is because loyalty to Canada among the nation's elites can no longer be taken for granted. Unlike those who were sympathetic to the United States or pro-American in past historical periods, the continentalists of today accept Canada's existence only as an established fact, not as a matter of conviction. Contrasting the outlook of Canadian with American capitalists makes the point. However wedded they are to the market, American capitalists are American to the core. So American are they that they cannot conceive of any other political loyalty apart from that which they gladly bestow on the United States of America. Any perceived or real threat against the United States calls forth a rapturous and unforced patriotism from American capitalists.

Canadian capitalists could not be more different. During the free trade debate, the large majority of the proprietors of small, medium and large businesses were solidly on the side of the Mulroney government and the FTA. The Business Council on National Issues (BCNI), the most influential business lobby organization in the country, was a major player in the drive for free trade. The BCNI, with its blue-chip membership of CEOs of top corporations in the financial, manufacturing and resource sectors, both Canadian- and U.S.-owned, was the authoritative voice of the major capitalists in the country.

Since free trade went into effect, business in Canada has gone over almost entirely to an agenda that favours ever closer integration with the United States. It is no exaggeration to say that business wants Canada to become a northern extension of the U.S. That does not mean that most business leaders would come out and proselytize on behalf of the annexation of Canada by the United States. Far from it. Business has no interest in provoking the upheaval that would come from an outright annexationist agenda.

In the mid-1960s, in his classic *Lament for a Nation*, George Grant depicted the Canadian predicament perfectly. "No small country can depend for its existence on the loyalty of its capitalists," he wrote. "International interests may require the sacrifice of the lesser loyalty of patriotism. Only in dominant nations is the loyalty of capitalists ensured. In such situations, their interests are tied to the strength and vigour of their empire."[9]

The problem, of course, is that the way of the economy is not a matter that exists in a vacuum, hermetically sealed from everything else. Economic organization has a considerable effect on the choices a society can realistically make about its own affairs. If Canada's economy is deeply integrated with that of the United States, can Canadians make choices reflecting their values—values that often differ from those of Americans—on other key questions?

———

Wolfe Island, the largest of the Thousand Islands, is located at the point where Lake Ontario flows into the St. Lawrence River. The island, which sits across from Kingston, Ontario, was once a strategic barrier against an American invasion of Canada. Along the waterfront of the old city of Kingston, with its unique limestone buildings and houses, are the remains of fortifications that date from the early nineteenth century. During the War of 1812, British possession of Wolfe Island helped guard crucial Kingston, whose seizure by the Americans would have cut Upper Canada off from the rest of British North America, and from military supplies and aid from Britain. When I was a student at Queen's University long ago, I often took the ferry with my friends across Kingston harbour and out to Wolfe Island for parties on the long beaches there. Recently, I boarded the ferry in my car for the twenty-five-minute ride out to the island. Historically, most of the 1,700 people who live on Wolfe Island have been farmers and a few of them merchants. Today, a fair number of people reside on the island and commute daily to their jobs in Kingston, riding on the free ferry provided by the Ontario government year-round.

Wolfe Island families have lived on their large, flat table of land for so long that they have their own accent, a sharper variation of the twang of Kingstonians. The visitor to Wolfe Island is greeted by a charming hamlet beyond the ferry wharf, with a small hotel, a bakery, a general store and a church with a handsome spire. With its network of lightly travelled roads, the island is a paradise for cyclists, who treasure the bucolic appeal of farmers' fields with frequent views of the blue lake and the great river. On its far side, Wolfe Island is much closer to New York State than it is to the Ontario mainland. Across a narrow stretch of water—the main channel of the St. Lawrence Seaway, and a throughway for enormous freighters—is the hamlet of Cape Vincent, New York. In the summer months, a car ferry covers the short distance across the water and the border. At the tiny customs post on Wolfe Island, the Canadian flag flies, and to remind visitors that this is serious business, there is a sign on the door of the building with the black image of a handgun and a red X drawn across it. Canadian gun laws apply here, the sign proclaims.

The Canada–U.S. border separates the realm of the Second Amendment of the U.S. Constitution from a regime of strict gun control regulation that includes firearms registration. Under the Second Amendment, as U.S. political leaders under pressure from the National Rifle Association have interpreted it, Americans are guaranteed a remarkably comprehensive right to acquire and carry firearms, both long guns and pistols. Today, there are over 200 million firearms in the United States, including assault rifles and automatic and semi-automatic weapons that are illegal in Canada.

While the murder rate has been falling in the United States in recent years as the population ages, it remains in a class by itself among advanced industrialized countries. A study released by Statistics Canada in December 2001 provided up-to-date figures that show the extent to which the United States is a vastly more violence-prone country than Canada. The homicide rate in Canada is 1.8 per hundred thousand per year, while south of the border it is more than three times as high, at 5.5 per hundred thousand per year. The rate of aggravated assault is more than twice as high in the United States as in Canada—324 per hundred thousand per year compared with 143 in Canada. Similarly, the robbery rate in the U.S. is 145 per hundred thousand per year compared with 88 in Canada. On the other hand, in both breaking and entering and motor vehicle theft, Canadian crime rates are higher than those in the U.S.—954 and 728 per hundred thousand per year, and 521 and 414, respectively.[10]

Firearms regulations vary widely from jurisdiction to jurisdiction in the United States. In some states, such as Virginia, it is much easier to acquire guns than is the case in other states, for instance Massachusetts. But since Americans are free to carry their property across state lines, the result is that there is no barrier against someone driving from Boston to Virginia to purchase a gun and then taking that gun back to Boston.

That's where the Canada–U.S. border becomes highly relevant. Porous as it certainly is, at the border Canada Customs is deployed to prevent the importation of illegal U.S. weapons into Canada. Even with Canada Customs in place, guns smuggled from the United States play a large role in crimes committed north of the border. Over half the handguns recovered following the commission of crimes in Canada have been smuggled in from the United States.

In fact, the problem of U.S. weapons showing up at crime scenes is a global, not merely a Canadian, problem. Eighty percent of the handguns recovered at crime scenes in Mexico have been smuggled in from the U.S. In the case of Japan, the figure is over 30 percent.[11]

Even though there is large-scale smuggling of U.S. weapons into Canada despite Canada Customs, the situation would be much worse without border checks. It is indisputable that a European-style system that would eliminate border checks would mean the full-scale importation of the U.S. gun culture into Canada.

The Canada–U.S. frontier is also a dividing line between a regime in which the death penalty exists in most states and at the federal level and one in which the death penalty has been abolished. When the Supreme Court of Canada ruled that Canada could not extradite those convicted of capital crimes to the United States without an undertaking by American authorities that they would not be executed, this issue was raised to the level of a high principle. Just as the European Union will not admit new member states that practise capital punishment, Canada has drawn a line between itself and the U.S. on the issue. In a short publication titled *Crossing the 49th*, which gives advice to Canadians travelling to the U.S., the government of Canada issues the following warning: "In the United States, you are subject to U.S. laws and regulations. Possession, use or trafficking of illegal drugs can lead to a lengthy jail sentence; serious violations can lead to the death penalty." Driving home this melodramatic statement, the next sentence is in bold type: "Canadian citizenship confers no immunity, special protection or rights to preferential treatment."

Just as the United States has refused to sign on to such initiatives as the International Criminal Court and the treaty to ban land mines, it has also taken a pass on the Kyoto environmental accord. North of the border, despite strong opposition to Kyoto from business lobbies and several provincial governments, the government has committed Canada to the accord.

Drafted in 1997, the Kyoto Accord was conceived as a vehicle by which nations would undertake to cut their emissions of greenhouse gases, as a way of combatting global warming. Targeted in the accord are carbon-rich gases that are the by-product of burning carbons, including oil, gasoline and coal. The theory behind the accord—supported by a preponderance of global scientific opinion—is that burning carbons release gases into the atmosphere, principally carbon dioxide. This creates a greenhouse effect that leads to rising temperatures around the world. Rising temperatures, in turn, can and will generate potentially catastrophic changes in weather patterns, including the expansion of deserts. Furthermore, as polar ice caps melt, sea levels will rise, threatening low-lying coastal regions and islands in many parts of the world.

The accord committed thirty-eight advanced industrialized countries—including Canada and the United States—to reduce their emissions of greenhouse gases by 5.2 percent by 2010, in comparison with their 1990 levels. Developing countries, while they were signatories to the accord, were excluded from the emission quotas on the grounds that this would be too burdensome for their economies.

A signatory to the Kyoto accord by the Clinton administration, the United States in March 2001 government announced that it was withdrawing from it. During the 2000 election campaign, George W. Bush included abandoning Kyoto in his election platform. Two months after being sworn into office, the new president pulled his country out of the agreement, stressing the potential economic damage it would do to the United States. One of Bush's main objections to Kyoto was that it did not restrict greenhouse emissions on the part of China and India, and therefore discriminated against American interests.

For the Bush administration, there were both ideological and venal reasons to oppose Kyoto. On the political right in the

United States, it has been fashionable to deny that the case for global warming has been proven. For many on the right, Kyoto was little more than an excuse for anti-free-market forces to interfere with the free functioning of the market system. Right-wing commentators regularly make the case that predictions of global warming are the unsubstantiated product of eco-extremists whose real goal is to undermine the American way of life. Another line of thought on the right accepts that global warming is occurring, but rejects accords such as Kyoto on the grounds that they will have such a minimal impact on climate change that they are not worth undertaking. Why hobble the economy in a vain effort to slow a process of climatic change that is already well under way? Those who hold this view maintain that it makes more sense to work out ways to cope with a changing climate than it does to try to slow or halt climatic change.

The sordid reasons for the Bush administration opposing Kyoto grew out of the very close connections between top administration members and the petroleum industry. Both the president and the vice president worked in the industry, have friends there, have received political support from Big Oil and share the thinking of the oil companies. No industry more strongly objected to Kyoto than the petroleum industry. For the petroleum industry, Kyoto posed both an immediate and an implicit longer-term threat. The immediate threat had to do with the cuts to greenhouse gas emissions required in the accord. Even though the cuts were far from dramatic, they were bound to exert pressure for much more efficient energy use, by automobiles and in the heating of homes and buildings. Greater efficiency would reduce the demand for petroleum. The long-term threat is likely to grow over time, as societies conclude that in a whole variety of ways it is time to develop the technology that will enable us to move beyond the carbon-burning age. For oil producers, who have been uniquely blessed during the 150-year petroleum age, this is not a happy prospect.

When the United States abandoned Kyoto, the reaction in Europe was harshly critical. In keeping with the general response, Swedish environment minister Kjell Larsson declared that "no individual country has the right to declare that a multilateral accord is dead," and French president Jacques Chirac called the American decision an "unacceptable challenge to Kyoto."[12]

In September 2002, at a global summit, Jean Chrétien announced that Canada would ratify Kyoto. The announcement came suddenly, catching many senior government ministers by surprise. The prime minister's announcement drew fire from political opponents, chief among them Alberta premier Ralph Klein. As it soon became apparent that the federal government did not have a clearly thought out plan for the implementation of Kyoto, along with an estimate of the costs to regions and economic sectors, major business organizations banded together to oppose ratification. Twin publicity campaigns, short on information and long on propaganda, were aimed at Canadians by the pro-Kyoto federal government and by Kyoto's opponents, who advocated what they called a "made in Canada" approach.

There was considerable irony in the business lobby's choice of the patriotic-sounding phrase "made in Canada" to win support for their go-slow approach to reducing greenhouse gas emissions. These were the same business groups that favoured deep integration of the Canadian and American economies. Indeed, their real concern was that with the U.S., the world's largest producer of greenhouse gases, outside Kyoto, Canadian business would be at a disadvantage against American competitors. As in their advocacy of a Fortress America approach to border security, business wanted to be inside the American perimeter when it came to Kyoto.

Wobbly though the Chrétien government's launch of Kyoto certainly was, it definitely drew a line between the Canadian and U.S. approaches to the accord. On one side of the line were Canada and Europe, and on the other side the United States.

The Canada–U.S. border is also the frontier between universal, government-funded health care and a mixed private-public health care system that leaves 40 million Americans with no health care coverage. In 1962, the government of Saskatchewan won the battle with the medical establishment and the insurance industry and established medicare in the province. Within a few years, the federal government set up a medicare program that was implemented by every province and territory. In the United States, all attempts to create a similar health care system—including the most recent initiative in the early 1990s, during the Clinton administration—have failed. In Canada, all political parties—even those that favour private clinics and hospitals—have to say they support the universal system. Canadians are committed to it, and anyone who aspires to political office knows it. South of the border, neither the Republicans nor the Democrats (with the exception of a few standouts such as Senator Ted Kennedy) support a universal, government-funded health care system.

———

On the crucial issues we have been examining—health care, gun control, capital punishment and environmental regulation— Canada occupies a position that is closer to that of Europe than to the United States. With the exception of the Kyoto Accord, where a change of administration in Washington resulted in a change of policy, the differences are long term, reflecting deeply rooted differences in societal values. Interestingly, a European country that insisted on taking the U.S. positions on gun control and capital punishment would actually be barred from membership in the European Union.

Today, Canadian business is committed to what we can call "functional continentalism." Step by step, it is the intention of the leading elements of business to integrate Canada ever further with the U.S. Each step creates what we can call a "spillover" effect, which establishes the preconditions for the next step. I have no doubt that if this agenda proceeds to a customs union, a common currency and harmonized visa, refugee and immigration policies, a decade or so down the road many voices will be raised in favour of political union as well. The argument will be made that integration has proceeded so far that Ottawa has little left to do. At that point, Canadians will wake up to a debate about whether to opt for admission to the American union or some other form of political association.

Not that it will be a simple debate. Canadians feel a deep loyalty to their country, and it will not be easily overcome. Historically, Canadian capitalists had a great deal to do with generating the notion that to be a nation, Canada required a national economy. Now they have abandoned that idea, but their nation-building legacy lives on as a momentous embarrassment to them. Yet the Canadian people have shown no inclination to jettison the idea of a Canadian nation.

Chapter 12 | **BORDER LIFE: After September 11**

I am driving north along the Saint John River on a hot, sunny afternoon. For a long way north of Fredericton, the Trans-Canada Highway goes up the west side of the river. At Hartland, the highway crosses the broad river via a bridge that affords a spectacular view of the world's longest covered bridge, beside it. Twenty-five years ago the covered bridge was open to traffic, and I will never forget the thrill of driving across it. Today, the bridge is there only to be seen. (New Brunswick is home to about two-thirds of the world's covered bridges.)

North of Hartland, the highway crosses again to the west bank of the river. At Grand Falls, the river becomes the frontier between New Brunswick and Maine, and the Trans-Canada Highway again crosses to the east side. I stay on the west bank and drive the very short distance to U.S. Customs at a little place called Hamlin, Maine. There is a sign on a post at the rustic customs office saying that if the post is closed, you can drive through, but you must drive directly to Van Buren, Maine, and report to the customs office there. The sign also says that if you fail to do this, your car will be seized. On this occasion, there is a customs officer present, a quiet, relaxed-looking man about fifty years old. He doesn't seem to think there's anything fishy about a Torontonian abandoning the comfort of the Trans-Canada Highway to travel through this remote part of Maine, a region whose main purpose seems to be to force Canadians to travel absurdly far north to stay in their own country while en route from New Brunswick to Quebec.

The date is August 11, 2001, one month to the day before the terror attacks that will alter the operation of even this quiet part of the border.

The highway from Hamlin to Van Buren is not a bad paved road, and it hugs the Saint John River, affording a fine view of the New Brunswick side and of the heavy traffic on the Trans-Canada. At this remove, trucks and cars stream in ghostly silence past farms and small communities. In this odd place, I am in backwoods U.S.A. gazing at Canada's major thoroughfare. En route to Van Buren, I cannot help thinking of this as one of numerous potentially illicit entry points into the United States from Canada. If you wanted to smuggle someone in here, what would you do? I suppose you'd bring the person with you and drop him or her off at a designated house along this route. Then it struck me that this was highly improbable, and that they probably had a video camera at the border point I'd just passed. Well, I guess you could hide the interloper in the trunk of your car to get around this problem.

Thirteen or fourteen kilometres later, I roll into Van Buren, a small town that looks half open and half shut down. There is a sign pointing off the main street to the customs post. I continue northward in the direction of Madawaska, the town across the river from Edmundston, where I will return to Canada. Most of the names on letter boxes in this part of Maine are francophone. Madawaska is a long, rather down-in-the-mouth-looking town. A big chunk of the main street is being repaved, which makes it look even rattier.

Acadian flags fly from the lampposts. In a few days, it will be August 15, Acadian Day. Despite the francophone names and the Acadian flags, all the signs on the buildings are in English only.

I find the bridge across the Saint John to Edmundston, a low, old-fashioned affair with metal girding overhead. Ahead of me is the Canada Customs post, which has three lanes to choose from. I fail to notice that only one of the lanes is open, and I pull into one of the wrong lanes. A female customs officer is leaning out of the window waving at me to come through the correct lane. In the meantime, two other vehicles pull up to the window and quickly get through. I back up and approach the customs window. "Are you importing alcohol, firearms, mace or tear gas?" says the young officer, in a tone that is distinctly cool. By this point I have already established that I am a Canadian citizen, and in answer to the question "How long have you been in the United States?" I say rather flippantly, "About half an hour." I'm regretting this answer as she runs through the list of undesirable items I might be importing. "Pull around the corner," she says as she hands me a piece of paper.

"Climb out of your car, sir, and step away from it," says the customs officer, who has rushed out of her office. A still younger female officer has now joined her. What is making me uneasy is that I'm driving a brand-new Camry, which I purchased in Moncton, New Brunswick, a couple of days ago when my old Camry, veteran of many adventures for this and earlier books, passed away. When I bought the new car, I simply shifted the Ontario plates to it. Perhaps not kosher, since the new car hasn't yet been registered in Ontario.

I am now sitting on the bench to which I have been waved as the two begin to go through my car, with tiny, narrow flashlights pointing into bags and under seats despite the fact that it is broad daylight. The older of the two discovers my laptop computer in its case on the floor of the car. "Do you have a customs form to prove you bought this computer in Canada?" she asks.

"Let's take a look at the computer," I reply, getting off the bench and opening the case. Triumphantly, I point to an Industry Canada sticker with a bright red maple leaf on the back of the computer.

"You could have upgraded the computer in the States," she shoots back. It didn't occur to me that I might add extra bells and whistles to my laptop in backwoods Maine on a Sunday afternoon.

The two intrepid officials turn their attention to the trunk of the car. They wheel out a long metal table on which they threaten to put all the contents of the trunk. I fear that they will soon be going through my wet running clothes. Frantically, I tell them that there's just laundry and other odds and ends in the trunk. At this point, the older one pulls a bottle of wine out of a paper bag. Aha, I've been caught. A bottle of rather inexpensive Italian wine. Again I'm saved by the peculiarities of my homeland. As I try to explain that I bought this bottle at the LCBO in Toronto, I find what I'm looking for—a bilingual label on the bottle. "They don't put French labels on wine bottles in the U.S." It is my great moment.

The younger official is looking less enthusiastic about continuing the interrogation, and even the older one is beginning to wane. The long metal table is wheeled back to the side. And they haven't even noticed the Ontario plates on my brand-new car side by side with the Acadia Toyota logo.

Letting bygones be bygones, we fall into a discussion about the people who live on the other side of the border. The older one tells me that while the people just across the river in Maine have French names, they don't speak much French. Acadians on this side of the border have relatives over there, people with the same last names. They've lived here for generations, but when it comes to language, they've grown apart. She goes on to say that in the more remote region west of Edmunston, many of the residents on the New Brunswick side of the line cross the border to have their babies in hospitals in Maine. As in the case of Campobello, those born across the line are dual citizens.

––––––

With all my border crossings prior to September 11, this brief and rather innocuous inspection is the most hassle I faced. While the ease with which I crossed back and forth had, no doubt, something to do with the fact that I am a white man of a certain age, most Canadians I talked to had similar experiences. Not all, to be sure. I remember the young man from Edmonton, a member of a rock band, who spoke nonchalantly of cavity searches at U.S. Customs. And there were people of colour who told me of tough questioning at the border every time they crossed. But for the most part, though, U.S. Customs officers waved Canadian residents into the country. And the Canadian customs officers grilled returning Canadians only briefly about the purchases they had made.

On September 11, however, the business of crossing the border changed dramatically for everyone, and it has remained troublesome ever since for landed immigrants and for Canadian citizens of Middle Eastern origin.

For twenty-four hours after the September 11 attacks, the border remained tightly shut. When it reopened, the lineups, particularly of commercial vehicles, stretched for many kilometres at key crossing points. AUTOPASS was suspended until further notice by the U.S. government. When traffic first resumed, passage through busy entry points into the United States took as much as twelve hours. A few crucial border crossing points— Surrey, B.C.–Blaine, Washington (south of Vancouver), Windsor–Detroit (tunnel and bridge), Sarnia–Port Huron, Buffalo–Fort Erie, and at Niagara Falls—accounted for nearly three-quarters of all crossings. At the Windsor–Detroit crossings, through which 61 percent of cross-border truck traffic passes, the situation was particularly critical.

Windsor is Canada's largest border city, with a population of over 200,000 people. The Metropolitan area has a population of 300,000. Whenever I drive to Windsor from Toronto along Highway 401, I always anticipate my arrival in Windsor by looking for the Detroit skyline, which shows up on the horizon far away, across the flat farmers' fields. Detroit comes into view well before Windsor does. Off the highway, I am heading downtown. The highest towers of Detroit, bundled together in a knot, loom over this Canadian city, so that I can't tell that the Detroit River lies between me and the American side. It always amuses me that I am heading north toward the United States. Because of the wide bend of the Detroit River to the northeast, Windsor is tucked in on the riverbank on the south side of the American metropolis.

When I have just about reached the entrance to the tunnel to Detroit, I turn onto Riverside Drive, the broad boulevard that runs along the river. I stop and get out to take in the unrivalled view of Detroit on the other side of the river. Downtown Detroit looks better from here than from any other vantage point. The Joe Louis Arena, home to the Detroit Red Wings, and the Renaissance Center are just across the river. So too are other buildings that have been a part of the effort to revitalize the city's heart over the past three decades.

You could easily imagine from the Windsor side that Detroit is one of those American success stories in which a hollowed-out, dangerous inner city has been brought back to health. When I drive through the tunnel and wander through the neighbourhoods on the other side, though, I find a mixed picture. There has been a revival in the heart of the city, and there are new commercial centres, restaurants and entertainment venues. But I've made periodic visits to downtown Detroit over the past thirty years, and many of the run-down neighbourhoods in the city centre are all too recognizably the same as they were in the days of the great social upheavals of the past.

One thing every older resident of Windsor remembers as though it happened yesterday is the great Detroit riot of July 1967. It was the summer of racial discontent in the United States. Full-scale urban riots erupted in Newark, New Jersey, New York City, Cleveland, Chicago and Atlanta. But the greatest and deadliest of the riots broke out in Detroit, a couple of kilometres from Canadian soil. What set off the explosion was a police raid on July 23 on an illegal African-American drinking establishment on 12th Street, across the river due north of Windsor. The police handcuffed the patrons and pushed them outside. When a crowd of black onlookers arrived on the scene, the police retreated, fearing for their safety. The riot, which began with the looting of white-owned stores, rapidly mushroomed to include the looting of black-owned premises as well. Rioters set fires, and both black and white businesses were burned to the ground. When fire trucks arrived to combat the fast-spreading blaze, snipers took shots at the firemen. Clouds of thick smoke billowed upward as the inner city was set alight. Gunfights broke out between snipers and police and National Guardsmen. The National Guard drove tanks through the heart of Detroit to quell the disturbance.

Among those listening and watching were the people of Windsor, thousands of whom came out of their houses to line up on Riverside Drive. They stood silently in horror, the young, the old, parents pushing baby carriages, and stared at the smoke rising from the city across the river. Residents of Windsor blessed the river and the border that tragic week.

Forty-three people died in the Detroit riot, nearly 1,200 were injured and over 7,200 were arrested. The riot prompted a flight of both whites and blacks out of the inner city, from which Detroit has never fully recovered. Not long after the riot, a friend from Windsor drove me through the gutted neighbourhoods of Detroit, past the burned-out buildings, past houses and stores where the bulletholes were all too visible. Windsor is one border city where the Canadian population is grateful to be separated from life on the other side.

That is not to say that the people of Windsor are not deeply interested in and attracted by Detroit. There is the Motown sound that makes Detroit a music capital and that draws Canadians across the river. Windsor is the first place I ever saw a young woman with the Stars and Stripes emblazoned on the rear end of her blue jeans. It is also the first city in Canada I ever visited where most people had air conditioners in their homes. There are people in Windsor who read the *Detroit Free Press* and watch nothing but U.S. television. I heard about a woman in Windsor who came upon the horrible tale in the *Detroit Free Press* of a murderer named Paul Bernardo who had tortured and killed two young women in St. Catharines, Ontario. While that seems unremarkable, what made it interesting was that she learned about the murders in the *Free Press* only at the time of Bernardo's trial, which was long after the story had become a sensation in the Canadian media.

With its close proximity to an American metropolis, Windsor is also a city in which Canadian nationalism is right at the surface. Over many years, people I have spoken to in Windsor—auto workers, students, academics—have been very upfront in their view that Canada should not allow itself to be dominated by the United States. When the CBC announced its intention to shut down its local station, fifteen thousand residents of Windsor marched down Riverside Drive in protest. They made the case that overwhelmed by Detroit media, Windsor needed a strong Canadian media voice. The CBC heard the message and took the local station off the chopping block.

No one who studies at the University of Windsor, located literally in the shadow of the Ambassador Bridge, which carries thousands of trucks in both directions every day, has to be told that Windsor and Detroit are linked by much more than proximity. Brian Etherington teaches law at the University of Windsor. He sees the bridge every day when he drives to his office. In the afternoon, as he heads home, he drives south away from the bridge along Huron, the road that leads to and from the bridge. Even in January 2003, the lineup of trucks waiting to cross the bridge to Detroit was often eight or nine kilometres long. This road and the bridge are the lifeline of Canada's most important manufacturing industry, the auto industry. What ties the industry together on the two sides of the border are not only the Big Three auto manufacturers, two of them American-owned, one German-controlled, but a totally integrated system of production. In the first days after September 11, the lineup of trucks stretched back twenty-five kilometres from the Ambassador Bridge, all the way out of the city to Highway 401, and back along the highway through the countryside.

Etherington reflects on how the lives of those in Windsor and Detroit were intertwined before September 11, and on the changes that have occurred since then. When he moved to Windsor with his family in the mid-1980s, he made frequent trips to Detroit. "You could get over there in a few minutes," he recalls. With his university colleagues, he would often drive over the Ambassador Bridge to Detroit's Mexican Village for lunch. During Etherington's first years in Windsor, the Canadian dollar was much stronger than it later became. Those were the days of widespread Canadian cross-border shopping in the United States. People crossed to fill their cars with gas, to buy groceries, to visit restaurants and to take in sporting events. In Windsor, while there are many Toronto Maple Leaf fans, they are outnumbered by Red Wing enthusiasts. Like many others in Windsor, Brian Etherington enjoyed much of what Detroit had to offer, attending a fair number of hockey and baseball games with members of his family. September 11 did not end

Etherington's cross-border peregrinations, but it cut them to a much smaller number. Relaxed lunches on the other side weren't worth it any more if he had to face the prospect of a huge tie-up at the border.

Well before September 11, the Canadian dollar plunged to a trading range of between sixty-two and sixty-eight cents to the U.S. dollar. Much of the Detroit market for residents of Windsor dried up. Now, it was Windsor that was drawing huge numbers of Americans across the border. Flashing signs on the Detroit side of the river beckoned people to cross over to Canada, "five minutes away." For ten or fifteen U.S. dollars, you could get a decent meal in one of Windsor's better restaurants. One Friday evening when I was driving back from Detroit to Windsor, there was a long line through the tunnel and a half-hour wait to get through Canada Customs. Almost all of the cars in the line carried Michigan plates. People were going to Windor's casino, and from there many of them would end up in a nearby restaurant or bar.

The terror attacks, of course, brought traffic between the two cities to a complete halt. When the flow of cars and trucks into the United States resumed, it moved at a snail's pace, with customs officers taking their time to check everyone with a fine-tooth comb. The designated lanes for frequent travellers were shut down as Washington put the system on Code One, Red Alert. As the weeks passed, the border delays became shorter, but during rush hour it could still take an hour or sometimes two to cross into Detroit from Windsor.

From the point of view of Canada as a whole, the border-crossing quandary at Windsor has to do with the well-being of the nation's automotive industry. It is now almost exactly a century since Sam McLaughlin, Canada's foremost independent auto manufacturer, began importing Buick engines from Detroit for installation in the horseless carriages he was assembling on the

Canadian side. In 1915, McLaughlin added Chevrolet engine imports to his operation, which was located in Oshawa, Ontario. A few years later, McLaughlin sold his two companies to General Motors, and General Motors of Canada was established. Superior American production of high-volume items such as auto engines and sub-assemblies quickly brought Ford and Chrysler into Canada as well.

Canada was launched on its career in the branch-plant manufacturing of cars and trucks for its own market and for the British Empire market. After World War II, the British Empire market for Canadian-assembled automobiles dried up. Canada was importing ever more auto parts and components from Detroit for its domestic auto assembly plants. The result was an industry that was uncompetitive and a sharply rising trade deficit for Canada in the auto sector. Following a fierce debate about whether Canada should opt for an auto industry that would produce cars and trucks for the Canadian market or for an industry that would produce for segments of a continental market, the Liberal government of Lester Pearson chose the latter option.

Over the decades since the Auto Pact went into effect in 1965, the integration of the Canadian with the U.S. auto industry has continued. Forty percent of Canada's exports to the United States are auto products, mostly assembled cars and trucks, and every year Canada runs up a massive trade surplus with the U.S. in the auto sector. As a consequence of medicare in Canada, which means the auto companies don't have to pay for expensive health plans as they do south of the border, and the cheap Canadian dollar, it has been extremely profitable for the auto giants to assemble vehicles in Canada.

Given the system of continental integration, however, no vehicle can be produced from start to finish in Canada. Auto design and development, and much of the production of auto parts and components for vehicles assembled in Canada, takes place in the United States. And with today's system of just-in-time inventory, thousands of trucks must cross the border every day in both directions to keep the industry humming. The majority of those crossings take place between Windsor and Detroit across the Ambassador Bridge. Indeed, if there is one piece of infrastructure on which the economic link between the two countries rests most heavily, it is the Ambassador Bridge. The governments of both Canada and the United States recognize that a terrorist attack on the bridge would do more damage to a vital industry and to trade between the two countries than any other single event.

Indeed, for the auto companies, with their just-in-time parts delivery systems, the first few weeks after September 11 were hell. Production schedules on both sides of the border were disrupted. Once the crossing times settled down and became more predictable, the companies were able to cope. The cost impact of having inventory sit on the road for an hour or two longer turned out to be negligible. In the first nine months of 2002, Canadian auto exports to the U.S. increased by 6.1 percent compared with the first nine months of 2001, despite the fact that the U.S. economy was weaker in the year following September 11. It turned out that the scare talk from border lobbyists about the threat of border slowdowns to the Canadian economy was just that—scare talk.

For individuals who lived in Windsor and worked in Detroit, it was a different story. Sitting in the car for an extra hour or more on the way to work every day is a hardship that few would accept with equanimity. Prior to the terror attacks, a large number of nurses who lived in Windsor were commuting across the border to work in Detroit. Many of them had been victims of job cutbacks in Ontario hospitals. A considerable number of hospitals in the United States had been actively recruiting Canadian nurses.

Detroit hospitals were happy to hire nurses from Windsor, and were in the unique position of being able to offer them jobs while not requiring them to move.

Prior to September 11, the commute to Detroit was no big deal, and the prospect of being paid in U.S. dollars was an added attraction. Some of the nurses even worked at two jobs, one on each side of the border. In the months following the attacks, however, with wait times of an hour or more, many of the nurses decided to seek work only in Windsor. This happened to coincide with a recruiting drive in Ontario for more nurses—the predictable and desperate response to the slashing of positions that had gone before.

The enormous tie-up of trucks crossing the Ambassador Bridge might not have had a serious impact on the well-being of the major auto manufacturers, but it certainly had a negative impact on Windsor neighbourhoods. A multi-kilometre line of idling trucks spewed pollution into the air. For many people, the trip to or from work involved driving past an endless parking lot of trucks sitting in a dedicated lane. Even before September 11, there was heated debate in Windsor about the need for a third vehicle route to link Windsor and Detroit. After September 11, the consideration of the third route turned to several competing proposals—each with its own backers, each potentially affecting Windsor neighbourhoods. One idea was to build a truck route under the river that would parallel the existing rail tunnel that runs between the Ambassador Bridge and the road tunnel. Other possible routes would run east of the existing tunnel or would run across the border from a point west and south down the Detroit River.

Although the economic stakes were highest at the Windsor–Detroit crossing points, other important border crossings were affected by delays after the attacks.

Not surprisingly, in my travels to write this book, I ran into a number of these traffic delays. One occasion, when I was driving to the border crossing point south of Vancouver, at Blaine, Washington, sticks in my mind.

———

Well before I reach the famed Peace Arch Park—a large green space that straddles the border—with its monument to fraternity between Canada and the United States ("May These Gates Never Close" reads the inscription) I am bumper to bumper in the long line to U.S. Customs. In the days immediately following the terrorist attacks on the United States, it took hours to enter the U.S. at this very busy crossing point. Within a few weeks, however, while the crossing at Blaine remained one of the slowest along the length of the border, crossing times were generally down to five to ten minutes, and at busy times of the day, thirty to forty minutes. Crossing times here, as along the rest of the border, continued to improve in succeeding months. On this Friday morning, however, I'm stuck in a lineup that is moving at a snail's pace. I have plenty of time to remember a little local history.

In Peace Arch Park, fifty years ago, on May 18, 1952, Paul Robeson, the renowned black American singer, performed for a crowd of between thirty and forty thousand people. Robeson, who had risen to fame as an all-star college football player, became the most highly praised black actor and singer of his day by the end of the 1920s. His involvement in labour struggles and in the cause of equal rights for blacks drew the suspicion and ire of U.S. authorities.

During the Cold War, it was Robeson's sympathy for the Soviet Union and his belief in Communism that brought the hand of Washington down on him. Called before a U.S. congressional committee during the reign of terror of Senator Joseph McCarthy, Robeson refused to say whether he was a Communist. In 1950, the U.S. State Department withdrew Robeson's passport, thus preventing him from leaving the country to perform abroad.

The State Department defended its action by saying that his travel to other countries was not in the interests of the United States. Two years later, the Mine, Mill and Smelter Workers Union in British Columbia invited Robeson to perform at its annual meeting. Even though Americans did not need a passport to enter Canada, the U.S. government barred him from making the journey to British Columbia. Mine, Mill responded by inviting Robeson to perform at a concert right on the border in Peace Arch Park. From the back of a flatbed truck, Robeson sang such classic labour songs as "Joe Hill" to his audience in two countries. The following year, the singer returned to the park on the border for another concert.

Three customs booths are open, and I pick the one on the left. As usual, I pick the wrong line, the one that is moving the slowest, but I'm stuck in it now. Up ahead, I see a man in U.S. military uniform coming out of the booth with a female customs officer and checking cars as they pass. One of the measures adopted by the U.S. government after September 11 was to deploy National Guardsmen on the border to reinforce U.S. Customs. We inch ahead. Trunks are being searched. The woman with the three kids in line ahead of me has her SUV thoroughly searched.

When I pull up to the booth, the military man does not come out. A male customs officer asks me, "How long have you been in line today?" I answer, "About forty minutes" and he waves me ahead. I've decided I'm the perfect demographic for a rapid passage through U.S. Customs—middle-class white male over fifty-five without sunglasses. Indeed, never once did I encounter the slightest difficulty entering the United States after the terror attacks. And I am not alone. For white Canadians, especially those who are middle class and were born in Canada, the aftermath of September 11 did not change things much at the border. The same cannot be said for Canadians of different ethnic origins or places of birth.

If delays were my worst experience, for Muslim residents of Canada from a swath of countries running from Pakistan to North Africa, crossing the border became a nightmare after September 11. For many, as the stories circulated about what had happened to others, the wisest course was simply to avoid travel to the United States. And that is what a lot of people—my friends, acquaintances, students, people I spoke to in preparation of this book—chose to do. Having no need to travel to the U.S., they stayed in Canada. If they wanted to go somewhere on vacation, they chose Mexican or European rather than American destinations.

Of course, some people of Middle Eastern origin did travel to the United States. Here is the account I received of one such journey.

It had occurred to Ariane, a single mother who lives in Toronto, that she might encounter problems if she took her two children to visit relatives in Vermont over the Christmas holidays. A Canadian citizen, Ariane was born in Iran. She wondered whether she ought to make the trip in the conditions that prevailed after September 11. Friends assured her, though, that she had nothing to worry about. She was a woman, travelling with two children. That was not the sort of thing that would alarm U.S. authorities, she became convinced. Since immigrating to Canada in 1997, she and her children had spent most of their summers in Vermont. How exciting it would be to visit in wintertime.

At Toronto's Pearson International Airport, a U.S. immigration officer told her she had to step into a side office to go through the special registration procedure. There, an officer from the U.S. Internal Revenue Service (INS) interviewed her. She was audio- and videotaped and digitally fingerprinted. The officer asked her to show her driver's licence, her passport and her Ontario health card. She was asked for her Social Insurance Number, her e-mail address, her parents' dates of birth and her Visa card information.

Although perturbed by all of this, she was really put on edge by the next step in the process. The officer handed Ariane documents to study on how to comply with her newly acquired status as a Special Registrant. The rules stipulated that as a Special Registrant, she had to exit the United States from a designated port of departure. The problem was that the airport in Hartford, Connecticut, where she was heading with her two children—and non-refundable tickets—was not a designated port of departure. The documents informed her of her legal responsibility to appear in person before an INS officer at a designated port of departure. Failure to do this could mean that she would be denied admission to the United States at a later date. When she asked the INS officer what she should do, he replied, "Sorry, ma'am, you have to comply."

Arriving at Hartford airport, she was met by her beaming relatives, but she found no sign of an INS officer. The next morning, she phoned the National Customer Service number of the Department of Justice and Immigration and Naturalization and was told that there was a designated point of departure at Highgate Springs, Vermont. Unfortunately, this is a four-hour drive north of where she was staying, and it is a land crossing point with no airport or rail service. When she asked how she was supposed to get back to Toronto from there, she was told once more, "We are sorry, ma'am, you have to comply."

Having reached the Canadian embassy in Washington on the phone, she was told that because these rules were new and not properly implemented as yet, the government of Canada had been advising Canadians in Ariane's situation not to travel to the U.S. for the time being. Next, Ariane turned to U.S. Air to see if she could switch her return flight to Boston, a designated port of departure. Since the tickets she held were non-refundable, she was invited to purchase three new one-way tickets from Boston to Toronto, US$275 each. She tried the INS in Hartford, but they were understaffed and offered no help. In the end, she flew back to Toronto from Hartford with her children.

Happy to be home, Ariane found that the drama was not quite finished. She received advice from her lawyer to write the U.S. consulate in Toronto and send them copies of all her travel documents to explain why she had been unable to comply with the U.S. port of departure regulation. She might later have to be interviewed by an INS officer at a designated port of departure to explain the whole affair. Ariane hoped she would not be banned from future U.S. travel. Hers was an experience all too common among Canadians born in the countries on the special U.S. hit list. And like so many others, she is disappointed that the Canadian citizenship of which she was so proud did not entitle her to the same treatment meted out to other Canadian citizens.

———

A few kilometres north of Point Roberts, Washington, is Steveston, B.C., once a sleepy little town in the rich alluvial flatland of the Fraser River delta, a place where intensive vegetable growing, aimed at the city market, predominated. The flatland is much prized because it is so rare in B.C. The delta is made up of soil that has been washed down from the mountains by the river over thousands of years. As it empties into the ocean, the Fraser, a wild, raging river in the interior of B.C., churns along slowly, muddy, brown and wide as it passes Steveston. From the bank of the river, if you look west, you can see shadowy grey mountains across the Strait of Georgia on Vancouver Island. I remember visiting Steveston in the early 1970s, when the local NDP MLA was Harold Steves, a descendant of the family after whom the town was named. It was the first week of March and the fields were already green. There were flowers, and the smell of fresh earth was in the air.

I return to Steveston on July 1, 2002, Canada Day, the year following September 11. The little town is now the southwest corner of Richmond, which, back in the seventies when I visited Steveston, was also a sleepy town. Today, Richmond is a vast growing edge city south of Vancouver, with a population largely of Asian origin. Indeed, Richmond is one of only two cities in Canada, the other being Markham, Ontario, that the 2001 Canadian census reported as having a non-white majority. This is a middle-class city with homes that range from comfortable to palatial. It is located a ten-minute drive south of the airport, which makes Richmond a true Pacific Rim city, with connections to Hong Kong, Beijing, Tokyo, San Francisco and Los Angeles.

Richmond is well known for its Hong Kong–style malls. On No. 3 Road, there is the Yaohan Centre, a huge mall with dozens of shops. The proportion of non-Asians in the mall is tiny, but there is no sense of exclusion here. The crowd is relaxed. Families intermingle with teens and the aged. On the first floor of the mall is an open area with about a dozen fast-food outlets, a typical feature of malls everywhere in North America. The difference is that the outlets all serve Asian food of one type or another. I opt for one that serves Chinese food. For $3.95, you get a heaping plate of rice with four choices of toppings. I pick two chicken dishes, a tofu with greens and an offering of Chinese vegetables. Hot and delicious, and a steal at the price. One shop upstairs in the mall has a large poster in the window advertising phone cards that feature calls to Hong Kong at a rate of one cent per minute. The Yaohan Centre is much like Hong Kong-style malls in Markham, on the northeastern edge of Toronto.

A few years ago, the burgeoning Asian population and the opening of malls whose clientele is overwhelmingly Asian provoked a furor of critical comments from some Vancouver Caucasians. The hubbub was fanned on the city's talk-radio shows. (Vancouver is the talk-radio capital of Canada.) The complaint against the Asians who were settling in Richmond and opening their malls was one that had been heard many times before in Canada over the past century. Much the same thing had been said in the past about the Jews who settled on the east side of Mount Royal in Montreal, the Ukrainians in Winnipeg and Edmonton, the Finns in Thunder Bay and the Italians in Toronto. These people are never going to assimilate to become a part of the wider Canada, the complaint went. Unlike earlier immigrants, those feeling threatened by the newcomers would say, these people are setting up communities and institutions that are for themselves alone. You don't hear a word of English spoken in their shops or malls or on the streets where they live, it was said. It was a calumny that earlier immigrants had had to bear, and a few years ago it was the turn of the Asians of Richmond to bear it.

On this sunny but not hot July 1, many thousands have turned out in the centre of historic Steveston to mark Canada Day. A parade is followed by other celebrations. Those out on the streets reflect the demography of Richmond. The crowd is Asian and Caucasian. Canadian flags and shirts featuring the maple leaf are everywhere. Many of those without flags are wearing red-and-white shirts or red shirts with white pants. Little children have Canadian flags stuck in their hair. Young men and women, and even several policemen I see, have maple leaves adorning their cheeks. Some young men with cut-off muscle shirts are sporting maple leaf tattoos on their biceps. Among the elderly are those with flags tucked into their belts. Some in motorized wheelchairs have flags flying from their vehicles. The celebration spills along Steveston's old main street, with its specialty food and clothing and craft shops. Outdoor cafés have Canadian flags adorning the tables, and special signs are posted welcoming people to come and enjoy Canada Day. At the tables, I see people arriving and wishing each other a "Happy Canada Day." Down along the wharves and the shops that look out over the Fraser River, the scene is the same—a sea of red and white in the sunshine. A Vancouver radio station is featuring a poll of its listeners saying that they want

Canada to be less like the United States, and that the thing they like most about Canada is that it is not the United States. The residents of Richmond seem to agree.

I am used to thinking of Canada Day as a time to flee to the cottage for a long weekend. July 1 in Richmond, B.C., is the most exuberant celebration of the day I have ever seen anywhere. It is completely natural, unforced. I cannot help thinking that this is the first occasion we have had to acknowledge our nationhood and independence since September 11, 2001.

Chapter 13 | **Good Fences**

A century ago, Sir Wilfrid Laurier boasted that the twentieth century would belong to Canada, as the nineteenth
century had belonged to the United States. Today, the
confident words of the former prime minister echo down to us as
hollow. From the standpoint of its nationhood, Canada now lives
in an age that is different from, and in some more ways more
threatening than, any that has come before.

It is odd that Canadian nationhood should be so severely at
risk today. With a population of over 30 million people, and technology that makes communication across distant spaces easier
than ever before, one could be forgiven for believing that
Canada's time has truly arrived. In some ways, it evidently has.
The last several decades have been a golden age of Canadian cultural expression. Writing about Canadian subjects, authors such
as Margaret Atwood, Robertson Davies, Michael Ondaatje, David
Adams Richards and Nino Ricci have been reaching audiences at
home and around the world. In social and material terms, Canada
is also a great success compared with other countries. In the

United Nations' annual ranking of nations in terms of human well-being, Canada consistently ranks in the top positions.

What threatens Canadian survival is the transformation of the United States from republic to global empire, and the response to that change from within the ranks of Canadian business, political and intellectual elites. The assertion by American leaders that the United States will exercise powers that eclipse the rights of other nations endangers the position of all small and middle-sized countries, Canada not least.

The shared heritage of Canada and the United States is enormous. English-speaking Canada and the United States are, if not sisters, then at least cousins. While the similarity of the two countries can be seen as evidence of the Americanization of Canada, this can be overstated. What has occurred has been the parallel development of two societies with much in common working out ways to live on territories where there is a wide overlap in the types of terrain and climate. The common patterns of land, sea and life in Maine, New Brunswick and Nova Scotia are there to be seen. The contiguous regions of Ontario, Quebec and New York State share much with each other. The Prairies of Canada and the Plains of the United States pose similar challenges. When I spend an evening with Saskatchewan and Nebraska farmers, I see how much their adaptation to the same problems has shaped an outlook that is not dissimilar. A West Coast culture, born of terrain and experience, binds the people of B.C. with those to the south in Washington and Oregon, and with those to the north in Alaska and the Yukon.

Despite the similarities, though, Americans today have a very self-centred view of the world and their place in it. Of all the "Middle Kingdom" outlooks in history, none has surpassed that of the United States at the beginning of the twenty-first century.

The contrast with the outlook of Canadians could not be more stark. Alone among the members of the G8, Canada has never been an imperial power. While Canadians have great pride in their country, they have never imagined it to be the centre of the world. Nor have they ever believed that they have a special mission, duty or right to export or impose their values or way of life on others. Quite the reverse. Canadians have assumed throughout their history that other countries—Great Britain in the nineteenth century and the U.S. today, and, if you go back far enough, France before the Conquest—are the natural leaders. As a country with profoundly important ties to outside, more powerful countries, the culture, values and political outlook of Canadians have been deeply affected and shaped by the influences of those countries. While Americans have the energy and confidence that goes with being at the centre of the world, Canadians are more cautious, less inclined to think they will blaze the path for the future. There is an element of the metropolis–hinterland, or imperium–satellite, relationship in the dealings between the United States and Canada.

But it is wrong to think of Canadians as merely mild-mannered Americans, or, as my friend in Seattle believes, "Americans without the jazz." Having been on the counter-revolutionary side in the great struggles of the eighteenth century, Canada is not simply a more northerly, gentle version of bourgeois society. Canada's continuing ties to Britain, after the U.S. severed its ties, opened Canada to Tory and later to socialist ideas. In that sense, Canada is an un-American nation.

The Canada–U.S. border has served as a filter that has allowed commerce, people and ideas to pass as freely as between any other two countries in the world. But on the northern side of the border, Canadians have fashioned a country with its own way of doing things, of achieving the public good, of resolving problems. Despite its ample shortcomings, Canada, it is fair to say, is a country admired, even envied, by much of the world.

Our neighbour occupies a very different space. Americans, leaders and people alike, are inextricably caught up in a great imperial undertaking. That blunt fact, as well as a history that has planted values which differ in important ways, has made the border between Canada and the United States much more consequential than a mere line between neighbouring jurisdictions.

For Canadians, it may be cold comfort to consider that we are not alone in having to adapt to the altered role being played in the world by the United States. Nevertheless, if Canada is not alone, there certainly are unique features that distinguish the Canadian case from any other. The question that now confronts us is whether a country, even as large and successful a country as ours, can stand and survive as more than a geographical expression next door to the superpower that expects the world to do its bidding.

Shortly after the attacks on September 11, President George W. Bush issued a directive ordering U.S. officials to work for the creation of a continental security perimeter with Canada. On this side of the border a powerful lobby, including Paul Cellucci, the U.S. ambassador—who regularly gives the Canadian government unsought advice, much in the manner of an imperial viceroy— along with the premiers of Ontario, British Columbia and New Brunswick, and the Alliance of Manufacturers and Exporters of Canada, headed by Perrin Beatty, has been pressuring Ottawa to move in the same direction.

Canadians should reject the Fortress North America concept. It risks an unacceptable loss of Canadian sovereignty and brings with it no guarantee that the U.S. will ease the security it now plans at the border. Instead we ought to take practical steps to meet Canadian and U.S. security needs so that border crossings can be as timely as possible for commercial and personal traffic.

Canadians are completely united around the goal of preventing terrorists from gaining access to Canada, either for the purpose of launching attacks against domestic targets or to use this country as a launch pad for cross border attacks against U.S. targets. The Ahmed Ressam case woke Canadians up to the need for greater communication and information sharing among Canadian authorities including CSIS, the Department of Immigration and police at all levels. It is entirely in our interest to ensure that terrorists cannot operate on Canadian soil. Information sharing between Canada and U.S. Customs and between Canadian and American law enforcement agencies, as well as with law enforcement authorities in other countries, to combat terrorism is something with which Canadians of all shades of opinion agree.

In addition, we ought to consider the advantages of a Frontier in Depth. By establishing an enhanced police and security presence within ten kilometres of major border crossing points, it should be possible to put less pressure on the border itself. This is one area where we can definitely learn from the Europeans, who operate a system of spot checks in areas near frontiers.

A few crucial border crossing points—Surrey B.C.–Blaine, Washington (south of Vancouver), Windsor–Detroit, Sarnia–Port Huron, Buffalo–Fort Erie, and at Niagara Falls—account for the large majority of crossings. These points require major new infrastructure investment on both sides of the border—more lanes, in some cases new bridges. Key industries, which account for the overwhelming bulk of our exports—the auto industry (assembly and parts), steel, chemicals, fabricated materials and forest products—should be singled out for special attention to ensure efficient border crossings, a vital interest to both countries.

On the other hand, Canada should reject the idea of having joint teams of American and Canadian Customs officials at key entry points into North America. Canada should refuse to harmonize its immigration, refugee and visa policies with those of the U.S. Harmonization would weaken our ability to pursue our own policies toward the rest of the world.

In all of this, let's not forget what is always overlooked by the proponents of Fortress North America—that Canada has its own security concerns. The U.S. has an enormous number of illegal immigrants, immensely higher than the proportional number of illegal immigrants and unaccounted for refugees in Canada. Canada has to be concerned about the importation of guns. Canada also needs to have the capacity to interdict illegal movements of toxic waste and explosives from south of the border.

Ottawa should guard against the temptation to weaken civil liberties in Canada in an effort to convince the Bush administration of the virtues of our security regime. In sum, Canada must retain control of its security, its territory and its ability to pursue an independent foreign policy. Fighting terrorism involves much more than military action and enhanced security. It rests, in the end, on helping to create a world in which resources and wealth are much more equitably shared, in which peoples have control over their own affairs and are not reduced to pawns in geo-political and resource struggles. Canada needs to retain its capacity to act on these propositions, something that could frequently put us at odds with the U.S.

Beyond these issues, bearing on the management of the border, the question of the hour for Canadians is how our country will survive the age of superpower America. All the other issues—globalization, the environment, the fate of medicare, control of our fresh water, the struggle for Canadian sovereignty in the High Arctic—are subsets of the dominant issue. In this country, real politics is waged between those who are pushing deep integration with the United States—the continentalists—and those who advocate a sovereign Canada. So far, the continentalists are winning.

It is no longer controversial to assert that the United States is the global successor to the British Empire and Imperial Rome. The gap between American military prowess and that of any other power is so huge that would-be allies vie for admission to the Bush administration's coalition rather than being courted by Washington. The long-term effect of September 11 has been to expose to the world an old-fashioned military empire that no longer bothers with the niceties of international covenants.

The traditional Canadian strategy—attempting to offset naked American power by encouraging multilateralism and by participating in structures such as NORAD that provide at least a nod to Canadian sovereignty—lies in tatters. In the new American command structure for homeland defence, Canada will be cut very little slack. We either place our forces under American command or we're left out. A century ago, a British general appointed by the British government commanded the Canadian militia. Unless we are prepared to sink back to that level of formal colonialism, we are going to have to think through a strategy for sustaining sovereignty.

The continentalists, who have dominated Canadian politics for the past two decades, can point to few ways in which their years at the helm have benefited Canadians. In terms of the trend of living standards, the 1990s—the decade that followed the free trade deal with the U.S.—was the worst decade of the twentieth century for ordinary Canadians, with the sole exception of the 1930s. Instead of the stronger, wealthier, more productive country the continentalists promised us, we have become more marginalized and relatively less productive. Putting us in an economic straitjacket where we can no longer fashion government programs to foster the excellence of Canadian companies has been a disaster for Canada. To be sure, Canada found a new basis for economic growth in recent years, but it was not at all the one the continentalists promised us. The sharp decline of the value of the Canadian against the U.S. dollar following the onset of free trade has ushered in a new period of crude protectionism for Canada. The cheap Canadian dollar lowered the cost of labour in Canada relative to that south of the border. The devalued dollar acted as a spur to our exports and as a barrier against excessive imports. Although we were pushed to a lower rung on the ladder of wealthy nations, Canada's economy has been growing more rapidly than the American economy for the past couple of years.

(In the spring of 2003, the Canadian dollar, for years locked in a trading range between 62 and 68 cents against the U.S. dollar, took off and had climbed to over 73 cents at the time of this writing. Rising roughly thirteen per cent against the U.S. dollar, the dramatic change foretold both promise and problems for the Canadian economy. Imports of food, energy, machinery and consumer goods would be cheaper and therefore, more attractive to Canadians. On the other hand, Canadian exports of autos and auto parts and of raw materials and semi-fabricated products would cost American importers more. The rise of the dollar brought with it the risk of a slowing economy. The dramatic change was the consequence of developments on both sides of the border. The U.S. economy was stalling, while the Canadian economy was growing. Washington was running a huge government deficit, while Ottawa enjoyed a surplus. Moreover, the U.S. was experiencing a massive trade and current account deficit and its international indebtedness was soaring. At the same time, Canada had a strong trade and current account surplus.)

The advocates of a sovereign Canada need to fashion policies in the interest of the majority of Canadians who have been left behind since the 1980s. That means dropping the free market religion that, followed to its logical conclusion, will reduce most of Canada to northern versions of Wyoming and Maine. Raising the living standards of Canadians, protecting medicare and widening access to higher education can never be entrusted to an economic regime that believes that markets and multinationals automatically act in our best interest. On national defence, our priority should be to rebuild the Canadian forces to patrol our extensive coasts, in particular our Arctic waters, which the U.S. insists do not belong to Canada. Placing our forces under a continental American command structure will reduce, not enhance, our sovereignty.

Canada is up against a hard-right assault on its very existence. The goal of the assault is no less than the complete neutering of Canadian sovereignty—the integration of Canada into the

American republic, either as a new band of states or as some kind of associate state. Make no mistake: this is a conscious and deliberate strategy, whose backers are some of the most powerful business leaders in the country. The opponents of Canada detest it as an enfeebled "Canadian system" that is hopelessly infected with "Canadian values," which are seen as irretrievably soft. Only through Americanization can we do away with the horrors of this bastard country. Those who espouse these views are truly adherents of a foreign power.

Stephen Harper is the most forceful of these within the political system. The paralysis and near death of traditional Canadian conservatism has created more influence for such extreme elements. The poison they direct into the bloodstream of Canadian politics is having its effect. On the other hand, the defenders of Canada are anything but single-minded in their approach. The left is often preoccupied with global issues and has done little thinking about this question for a generation. And the centre is weakened by the ideology of globalization, which has convinced many that the nation-state is bound to wane.

What makes this truly galling is that people with this outlook have done everything in their power over the past couple of decades to bring Canada to its knees as a nation, and now they don't like what they see around them.

There have always been Canadians who have longed for what they imagine to be the greener grass on the other side of the border and there always will be. In the more than thirty thousand kilometres I have traveled to write this book, however, I have found Canadians hopeful about their country.

In the more than thirty thousand kilometres I travelled to write this book, I found Canadians serious and hopeful. This is a land of multiple identities, but these identities do not close Canadians off from one another. Rather, they are starting points for dialogue, for discovery. Canadians are saying to one another, "Here is who I am, where I begin," and they want to know who you are and what you have to add. I remember a forty-year-old man from Nova Scotia on the train in Saskatchewan talking about how wonderful this country is; a Canadian customs official in British Columbia dismissing the idea of a union with the U.S. with the comment "I'm a Canuck, and that's it for me"; and an auto worker in Windsor who muttered on the same subject, "Why not stick with goddamn Canada." This is a deeply loved, but still unknown, country. It is North American, having thrown off European modes of judging people according to their accents and other external cultural trappings. In the vastness of our country, we have no appetite for empire. Canada is a country of generous space, and that space is not merely physical, although physical space should never be discounted as a factor in making us who we are. The deepest instinct of Canadians is toward tolerance, toward an acceptance that no single synthesis that works for everyone is available among cultures and lifestyles. And in a land that remains unknown, there is a sense that the future will reveal the truth. A northern country can never easily be optimistic, but an irreducible hopefulness is a part of what it is to be Canadian. Among all the nations of this hemisphere, Canada has been the most successful in creating an egalitarian life for its people—and we have a very long way to go. Among the nations of this hemisphere, Canada is closer than any other to a peaceable kingdom. Canada is one of the few countries on earth in which all of the elements needed to create a civilization are present. It is no preposterous conceit to believe that the greatest days of our country lie before us, even a long, long way before us.

During our history, Canadians have withstood numerous invasions from the south—and I do not mean invasions by arms alone. In the 1950s, the shrill blare of McCarthyism had its effect in Canada, but it was modulated here. In 1961, when President John F. Kennedy regarded selling wheat to China as trading with the enemy, the government of John Diefenbaker stood its ground and went ahead with a massive sale that transformed the prairie economy. Again, when Kennedy mounted his naval blockade around Cuba during the 1962 Cuban Missile Crisis, Diefenbaker called for a cooling-off process during which the facts could be verified. Although Diefenbaker was to pay with his political head for standing up to Kennedy, he stood up nonetheless. And later in the 1960s, when Lyndon Johnson applied pressure on Canada to send troops to Vietnam, the government of Lester Pearson did not buckle. No Canadian troops were sent.

On March 17, 2003, Prime Minister Jean Chrétien rose in the House of Commons and announced that in the absence of a resolution of the UN Security Council authorizing it, Canada would not participate in the Anglo-American military assault on Iraq. After months of wavering and giving signals that could be interpreted one way or the other, Chrétien took his stand. His position rested on the premise that going to war to change a country's regime, without an explicit UN mandate, posed a dangerous threat to international law. "Who's next?" he retorted on more than one occasion when asked why he had kept Canada out of the conflict. Although his stand was condemned by Stephen Harper as "gutless," Chrétien's crucial decision showed that Canada was capable of acting in pursuit of its values even when those brought it up sharply against Washington's course. The Chrétien government decided that it was not in the interest of Canada to participate in an illegal assault on a small country that posed no direct threat to the United States. For a middle-sized country like ours, multilateralism and respect for international law are essential to our survival as a sovereign nation. The government of Canada was acting in our national interest.

Ottawa's decision, taken one day before cruise missiles were launched against Baghdad, quickly brought the wrath of Washington down on Canada. The Anglo-American assault was a week old when Paul Cellucci, the U.S. ambassador to Canada, told a Toronto business audience that the Bush administration was "disappointed" with the Chrétien government's decision to stay out of the war. In his speech to the Economic Club of Toronto, Cellucci hinted at possible U.S. economic reprisals when he said, "We'll have to wait and see if there are any ramifications." Cellucci's speech energized the Canadian Alliance, whose members flayed the government in the House of Commons for not taking the side of the United States in the war and for endangering Canada's most important external relationship. Two premiers, Alberta's Ralph Klein and Ontario's Ernie Eves, declared that Canada should have entered the war.

On the other side were those Canadians who were sympathetic to the views of many millions of people around the world who had opposed the war before it was launched. On February 15, a month before the conflict began, 10 million people participated in demonstrations in opposition to the war in several hundred cities around the world. In Canada, on that day, there were demonstrations in many cities, with eighty thousand marching in Toronto, and an extraordinary two hundred thousand taking to the streets in Montreal.

In its drive to war, the United States faced not only the opposition of France, Germany, Russia and China in the UN Security Council, it was also up against an unprecedented global expression of popular wrath. In the world, it was said, there were now two superpowers, the United States, and an energized global public opinion. Three weeks after the war began, the Americans were in Baghdad. Time would tell whether this was to be only the first in a series of pre-emptive American wars, and how the peoples of the Middle East would respond to the American occupation of a major Arab country.

In Canada, the divisions over the war brought into sharp focus the great debate about Canada's future that had become the dominant item on the nation's agenda. Would Canada seek deep integration with the United States, or would it choose the path of national independence?

———

Canada can survive next door to the United States as long as the people and our political leaders are determined not to give up our sovereignty. At times, choosing sovereignty will mean that our leaders will not be the intimates of America's leaders. Invitations to play golf at Kennebunkport could be scarce. But we will survive, and we will prosper.

If we listened to the continentalists, we would believe that any assertion of Canadian sovereignty will mean economic disaster for Canada—that the Americans will retaliate against us. What is completely ignored in this counsel of helplessness is that American interests are so deeply entrenched in Canada because it is hugely profitable for them to be here. Canada is a vast source of materials needed by American industry. Canadians are a huge market for American multinationals. U.S.-owned auto plants in Canada are facilities in which billions of dollars have been invested because it is more profitable for the U.S. auto giants to assemble cars and trucks here than south of the border. All of those factors give us more freedom to manoeuvre than our timorous elites imagine. The U.S. multinationals will stay in Canada just as they did during the years when Ottawa refused to send Canadian troops to Vietnam. The sky will not fall. We do not have to listen to our homegrown Chicken Littles.

A sovereign Canada can be sustained next to the heart of the American Empire. The United States will leave us in peace because it cannot afford to do otherwise. Interference in Canadian affairs from south of the border can be expected. At times, Canada will be subjected to intense pressure to go along with Washington. How Canada stands up to the pressure will depend on Canadians themselves. The groups that espouse tighter ties with the U.S. will be a continuing presence. The C.D. Howe Institute and the Fraser Institute will pour out their streams of studies in which Canada is portrayed as having no choice but to adhere to the American position on great questions and to adopt a social system virtually indistinguishable from that south of the border. The continentalists can count on the ongoing allegiance of the Canadian Alliance to their cause. And they will have great sway in the Canadian media.

To counter this, the advocates of a sovereign Canada need to be much more assertive than they have been since the free trade debate of the eighties. The large majority of Canadians want Canada to survive as an independent country with its own political values and its own social system. But Canadians have not been alerted to the mounting dangers that threaten our independence. Regardless of party, those who oppose the continentalist agenda need to be ever present in the great debates in Canada, to prevent the nation from being compromised out of existence.

No one can foresee how long the United States will run amok, pursuing unilateralist policies in the world. The global campaign to make the world safe for America, begun by the Bush administration after September 11, will run on until its costs become too high for the American people and American business to absorb. The turning point may come when a foreign policy adventure goes awry, when a bloc of important states stands up to Washington's splendid isolation in a telling way, or when the American people decide they want to change the subject to health care or the health of the economy.

The lesson of history teaches that nations outlive empires. During the centuries of our national story, we have survived the decline and fall of the French and British empires. What destroys empires is imperial overstretch, the unwillingness of rulers to understand the limitations of their sway. That is the likely fate of the American Empire in the twenty-first century. The United States is like a supernova in today's world. In explosive fashion, American armed forces intervene around the globe; in the world's councils, the U.S. government arm-twists other nations into acceding to its variety of capitalism; American cultural missionaries, from

Hollywood filmmakers to media ideologues, sell the American line to humanity. And much like a supernova that is consuming itself rapaciously, the United States is more in debt to other countries than any other nation. Meantime, George W. Bush's twin policies of military adventures abroad and tax cuts for the rich at home are driving the U.S. government's deficit to stratospheric heights.

Living next door to a supernova is not a pleasant prospect. If we follow the advice of those who counsel deep integration with the United States, we could be consumed. With judicious realism, though, Canada has every prospect of surviving as a country and not merely as a geographical expression.

How Canada behaves in this period matters to the world. It is easy to be sucked into the view that Canada is such a small player on the global stage that by going along with Washington on everything, we'll be feathering our own nest without really changing the direction of global affairs. The continentalists who counsel us to take this course assume that even those Canadians who do not believe deeply in the American cause will follow the U.S. lead for reasons of what can be called cynical realism. If the U.S. is going to follow a particular course in any event, why not be onside?

That reasoning sells Canada short. When a great North American nation with much in common with the United States eschews American unilateralism and its drive for empire, it will make its mark on the world. Canadian positions on peacekeeping, on the nuclear test ban, on the abolition of land mines and on the International Criminal Court have left their mark. A peaceful, non-imperial Canada will have a welcome place in the world of the twenty-first century.

Naysayers have predicted the demise of Canada throughout our history. I believe we will prove them wrong once again.

Appendix | **The Making of the Border**

The Revolutionary War of the Thirteen Colonies against Great Britain led to the drawing of much of the line between the United States and Canada that remains in place to this day. On November 30, 1782, Britain and the United States signed a preliminary peace in Paris. The treaty recognizing the independence of the United States was signed for Great Britain by Richard Oswald, and for the United States by John Adams, Benjamin Franklin, John Jay and Henry Laurens. Article II of the preliminary treaty, which appears word for word in the definitive Treaty of Paris, signed on September 3, 1783, lays out the border between British and American territory all the way from the East Coast to the Lake of the Woods, northwest of Lake Superior.

The words in the treaty that describe the border are deceptively clear, considering that they were to lead to disputes that festered for many decades, and that came perilously close to generating a new war between Britain and the United States. Bear in mind that the treaty was signed in Paris by men on both the American and

British sides who had, to put it mildly, an imperfect knowledge of the geography of North America.

The 1783 Treaty of Paris was substantially based on what was known as Mitchell's map, one of North America completed in 1755. While Mitchell's was superior to maps of an earlier date, much of the continent remained unexplored, and important information obtained by the French was not available in the production of the map. As a consequence, accuracy of the kind we take for granted today was not to be expected. Both sides were determined to use the ambiguities of the settlement to champion their interests in subsequent disputes, which continued for many decades.

The peace treaty of 1783 left a number of questions requiring quick resolution. For one thing, the new boundary between the United States and British North America cut Canada off from an immense fur-trading territory south of the Great Lakes. While the Americans offered Britain a reciprocal free trade deal at the end of the Revolutionary War, Britain turned down the idea. For a number of years after the war, British forces held on to western posts on the American side of the border, posts that were in the fur-trading area to which Canadian traders had long had access. Continuing British occupation allowed the Canadian fur traders to remain active in the area. In 1794, however, a new treaty, Jay's Treaty, was negotiated between the United States and Britain to deal with these matters. As a consequence, Britain surrendered the posts on U.S. soil, and free trade was established across the border between the American republic and British North America. In theory this meant the Canadian fur traders should have had continued access to the fur-trapping territory south of the Great Lakes, but in practice U.S. regulations and transit tolls shut them out. With Jay's Treaty and the departure of the British from the western posts on American soil, the Canadian fur trade south of the border was ended for practical purposes.

QUAGMIRE: the Maine–New Brunswick Boundary

It is difficult today to imagine that the line dividing New Brunswick from Maine proved to be a powder keg that very nearly triggered a war between Britain and the United States.

To begin with, there was the issue of the St. Croix River, on which much of the border between Maine and New Brunswick was to be based. According to the treaty, the boundary was to be "formed by a line drawn due north from the source of St. Croix River to the Highlands." Mitchell's map showed the St. Croix flowing from a large lake called Kousaki into an unnamed bay, which most likely is the one now named Passamaquoddy. Since no one was quite sure which of several streams was the true St. Croix, the British and the Americans each nominated as the St. Croix a river that would give them a claim to the greatest possible amount of territory. The British claimed that the westernmost branch of a stream still called the Schoodic was the true St. Croix, while the Americans insisted that the Magaguadavic, almost eighty kilometres to the east, was the river referred to in the treaty. At stake, therefore, was a strip of territory almost eighty kilometres wide, extending from the Bay of Fundy all the way to the northern boundary of Maine.

In 1783, the division between U.S. and British territory—which was to become the boundary between Maine and New Brunswick—separated Massachusetts from Nova Scotia. Indeed, in 1763, when an earlier Treaty of Paris ceded New France to Britain, a boundary dispute was triggered between what were then two British possessions—the Massachusetts Bay Colony and Nova Scotia. That dispute, prior to the American Revolution, helped set the terms for the altercations that followed once the United States became an independent country.

Within a year of the treaty ending the American Revolutionary War, U.S. authorities accused the British authorities in Nova Scotia and the newly founded province of New Brunswick of sponsoring the creation of settlements across the line in American territory. The wave of immigrants from the United States to British North America in the first years after the Revolutionary War increased the population on the northwest shore of the Bay of Fundy and up the Saint John River from a few hundred to about 14,000. In 1784, this territory was separated from Nova Scotia to create the province of New Brunswick. In part, the motivation for establishing New Brunswick was political. With a population heavily drawn from Loyalists, who had suffered at the hands of the American patriots, the British believed the new province would provide a bulwark against American influence.

More than that, the Loyalists were Canada's first immigrants who had a grudge against the neighbouring republic, which would alter over time but never completely disappear.

The border between New Brunswick and Massachusetts (later Maine, when that state was established) remained a potential flashpoint in Anglo-American relations until the 1840s. In 1794, Great Britain and the United States appointed commissioners to decide which stream was the true St. Croix River. On October 25, 1798, the commissioners signed a declaration concluding that the Schoodic River that flowed into Passamaquoddy Bay was the one intended in the treaty to be the St. Croix, and therefore formed this part of the boundary.

The Anglo-American commission that settled this boundary quandary left unsettled the question of the ownership of the islands in the St. Croix River, a matter not resolved for more than a century, until a treaty was signed in Washington on April 11, 1908. The much more important matter of who owned the major islands in Passamaquoddy Bay arose in the years following the War of 1812. Under the Treaty of Ghent, signed on December 24, 1814, which ended the war, the United States and Britain were left in possession of the islands in the bay that they held at the conclusion of the conflict. The treaty provided that both sides would appoint commissioners to resolve the matter of the islands, in conformity with the true intent of the Treaty of Paris of 1783. Negotiations turned on the territories that had been included in the British grant of Nova Scotia to Sir William Alexander in 1621, a grant that had originally been drafted in Latin. In the agreement reached in the autumn of 1817, Britain won the greater share of the islands. The U.S. was awarded Moose Island, which had been occupied by the British military during and following the War of 1812. (Moose Island, which encompasses the town of Eastport, is now connected to mainland Maine by tidal dike causeways.) Adjacent to the coast of Maine, Britain won Campobello, Deer Island and, a little farther to the south and east, Grand Manan, the largest of the islands.

The settling of the southern boundary of Maine and New Brunswick left the question of the boundary between the source of the St. Croix River and the St. Lawrence River to be resolved. This is the story of how Maine got its infamous northern hump. The issue at stake was the boundary to be established between northeastern Maine and New Brunswick. The problem grew out of the wording of the Treaty of Paris of 1783, which defined this portion of the boundary as follows:

> From the north-west angle of Nova Scotia [including New Brunswick], viz., that angle which is formed by a line drawn due north, from the source of Saint Croix River to the Highlands; along the said Highlands which divide those rivers that empty themselves into the River St. Lawrence, from those which fall into the Atlantic Ocean, to the north-westernmost head of Connecticut River; thence down along the middle of that River, to the forty-fifth degree of north latitude; from thence, by a line due west on said latitude, until it strikes the River Iroquois or Cataraquy; thence along the middle of said river . . . East, by a line to be drawn along the middle of the River St. Croix, from

its mouth in the Bay of Fundy to its source, and from its source directly north to the aforesaid Highlands which divide the Rivers that fall into the Atlantic Ocean from those which fall into the River St. Lawrence, etc."

Since the source of the St. Croix had already been determined in the settling of the southern Maine–New Brunswick boundary, it should have been a simple matter to draw a line due north from that point. The meaning of the term "Highlands" ought also to have been plain. It should have been construed as referring to lands high enough to form a divide between waters flowing north into the St. Lawrence and waters flowing south into the Atlantic Ocean.

The border dispute that developed between New Brunswick and Maine, and therefore between Great Britain and the United States, was chiefly about possession of the Madawaska region of northwestern New Brunswick. Strategically at stake as well in the controversy was the question of a direct line of communication between Halifax and Quebec. During the peace negotiations that led up to the conclusion of the War of 1812, British negotiators put on the table the idea of agreeing to "such a variation of the line of frontier as may secure a direct communication between Quebec and Halifax." The American negotiators soundly rejected this idea, stating that they had "no authority to cede any part of the territory of the United States, and to no stipulation to that effect will they subscribe."

Both the British and the Americans dug in their heels and surveyed the terrain. Each came up with a claim about which "Highlands" were intended in the Treaty of 1783 that was highly favourable to their own particular interests. Overall, about 31,147 square kilometres of territory was in dispute. The U.S. claimed a sickle-shaped slice of territory stretching about thirty kilometres east of the present boundary, and going north the full length of

New Brunswick and into Quebec. From there, the blade of the sickle turned southwestward to take in a large swath of territory north of the present boundary. If the U.S. had got the full claim it wanted, the towns of St. Andrews in the south and Edmundston in the north of New Brunswick would have ended up in the U.S., as would Hartland, Perth and Grand Falls along the Saint John River. The U.S. claim would have meant that the direct route from the Maritimes to Central Canada on Canadian territory would have been even more tortuous than the one we have with the present boundary. The British claimed a chunk of territory that ran from south to north well west of the Saint John River, encompassing the town of Houlton, Maine. Most important, the British claimed the northern hump of present-day Maine, from east to west, stretching southward from the present border about eighty kilometres. If the British had got their full claim, the all-Canadian route from the Maritimes to Central Canada would have been more direct.

The boundary quandary dragged on into the 1820s, with the danger of conflict increasing as both sides began issuing licences to cut timber in the disputed territory. As population and economic activity increased in the region, the danger of a trivial incident blowing up into an international crisis grew ever greater. In 1827, when New Brunswick authorities arrested a certain John Baker in the disputed territory, the United States demanded that he be set free and paid "a full indemnity for the injuries which he has suffered." In reply, the British government asserted that Baker had interrupted the mail from Canada, hoisted the U.S. flag and conspired with others "to transfer the territory in which he resided to the United States."

That same year, the British and the Americans signed a treaty undertaking to seek the arbitration of a friendly sovereign or state to come up with an even-handed settlement to the dispute. In the spring of 1828, London and Washington agreed on the king of the Netherlands as arbitrator. On January 10, 1831, the king released his decision. Arguing that the criteria in the 1783 treaty and arguments based on the boundaries of British provinces out of the past led nowhere, the king proposed a boundary based on convenience. Of the total of about 31,147 square kilometres in dispute, the king's decision awarded about 20,500 to the U.S. and 10,600 to Britain. While the British were inclined to accept the settlement, the Americans were not.

One reason a settlement was so difficult to reach was that sharply different opinions were held by U.S. decision makers. President Andrew Jackson wanted to reach a deal with the British on the issue before the end of his term in March 1837, but he was concerned that a treaty might be turned down in the Senate, where a two-thirds vote was required for ratification. Moreover, the State of Maine was adamant on the issue. In an era when U.S. senators were appointed by the states, the Senate was especially sensitive to the opinions of state administrations.

Haggling continued and the risk of conflict increased. Both Maine and New Brunswick attempted to administer the disputed region. For example, the U.S. census records for Maine for the year 1840 include the part of Madawaska County, New Brunswick, that lies north of the Saint John River. In 1831, a number of people tried to hold a U.S. election in the Madawaska settlement and were arrested by New Brunswick authorities. After their convictions, they were set free when authorities in Maine repudiated their actions. In 1836, the New Hampshire militia arrested a Canadian justice of the peace for attempting to carry out his functions in disputed territory. The following year, New Brunswick authorities arrested an officer who was taking the census for Maine in the Madawaska settlement. In 1838–39, the so-called Aroostook War broke out. The State of Maine sent an agent to arrest British subjects for cutting timber in the Aroostook region. In turn, New Brunswick authorities arrested the agent. Brawls broke out between opposing gangs of New Brunswick and Maine lumberjacks.

From this point, the conflict lurched in the direction of war. The State of Maine appropriated $800,000 for military operations, assembled an armed civil posse and constructed fortifications in the disputed territory. The U.S. Congress voted $10 million dollars to be used if war broke out, and authorized the president to call out the militia and raise fifty thousand volunteers. With war in the air, the two sides backed away from the brink. They agreed that the State of Maine should remain in possession of one part of the territory and the British should hold on to the rest, with such possession not to detract from claims to be made in ongoing negotiations. Despite the agreement to cool things off, the State of Maine sent three hundred men, described as a "civil posse," to erect a blockhouse on the Saint John River.

In March 1841, Daniel Webster, the new U.S. secretary of state, informed the British minister at Washington that the U.S. was willing to try again to reach a compromise settlement with Britain. The British government, also in the mood for an agreement, sent Lord Ashburton to Washington with full powers to settle all the outstanding issues between the two countries. His Lordship, a son of Sir Francis Baring, the founder of the major bank Baring Bros. and Co., was married to an American and well disposed toward the United States. Arriving in the U.S. capital in April 1842, Lord Ashburton had to contend with uncompromising resolutions on the border question that had been passed by the legislatures of Maine and Massachusetts (which also took an interest, since it had claimed the disputed territory prior to the creation of Maine in 1820). After three months of negotiations that went nowhere, Webster and Ashburton decided they had to meet in face-to-face conferences instead of exchanging written communications. Using this method, the negotiators reached a tentative agreement, under which 18,167 square kilometres of the 31,147 in dispute would go to the United States and 12,980 to Britain. Even though the U.S. was getting 2,312 fewer square kilometres of territory in this deal compared with the award of the king of the Netherlands, Secretary of State Webster claimed in letters to Maine and Massachusetts that the seven-twelfths awarded to the U.S. was "equal in value to four-fifths of the whole."

In addition to the land settlement, Britain conceded to the United States the right to float timber down the Saint John River, free of any discriminatory tolls. The U.S. for its part granted to British subjects the same right on the upper Saint John River, which flowed through U.S. territory. The agreement conceded minor tracts of territory to the states of New Hampshire, Vermont and New York. As a consequence of this, Webster offered to pay a sum of $250,000 each to Maine and Massachusetts for the expenditures they had undertaken in dealing with the case, including the raising of a civil posse.

The treaty, signed in Washington on August 9, 1842, was strongly condemned in both the U.S. and Britain, and prompted scorn for both Webster and Ashburton in their own countries. In the U.S. Senate, Webster was accused by one senator of "victimizing that deserted and doomed State," Maine. In Britain, Lord Palmerston called the treaty "Lord Ashburton's capitulation," suggesting that he should receive the new title of "Earl Surrender."

A curious "battle of the maps" helped bring the matter of the Maine–New Brunswick border to a close with the ratification of the treaty by the U.S. Senate and the British Parliament. An early French map, with a red line drawn on it, supposedly by Benjamin Franklin, was discovered in Paris and sent to Daniel Webster. The map supported the British claim in the dispute. Judicious use of the map in the U.S. by Webster helped convince senators and authorities in Maine and Massachusetts that the U.S. had not done badly in the outcome. A map unearthed in the British

Museum lent support to the American claim and was used by Lord Aberdeen, the British foreign secretary, to demonstrate how well Ashburton had done in crafting the treaty.

The chief outcome of the Webster–Ashburton Treaty was to settle once and for all the issue of the Maine–New Brunswick border. It also made some minor amendments to the border between New Hampshire, Vermont and New York on the U.S. side and the Province of Quebec on the British side. Perhaps the most noteworthy case of a minor adjustment in favour of the United States was the moving of the border a short distance north at Rouse's Point, New York. At this point, the boundary between Quebec and the United States had been fixed to run along the forty-fifth parallel. Based on a faulty calculation, the U.S. had built an expensive fortification at Rouse's Point, believing the fort to be just south of the border. Later reckoning disclosed, however, that the fort was just north of the forty-fifth parallel, and therefore, according to the Treaty of 1783, on British soil. The Webster–Ashburton Treaty rejigged the line a little northward to keep Rouse's Point—and more important, the fortification—on U.S. soil.

To the Rockies

The Webster–Ashburton Treaty also largely confirmed the border between the United States and British North America west past the Great Lakes to the Lake of the Woods, which forms a part of the present boundary between northwestern Ontario and Minnesota. The Treaty of Paris of 1783 had laid the border for the territory west of Maine so that it would run along the forty-fifth parallel to the St. Lawrence River and then down the middle of the river to Lake Ontario. From there, the treaty described the boundary as running through the middle of lakes Ontario, Erie and Huron and the water communications between them. Beyond that point, Article II of the treaty reads as follows: "thence through Lake Superior, northward of the Isles Royal and Phelipeaux, to the Long Lake; thence through the middle of said Long Lake, and the water-communication between it and the Lake of the Woods, to the said Lake of the Woods; thence through the said Lake to the most north-western point thereof, and from thence on a due west course to the River Mississippi."

The Treaty of Ghent (1814) reiterated this language and dealt with difficulties that had arisen in determining the location of the middle of the lakes in question and the middle of the water communications between them, as well as deciding on the division of the islands in the boundary waterway. A commission was set up by Britain and the United States to grapple with these questions. One problem with drawing the boundary through the middle of the rivers is that in some cases this would mean the boundary would intersect islands. Another problem was that in many cases the middle of the river—the point equidistant from the two shores—did not coincide with its deepest channel.

As a way to avoid future friction, it was agreed that in cases where the line would have intersected an island, one side or the other would be granted the island whole. In these negotiations, which were concluded in June 1822, the British were successful in obtaining Wolfe Island, the largest of the Thousand Islands, located strategically at the point where Lake Ontario flows into the St. Lawrence River. The British were deeply concerned that if Wolfe Island were in American hands, a fortification could be built there that would threaten naval installations and fortifications in Kingston, just opposite the island. In return for allowing Britain to obtain Wolfe Island, the U.S. was able to bargain for control of Grand Island, just above Niagara Falls in the Niagara River, as well as Barnhart and other islands in the St. Lawrence, near Cornwall. An accommodation was also reached on the details of the boundary through lakes Ontario, Erie and Huron and their interconnecting waterways.

Further negotiations between the two sides were required to settle border issues that remained outstanding for the line between northern Lake Huron and the Lake of the Woods. First, there was the question of whether Britain or the United States was to obtain St. George (Sugar) Island in the St. Mary River, which flows from Lake Superior into Lake Huron. After wrangling over the matter, the island was eventually assigned to the U.S. in the Webster–Ashburton Treaty. Second, there was an important disagreement over where the line was to run from Isle Royale in Lake Superior to the Lake of the Woods. On this issue, the treaty of 1783 referred to a "Long Lake" that emptied into Lake Superior. The British claimed that the waterway mentioned was the St. Louis River, which flows into Lake Superior at the point where the present city of Duluth, Minnesota, is located. The Americans insisted the border should follow the Kaministikwia River, which empties into the lake at the location of the present city of Thunder Bay. Ashburton and Webster also resolved this issue. Ashburton proposed to Webster that the border should run off Lake Superior at the location of the Grand Portage, which is about two-thirds of the way from Duluth to Thunder Bay on the northwest shore of the lake. Webster accepted the proposal with the caveat that the waterways and portages along the border would "be free and open to the use of the subjects and citizens of both countries." On this basis, the parties incorporated these terms into the treaty of 1842.

From the northwest angle of Lake of the Woods, the treaty of 1783 stipulated that the boundary was to be drawn on a "due west course to the River Mississippi; thence by a line to be drawn along the middle of the said River Mississippi . . ." The problem with this wording, based on an inaccuracy found in Mitchell's map, is that it is at odds with the geography. Not long after the treaty was signed, it was discovered that a line drawn west from the Lake of the Woods would not intersect the Mississippi. At issue here was no less than the border to be drawn between U.S. and British territory all the way from Lake of the Woods to the Rocky Mountains. Or, more accurately, this became the issue once Thomas Jefferson made a spectacular deal with France in 1803—the Louisiana Purchase. The purchase, which transformed the United States from an Eastern Seaboard nation to a continental one, gave it a whole new set of territorial and boundary interests. Among these was the border to be drawn between the northern boundary of the Louisiana Territory and the British territories held by the Hudson's Bay Company.

The forty-ninth parallel, which was ultimately to become the border between western Canada and the United States, first made its appearance as a boundary well before the American Revolution. Following the Treaty of Utrecht of 1713, British and French commissioners negotiated over the boundary between the territories of the Hudson's Bay Company and the French territory to the south. In these talks, British commissioners made a case for the forty-ninth parallel as the southern limit of British territory, while French commissioners insisted that their territory ought to extend to within about eighty kilometres of Hudson Bay. These talks came to naught, but British geographers made it their practice to locate the southern boundary of the Hudson's Bay Company territories at the forty-ninth parallel.

After several failed attempts to resolve the border between U.S. and British territory west of Lake of the Woods, the matter was resolved as part of a convention in 1818 dealing with fisheries and boundaries. In these negotiations in London, the U.S. representatives proposed that the forty-ninth parallel be made the boundary between Lake of the Woods and the Pacific. The British replied that they would not settle for a boundary that did not give them the territory down to the mouth of the Columbia River on the Pacific coast. Later, the British proposed the addition of an article by which the boundary to the Rocky Mountains (still called the Stony Mountains at the time) would be the forty-ninth parallel, and that beyond the mountains citizens of both countries would be free to settle between the forty-fifth and forty-ninth parallels for a period of ten years. To this, the Americans agreed.

The Oregon Country

Beyond the Rockies, two crucial border disputes remained to be settled. The first one, over what was called the Oregon Country, would determine who controlled an immense stretch of the Pacific coast. The second, about the boundary between Alaska and Canada, became acute at the end of the nineteenth century because of the discovery of a motherlode of gold in the Yukon.

European territorial claims on the Pacific coast of North America extended all the way back to the earliest years after Columbus's first voyage to the Western Hemisphere. On June 7, 1494, Spain and Portugal signed their famous treaty of Partition of the Ocean, by which Portugal was granted exclusive territorial rights east of the meridian line that passed 370 leagues west of the Cape Verde Islands. Spain was granted the same rights west of that meridian. This arrogant grab for territorial rights over much of the globe received the imprimatur of the papacy. England, though, ignored the Spanish and Portuguese claims and the weight of papal authority and carried out its own expeditions in the quest for territory.

Over the next three centuries, Spanish, British and Russian expeditions to the west coast of North America resulted in claims being made to territory—claims that would affect the settling of the Canada–U.S. border in the nineteenth century.

Once Britain and the United States sought agreement on the border between them, the struggle for territorial advantage on the West Coast was rendered more uncertain and precarious because it also involved Russia and Spain. At the end of the eighteenth century and the beginning of the nineteenth, British and American expeditions across the continent by land played a role in buttressing each country's claims. In 1793, Alexander Mackenzie made his way from British territory to the Pacific. Seven years later, Duncan McGillivray, a British fur trader, was the first European to discover the upper waters of the Columbia River. In 1804, following the acquisition of the Louisiana Territory by the United States, President Thomas Jefferson engaged Lewis and Clark to explore the Missouri River to its source and to discover a water route to the Pacific. In 1805, the intrepid pair followed the Snake and Columbia rivers to the Pacific.

Over the next few years, the British and the Americans established trading posts in the Oregon Country. The North West Company, a British concern, set up several posts south of the forty-ninth parallel. In 1811, the Pacific Fur Company, an American enterprise, established Fort Astoria at the mouth of the Columbia River. Two years later, when Britain and the U.S. were at war, the U.S. company sold Astoria to the North West Company so that the post would not be seized by a British warship. With the Treaty of Ghent, which ended hostilities in 1814, both sides agreed to restore possessions that had been seized during the war. The British handed Astoria back to the Americans, even though the post had been acquired by purchase and not as an act of war.

A note from U.S. Secretary of State John Quincy Adams in 1818 to the U.S. ambassador to Britain, Richard Rush, showed that the American government had already developed the view that the United States had a very special role to play in North America:

> If the United States leave her [Great Britain] in undisturbed enjoyment of all her holds upon Europe, Asia, and Africa, with all her actual possession in this hemisphere, we may very fairly expect that she will not think it consistent either with a wise or a friendly policy to watch with eyes of jealousy and alarm

every possibility of extension to our natural dominion in
North America . . .

For the British, then at the height of their imperial power, to be
faced with such an upstart was an early warning from a future
global challenger. The note presaged the Monroe doctrine by
five years. Indeed, John Quincy Adams, secretary of state, heavily shaped the Monroe doctrine, which was put into words by
President James Monroe in his annual message on December 2,
1823. He stated that the time had been "judged proper for asserting as a principle . . . that the American continents, by the free and
independent conditions which they have assumed and maintain,
are henceforth not to be considered as subjects for future colo-
nization by any European powers."

When Lord Ashburton arrived in Washington in 1842, as we
have seen, he had instructions to reach a settlement of the boundary between the U.S. and Britain in the Oregon Country, as well
as the Maine boundary. Fearing that a failure to settle the Maine
boundary could lead to hostilities, Webster and Ashburton con-
centrated their efforts on this issue, leaving the Oregon question
to be settled later.

Two years later, the Oregon issue exploded onto the scene in
a new and volatile way. At the Democratic Party's convention in
May 1844 in Baltimore, the party adopted a plank on Oregon that
was soon translated into combative language: "Fifty-four-forty or
fight." The latitude in the slogan was the initial boundary
between Russian Alaska and the Oregon Country. With this truc-
ulent stand, the Democratic presidential candidate, James Polk,
was able to offer his supporters the prospect of new land on the
far side of the Rockies. Of critical importance, Oregon would be
"free territory," unlike slave-owning Texas, which Polk was also
determined to annex. The fight for all of Oregon, which meant
taking a belligerent stand against Britain, helped Polk on his way

to the White House. Polk used the opportunity of his inaugural address, on March 4, 1845, to state that his policy would be to "assert and maintain by all constitutional means the right of the United States to that portion of our territory which lies beyond the Rocky Mountains. Our title to the country of the Oregon is clear and unquestionable."

Polk, who had expansionist ambitions to the south as well as the north, had boxed himself in with his tough talk that made it seem that he would be satisfied with nothing less than the whole of the Oregon Country. Throughout 1845, Polk pushed ahead with his aggressive stand toward Britain. On April 28, 1846, the president gave notice that the United States was abrogating the convention of 1818 under which the two countries jointly occupied the disputed territory. While publicly belligerent, Polk let it be known behind the scenes that he was prepared to accept a compromise settlement with Britain. Two weeks later, the United States declared war on Mexico.

Lord Aberdeen, the British foreign minister, instructed the British ambassador in Washington, Richard Pakenham, to propose the forty-ninth parallel as the boundary from the Rockies to the Pacific, with Britain to retain the whole of Vancouver Island and the right to navigation on the Columbia River. On June 15, 1846, the so-called Oregon Treaty was signed at Washington, with these as the terms. By the time the treaty was signed, American settlers in the Oregon Territory numbered about seven thousand, compared with only about four hundred British setters. Time was clearly not on the British side.

While the treaty settled the main issues arising out of the Oregon dispute, it was quickly followed by a new set of differences over the boundary between Vancouver Island and the U.S. mainland. The question was, Which was the main channel separating the island from the continent? The British claimed Rosario Strait, the eastern channel, while the U.S. insisted that the boundary should run through Haro Strait, the western channel. An attempt to settle the matter through the appointment of commissioners from both sides failed. In 1859, an absurd issue on San Juan, one of the channel islands in dispute, brought matters to a boil. An American citizen shot a pig that belonged to the Hudson's Bay Company. The shooter claimed that an officer of the Hudson's Bay Company threatened to arrest him and take him to Victoria for trial. In retaliation, the U.S. general in charge of the Oregon Territory dispatched troops to the island. The risk of a skirmish between the Americans and the British, which could have led to wider hostilities, passed when the local British commander did not rise to the bait. A deal was reached for a joint occupation of San Juan Island by one hundred American and one hundred British troops.

Following several futile efforts to resolve the border issue, the Treaty of Washington of 1871, which resolved a number of other issues of importance to Canada, stipulated that the question should be submitted to the German emperor for arbitration and an award. After receiving the cases of both sides, on October 21, 1872, the emperor issued his award, which favoured the U.S. claim for Haro Strait as being "most in accordance with the true interpretations of the treaty" of 1846. In Washington the following March, the U.S. and Britain signed a protocol putting the issue to rest on the basis of the German emperor's award.

The Alaska Boundary Dispute

Settling the great dispute over the Oregon Country left one significant land question unresolved: the boundary between Alaska and British North America.

In 1821, the czar of Russia issued a ukase forbidding "all foreign vessels not only to land on the coasts and islands" between the Bering Strait and the fifty-first parallel "but also to approach them within less than a hundred Italian miles." Violators risked the seizure of their vessel and cargo. Britain and the United States protested this Russian territorial claim to a sizable slice of the west coast of North America stretching nearly as far south as the northern tip of Vancouver Island. On February 22, 1819, two years prior to the czar's startling claim, the United States had signed the Treaty of Florida Blanca with Spain. This treaty had ceded to the U.S. all the territorial rights of Spain north of the forty-second parallel on the West Coast. The U.S. government asserted that no Russian settlements should be allowed south of the fifty-fifth parallel, and no British settlements north of the fifty-fifth parallel or south of the fifty-first. Moreover, U.S. settlements should not be established north of the fifty-first parallel.

The British regarded this American position as the height of effrontery. George Canning, the British foreign secretary, wondered on what basis the U.S. was inserting itself into affairs that were hardly its concern. The British rejoinder was to claim the right to establish British settlements on the Pacific coast between the forty-second and fifty-first degrees of latitude, in addition to other "unoccupied" portions of America. Adopting a more conciliatory tone, the British then proposed the forty-ninth parallel as the boundary with the U.S. as far west as the intersection of the Columbia River. From that point to the Pacific, the British wanted the boundary to be drawn along the centre of the river. The American response was negative to this idea, but Richard Rush, the U.S. ambassador in London, did offer to shift his government's position to the acceptance of the forty-ninth rather than the fifty-first parallel as the border.

On December 2, 1823, as we have noted, in his message to Congress, President James Monroe focused on the U.S. negotiations with Russia. This was also the occasion when he issued his famous doctrine, a cornerstone of U.S. foreign policy ever since.

Deals between the U.S. and Russia in 1824 and Great Britain and Russia in 1825 eliminated the three-way power struggle over the Oregon Country. The U.S. and Russia agreed in a treaty that U.S. citizens would not establish settlements north of latitude 54 degrees 40 minutes, and the Russians undertook that they would not settle the territory south of that point. The British treaty with Russia limited the southern point of Russian settlement to latitude 54 degrees 40 minutes and on the east by the first range of mountains and the 141st meridian.

The triangular conflict then led to separate negotiations between the Americans and the Russians and the British and the Russians. When the Crimean War broke out in 1854, there was a serious risk that the conflict between Britain and Russia would extend to Russian Alaska. The Russian American Company and the Hudson's Bay Company convinced their respective governments that the west coast of North America should be considered neutral territory during the conflict. Although a few incidents occurred, the British and Russians stuck to the arrangement.

In 1867, the situation on the northwest Pacific coast was dramatically and permanently altered when Russia sold its American possessions to the United States for the grand sum of $7.2 million. That same year, of course, brought Canadian Confederation. By 1871, the fledgling Dominion had expanded to include the territory of the Hudson's Bay Company and British Columbia. From that date forth, although Britain was still very much involved, the boundary to be determined was between American Alaska and Canada.

A first attempt in 1872 to set up a commission to define the border between Alaska and British Columbia came to nothing. As in the case of the earlier dispute over the Maine–New Brunswick boundary, the Alaska–B.C. boundary would prove extremely difficult to settle. The problem lay in the vagueness of the description of the extent of Alaska when the Russians sold the territory to the Americans. At issue was the Alaska Panhandle, the narrow strip of territory, flanked by a string of islands, that pushes down the coast from Alaska proper to 54–40 latitude, just north of Prince Rupert,

B.C. The argument turned on the interpretation of two treaties: the 1825 treaty between Britain and Russia and the 1867 treaty by which Russia sold Alaska to the United States. Disputes continued over the years until July 1892, when a convention was signed between Britain and the United States that provided for a survey of the border area. When the two-year deadline passed without the completion of the work, the timetable was extended to December 31, 1895. Although a report was drafted and maps were forwarded to the British and American governments on the appointed date, the dispute again remained unresolved.

What had been a relatively tepid dispute over a remote territory exploded into serious conflict in 1896 with the discovery of gold in the valley of the Klondike River in the Yukon. Tens of thousands of miners set out for the new eldorado. In 1898, the population of Dawson, the centre of the gold rush country, soared to forty thousand, making it, for a time, the biggest town in Canada west of Winnipeg. The great issue at stake was whether the U.S. or Canada would control the gateway to the gold.

Under the circumstances, it became a matter of vital importance to fix the boundary, especially in the area where the influx of miners was greatest. The ports of Dyea and Skagway, entrance-ways to the Upper Yukon via the Lynn Canal (channel) and to the Chilkoot and White passes, became vital passage points. Temporary agreements about the border needed to be superseded by a permanent settlement. In May 1898, at a meeting in Washington, Britain and the U.S. decided that each side should communicate to the other its views on the subject. On October 20, 1899, Britain and the U.S. agreed on a provisional boundary, fixed at the summits of the White and Chilkoot passes, and on the Chilkat River at the mouth of Klehini River.

It was not until January 1903 that Great Britain and the United States signed an agreement in Washington to establish a tribunal to arrive at a permanent settlement of the boundary. The

British had suggested a tribunal of seven jurists, three from each side and one from a neutral country. The U.S. refused this proposal, and so, in the end, the tribunal was to be made up of "six impartial jurists of repute," three to be appointed by the U.S. and three by Britain. The U.S. appointed Elihu Root, the U.S. secretary of war, himself a member of the administration that had advanced its case on the Alaska boundary; Henry Cabot Lodge, a senator, who was reported to have stated that the Canadian claims regarding the Alaska boundary were "baseless"; and George Turner, a senator from Washington State. It was said of Turner that to take Canada's side in the case would have been easier for anyone else in the U.S., members of the administration aside, with the exception of "a politician of the state of Washington and a resident of Spokane." All three of Theodore Roosevelt's appointments were shockingly partisan, and were viewed as such by the Laurier government in Ottawa. The imperial government decided to go ahead with the case on the basis of the agreement, despite the fact that in both Ottawa and London it was felt that Washington had grossly violated the undertaking to appoint "impartial" jurists.

The British appointed two Canadians—Sir Louis Jetté, lieutenant-governor of Quebec, and J.D. Armour, a judge of the Supreme Court of Canada—along with Lord Alverstone, chief justice of England. When Armour died, another Canadian, A.B. Aylesworth, a prominent lawyer (later to be minister of justice), replaced him.

There were three chief points at issue, to be settled by a majority vote of the members of the tribunal. First, there was the question of the initial point of the boundary in the disputed sector. Second, there was the matter of whether the boundary should pass north or south of Wales, Pearse, Sitklan and Kannaghunut islands, a settlement that was to be based on identifying which channel was truly the Portland Canal. Third, and the heart of the dispute, was to agree on the boundary down the length of the Alaska Panhandle—the mountain, or so-called *lisière* (strip), boundary.

The first issue was disposed of without difficulty. All six members of the tribunal agreed that Cape Muzon was the initial point of the boundary.

The second question proved more thorny. Located just south of Dall Island, Cape Muzon marks the southern limit of the Alaska Panhandle. With the U.S. arguing that the true Portland Canal passed south of the islands in question and the British insisting that it passed north of them, the result was a clear victory for the United States. The three American members of the tribunal were joined by the British member, Lord Alverstone, and were opposed by the two Canadians on this matter. By a vote of four to two, the tribunal ruled that the Portland Canal passed south of Sitklan and Kannaghunut islands, which went to the U.S. and north of Wales and Pearse islands, which were awarded to Canada.

In a toughly argued dissenting opinion, Aylesworth set out to show that the majority opinion was the product of politics rather than a fair attempt to interpret the words of the treaties at issue. In his dissent, he rested his case on the claim that in his 1793 voyage in the region, the English navigator Captain George Vancouver had made it clear that the passage he called Portland's Canal lay to the north of the four islands in question. The boundary agreed on by Lord Alverstone and the three Americans, Aylesworth stated, had never been suggested by anyone. In his mind, it was clear that the British lord had voted with the Americans solely to ensure a settlement. The Canadian jurist wrote:

> Upon such findings of fact as those above described, and after a solemn adjudication that the Portland Channel of the Treaty lies to the north of Pearse and Wales islands, the taking of the two important islands Sitklan and Kannaghunut, from Canada,

and giving them to the United States by a proceeding said to be judicial, is, "according to my true judgment," nothing less than a grotesque travesty of justice.

The third issue, the tribunal's most important task, was to decide on the boundary between the head of Portland Canal and the 141st meridian in the vicinity of Mount St. Elias. The 141st meridian forms the north-south boundary between the main body of Alaska and the Yukon. At stake here was where the boundary would run along the full length of the Alaska Panhandle, from Portland Canal in the south to Mount St. Elias in the north, a stretch of over five hundred kilometres. The question of substance was whether the American boundary would be a continuous one, along the full length of the Panhandle, or whether at one or several points the line would be breached by Canadian enclaves on the coast. It was precisely the acquisition of ports by Canada along the line of the Panhandle that the American negotiators were determined to prevent.

The treaties referred to the boundary running along the line of mountains parallel to the coast, and in the absence of such mountains the extent of the strip, or *lisière*, was to extend to a depth of ten leagues from the coast. The British, and therefore Canadian, case was that the width of the strip ought to be measured along a line that ran at right angles to the trend of the coast in the area. Where there was an absence of mountains, the case went, and where an inlet extended inland for more than ten leagues, the upper portion of it would be Canadian territorial waters.

The U.S. case, mounted on the strength of the Russian claim prior to 1867, maintained that the Russian position, which was secured in the Anglo-Russian Treaty of 1825, was to establish a territorial barrier between the Russian coast and the British interior. The Americans concluded that the intention of the 1825 treaty was to affirm Russian sovereignty over a continuous strip of territory from Portland Canal to the 141st meridian. They rejected the British argument, insisting that the width of the strip was to be ten marine leagues, measured not from the coast but from the heads of all the inlets—a position that guaranteed there would be no Canadian port in the Panhandle. They further maintained that this was the basis on which the United States purchased Alaska from Russia in a deal that was open for all to see, and to which the British had raised no objection.

On this critical issue before the tribunal, the deciding vote, once again, was four to two—with Lord Alverstone joining the three American jurists. The four decided on a mountain boundary that was very closely in accordance with the case presented by the United States. The two Canadian jurists, Jetté and Aylesworth, vigorously dissented and refused to put their names to this section of the award, as well as the section on the Portland Canal.

Although the tribunal succeeded in settling a thorny border dispute, it created a political firestorm in Canada. The Laurier government and the Canadian public were outraged at the outcome. There was understandable anger at the United States for the unwillingness of the Roosevelt administration to sanction a compromise with Canada that would have allowed for a Canadian port at the head of the Lynn Canal, the best point of access to the Yukon goldfields. Canadians believed that the attitude of the U.S. government toward Canada was one of pure malevolence. More novel was the fury at Britain because Lord Alverstone had sided with the Americans on the key issues. Many Canadians asked what the point was of being an integral part of the British Empire if it meant that Britain would sell out Canadian interests so as not to undermine Anglo-American amity. In the House of Commons, the prime minister, Sir Wilfrid Laurier, concluded:

> I have often regretted . . . that we have not in our own hands
> that treaty-making power, which would enable us to dispose of

our own affairs . . . so long as Canada remains a dependency of the British crown the present powers that we have are not sufficient for the maintenance of our rights. It is important that we should ask the British Parliament for more extensive power, so that if ever we have to deal with matters of a similar nature again we shall deal with them in our own way.

In French Canada, where opinion had always been lukewarm about the British connection, the reaction to the Alaska settlement was sulphurous. In Quebec's highly partisan press, those who were pro-Laurier attacked Britain, while those who were anti-Laurier condemned the prime minister as a weakling who was not prepared to stand up to the British. The net effect, in all parts of Canada, was to call into question the benefits of the alliance with Britain where matters of Canadian-American relations were at issue.

Arctic Waters: Today's Major Territorial Question

With trivial exceptions, the land-border issues between Canada and the United States have been resolved. What remains unresolved, however, is a matter of exceptional importance: the question of whether Canada owns the waters it claims in the High Arctic, including the waterway known as the Northwest Passage. The problem is that the United States does not recognize Canada's claim that these are domestic waters. The dispute over the issue has gone on for several decades in an active way, with neither side showing any willingness to back down. The dispute highly significant for the twenty-first century because the waters of the High Arctic have been warming in recent decades. This makes it likely that in the future, the Northwest Passage will become a major global shipping route. In this event, who will control the shipping lanes through these northern waters? Will it be Canada, or will the Northwest Passage become an international shipping route, with all the risks this could entail for the environment of a highly sensitive region? Furthermore, as Canada integrates its armed forces ever deeper with those of the United States, will Canada be in a position to resist American claims on the issue when they are forcefully put?

Canada's claim to the High Arctic goes back to two British transfers of territory to Canada in the late nineteenth century. The first occurred in 1870, when Britain transferred Rupert's Land, the territory of the Hudson's Bay Company, to the new Dominion of Canada. In 1880, Britain surrendered its rights to its remaining territories and waters in the High Arctic to Canada. From that point, Canada moved slowly to make good its jurisdiction over the North. In 1895, an Order-in-Council created four districts: Yukon, Mackenzie, Ungava and Franklin, the last defined as extending north for an "indefinite extent." By the 1930s, Canada had successfully asserted its claim to the land territory that makes up the Arctic archipelago. It had settled a dispute with Norway over ownership of the Sverdrup Islands in 1928 by paying Norway $67,000 for the maps and charts of the Norwegian explorer who had claimed the islands for Norway. The only remaining land dispute today is over ownership of Hans Island, a small island between Baffin Island and Greenland. The government of Denmark contests Canada's claim to ownership of the island.

In 1925, Canada made a claim to the waters as well as the lands of the Arctic, to everything between 61 degrees west longitude and 141 degrees west longitude, north all the way to the pole. As John Honderich notes in his book *Arctic Imperative*, "this dramatic claim for a giant slice of the Arctic pie was known as a 'sector claim.'" Both Britain and Russia made sector claims in the early nineteenth century, and they agreed that the boundary between British North America and eastern Siberia extended as far as the "Frozen Ocean." Australia, New Zealand, Argentina, Chile and France have made sector claims to slices of Antarctica, some of the claims in conflict with one another. Significantly, the United States has never accepted as valid any of these sector claims in the Arctic or Antarctic.

While various Canadian cabinet ministers reiterated the sector claim over the decades, in 1956 the theory was put aside when Jean Lesage, the minister of northern affairs, weighed into a controversy about whether Canadians should regard a Soviet ice-floe station that drifted into the Canadian sector as an invasion of Canada. Lesage declared that "we have never subscribed to the sector theory in application to the ice. We are content that our sovereignty exists over all the Arctic islands."

Dropping the sector theory as the basis for a Canadian claim to the waters of the Arctic did not mean dropping the claim itself. In the House of Commons on September 10, 1985, Joe Clark, Canada's external affairs minister, made the most comprehensive statement to the effect that Canada assumed full sovereignty over the Arctic waters and, most important, the Northwest Passage. Clark stated:

> Canada's sovereignty in the Arctic is indivisible. It embraces land, sea and ice. It extends without interruption to the seaward-facing coasts of the Arctic Islands. These Islands are joined and not divided by the waters between them. They are bridged for most of the year by ice. From time immemorial Canada's Inuit people have used and occupied the ice as they have used and occupied the land.

Noteworthy in the statement was the linking of the claim to the fact that for most of the year the islands of the Arctic are bridged by ice. The implication is that the Northwest Passage is a unique waterway because of the historic habitation of the Inuit on the ice.

Joe Clark's declaration on Canadian sovereignty in the Arctic was not made in a vacuum. It was delivered at a time of high emotion in Canada, in the aftermath of the voyage of the U.S. ice-breaker *Polar Sea* through the Northwest Passage in the summer of 1985. The U.S. government sent the *Polar Sea* through the Passage without seeking Canadian permission. The United States has never recognized Canadian sovereignty over the Northwest Passage, insisting on regarding it as an international strait. The American dispute with Canada over the Northwest Passage is an integral part of the U.S. position on what it insists are international waterways in many parts of the globe. As the world's leading naval power, the U.S. wants to be able to sail its warships wherever it likes, and that includes the right to navigate narrow straits of strategic importance. In the 1980s, the U.S. sent warships into the Gulf of Sidra, off the coast of Libya, to forcefully deny Libyan claims that the Gulf lay within that country's internal waters. In early 1986, the U.S. sent two warships into the Black Sea on a route that deliberately took them inside the twelve-mile limit claimed by the Soviet Union as internal waters.

When it dispatched the *Polar Sea*, the U.S. was asserting a right to "innocent passage" through the Northwest Passage. If the U.S. view of the dispute prevailed, this would allow the ships of any nation to sail through the Passage without Canadian permission and without subjecting themselves to Canadian environmental and safety rules and regulations. The voyage of the *Polar Sea* was not the first time an American vessel had traversed the Passage and challenged Canada's claim to sovereignty. In the summer of 1969, the supertanker *Manhattan*, owned by Humble Oil, sailed through the Passage without first seeking the permission of the Canadian government. The purpose of the voyage was to determine whether it would be feasible to ship large quantities of Alaskan oil to market by tanker through the Northwest Passage. The 155,000-tonne *Manhattan* was heavily reinforced to deal with the ice. The ship was as long as the Empire State Building laid on its side, and displaced twice as much water as the *Queen Elizabeth 2*. Ironically, during the voyage, the *Manhattan* twice became stuck in the massive ice jams of the Passage and was forced to call for help from a Canadian icebreaker, the *John A. Macdonald*.

Between the voyages of the American ships in 1969 and 1985, three other vessels, the Polish *Gdynia* and the Swedish *Lindblatt Explorer* and *World Explorer*, made full or partial journeys in the Passage. In all three cases, Ottawa's permission was sought and granted. In 1999, a Russian company sold a dry dock in Vladivostok to new owners who wanted to move it to Bermuda. The dry dock was successfully towed through the Northwest Passage with the assistance of a Russian icebreaker and an ocean-going tug. Also in 1999, a Chinese research vessel made a voyage to Tuktoyaktuk. The Canadian embassy in Beijing had been notified of the planned expedition, but no one had bothered to inform the local officials, who were more than a little surprised when the Chinese vessel arrived. Canada's very limited monitoring of the Arctic was laid bare for all to see when the first inkling Canadian officials had of the vessel's arrival in Canadian waters was when it sailed into the harbour.

Joe Clark's 1985 declaration on Arctic sovereignty made explicit mention of the fact that the islands were bridged "for most of the year by ice." In the early years of the twenty-first century, however, as the average temperatures in the Arctic rise at a more rapid rate than in any other region of the world, the ice cover in the Northwest Passage has been thinning. As Rob Huebert, a strategic studies specialist at the University of Calgary, noted in an article on climate change and Canadian sovereignty, Arctic warming "is evidenced by the thickness of the ice cover; the occurrence of both the melting and freezing of the Arctic Ocean and its surrounding waterways; and from the samples of ice cores." Whether the decreasing ice cover in the Arctic is explained by global warming or some more local cause, the consequence is that it is becoming easier to navigate the waters of the Northwest Passage for longer periods of time. Melting ice may both dissolve a portion of Canada's claim to sovereignty and make the Northwest Passage a more attractive waterway for those who inclined to challenge Canada's claim. It was a sign of the growing interest in the region that the U.S. navy held a symposium in April 2001 on the subject of conducting surface-vessel operations in Arctic waters.

It is certainly not the case that Canada has made ice the overriding factor in its claim to sovereignty. Indeed, on January 1, 1986, the Canadian government decided to fortify its claim by enclosing the Arctic Archipelago in a perimeter of what are called "straight baselines." A problem with this proclamation of straight baselines is that in 1982 Canada signed the United Nations Law of the Sea Convention, which includes article 8(2), stating that a nation cannot close an international strait by declaring straight baselines.

Canada's effort to secure sovereignty over the Arctic waters is opposed not only by the United States but by the European Union as well. As the attractions of the waterway grow both for commercial interests and for those, especially the Americans, who see the Northwest Passage as a military thoroughfare, the pressures on Canada are likely to build. If Canada is going to hold on to the sovereignty it has proclaimed, it will have to invest considerable resources and muscle into making good its claim. Of central importance will be increasing the capacity to monitor the Arctic. Until now, the Canadian government has often been in the embarrassing position of not really knowing who is passing through the waters of the Northwest Passage. The example we have seen of the Chinese vessel arriving at Tuktoyaktuk is a case in point. During the Cold War, it is highly likely that both U.S. and Soviet submarines passed through the waterway without informing anyone. There is no reason to believe that the

American navy does not continue submarine voyages through the Passage today.

Patrolling Canada's immense coasts, including those in the Arctic, will have to be a primary, arguably *the* primary, task of the Canadian military in the twenty-first century.

Notes

Chapter 1: The Meaning of the Border

1. Cited in Carl Berger, *The Sense of Power: Studies in the Ideas of Canadian Imperialism 1867–1914* (University of Toronto Press, 1970), 155.

Chapter 2: Bookends: Point Roberts and Campobello

1. Mark Goldman, *High Hopes: The Rise and Decline of Buffalo, New York* (Albany, NY: State University of New York Press, 1983), 273–75.

2. U.S. Department of Commerce, *State and Metropolitan Area Data Book, 1997–98* (Washington: U.S. Department of Commerce, 1998), 60.

Chapter 3: Remote Frontiers

1. Claus-M. Naske and Herman E. Slotnick, *Alaska: A History of the 49th State* (Norman, OK: University of Oklahoma Press, 1994), 28.

2. Ibid., 59.

3. Ibid., 73.

4. Ibid., 95.

5. Ibid., 135.

6. Ibid., 147.

7. *International Herald Tribune*, 20–21 July 2002.

8. Pierre Berton, *The Klondike Fever: The Life and Death of the Last Great Gold Rush* (New York: Carroll and Graf, 1985), 318.

9. Ibid., 161, 164.

10. Ibid., 359, 360.

Chapter 4: Seeking Refuge

1. *Globe and Mail*, 15 March 2003.

2. Ibid.

3. see Rick Hornung, *One Nation Under the Gun: Inside the Mohawk Civil War* (Toronto: Stoddart, 1991).

4. Cheryl MacDonald, "Last Stop on the Underground Railroad," *The Beaver* (February–March 1990).

5. Ibid.

6. Ibid.

7. Ibid.

8. Ibid.

9. Samuel Eliot Morison and Henry Steele Commager, *The Growth of the American Republic*, vol. 1 (New York: Oxford University Press, 1962), 624–627.

10. MacDonald, "Last Stop on the Underground Railroad."

11. Ibid.

12. Ibid.

13. Garry Wills, *Certain Trumpets: The Call of Leaders* (New York: Simon and Schuster, 1994), 48.

14. Ibid., 41.

15. Ibid., 45.

16. Ibid., 47.

17. *The Nation*, 3 December 2001.

18. Ian Anderson, "Sitting Bull and the Mounties," Wild West website, February 1998.

19. John Hagan, *Northern Passage: American Vietnam War Resisters in Canada* (Cambridge and London: Harvard University Press, 2001), front page.

20. Ibid., 204.

21. Norman Penner, *Canadian Communism: The Stalin Years and Beyond* (Toronto: Methuen, 1988), 166.

22. Ibid.

23. Ibid.

24. Stanley Ryerson, *Unequal Union: Confederation and the Roots of Conflict in the Canadas, 1815–1873* (Toronto: Progress Books, 1968), 129, 130.

Chapter 5: Border Riches: Customs and Smuggling

1. Dave McIntosh, *The Collectors: A History of Canadian Customs and Excise* (Toronto: New Canada Publications, 1984), 185.

2. Ibid., 56–59.

3. Canada Customs and Revenue Agency, "The Canada Customs and Revenue Agency—an evolution," www.ccra-adrc.gc.ca, 4 January 2002.

4. McIntosh, *The Collectors*, 109, 111.

5. Ibid., 153.

6. Lita-Rose Betcherman, "The Customs Scandal of 1926," *The Beaver* (April–May 2001).

7. Ibid.

8. McIntosh, *The Collectors*, 254.

9. Ibid.

10. C.W. Hunt, *Booze, Boats and Billions* (Toronto: McClelland and Stewart, 1988), 70, 71.

11. Betcherman, "The Customs Scandal of 1926."

12. Ibid.

13. Ibid.

14. Ibid.

15. Ibid.

16. McIntosh, *The Collectors*, 268.

17. Ibid., 267, 268.

18. Ibid., 269, 270.

19. Ibid., 271–273.

20. Ibid., 277.

Chapter 6: Modern-day Rum-runners

1. *Gazette*, published by the RCMP, 63, no. 3 (2001).

2. *Canadian Press*, 7 October 2002.

3. Ibid.

4. *New York Times*, 27 February 2000.

5. *Globe and Mail*, 11 September 2002.

6. *Globe and Mail*, 28 November 2002.

7. Ibid.

8. *BBC News*, 12 August 1999.

9. *New York Times*, 27 February 2000.

10. *National Post*, 15 April 1999.

11. *National Post*, 17 May 2002.

12. Ibid.

13. *Herald American* (Syracuse), 7 June 1998.

14. Ibid.

15. Statement of Robert A. Robinson, Director, Food and Agricultural Issues, Resources, Community, and Economic Development Division, Cigarette Smuggling, in testimony before the Senate Task Force on Tobacco, United States General Accounting Office, 4 May 1998.

16. Reuters, 4 November 2002.

17. Canadian Cancer Society, Non-Smokers' Rights Association, Physicians for a Smoke-Free Canada, and Quebec Coalition for Tobacco Control, *Surveying the Damage: Cut-Rate Tobacco Products and Public Health in the 1990s* (Ottawa, October 1999), 29.

18. Ibid., 47, 24, 3.

19. Ibid., 23.

20. *Globe and Mail*, 20 February 2002.

21. Ibid.

22. "Drugs with borders: When prescription drugs go over the line," amednews.com, 22/29 October 2001.

Chapter 7: Canadians and Americans up against the Red River

1. C.A. Coates, "A Preacher of the Old School" (Middlesex, England: Bible and Gospel Trust).

2. Kimberly K. Porter, *Uncommon Heroes: The City of Grand Forks Flood Fight, 1997* (Grand Forks, ND: North Dakota Museum of Art, 2001), 21.

3. Ibid., 1, 2.

4. Ibid., 21.

5. Ibid., 4.

6. Ibid., 123.

7. Ibid.,127.

8. Ibid., 129, 130.

9. Ibid., 131.

Chapter 8: Other Borders

1. U.S. Census Bureau, *Statistical Abstract of the United States: 1998* (Washington, DC, 1998), 8, 14.

Chapter 9: Down the Dark Road

1. *Globe and Mail*, 31 October 2002.

2. *Globe and Mail,* 16 October 2002.

3. *Globe and Mail,* 31 October 2002.

4. *Globe and Mail,* 1 November 2002.

5. CBC Newsworld, 7 November 2002.

6. *Toronto Star,* 4 November 2002.

7. *Globe and Mail,* 2 November 2002.

8. *International Herald Tribune,* 29 and 30 September 2001.

9. American Council of Trustees and Alumni, "Defending Civilization: How Our Universities Are Failing America and What Can Be Done about It" (November 2001).

10. *The Nation,* 3 December 2001.

11. *National Strategy for Homeland Security,* (Office of Homeland Security, July 2002, Washington, DC) 69.

12. President, State of the Union address, 29 January 2002.

13. *International Herald Tribune,* 14 February 2002.

14. *Globe and Mail,* 18 February 2002.

15. *International Herald Tribune,* 18 February 2002.

16. Ibid.

17. *International Herald Tribune,* 22 February 2002.

18. *International Herald Tribune,* 12 March 2002.

19. *International Herald Tribune,* 14 March 2002.

20. *International Herald Tribune,* 13 March 2002.

21. *New York Times,* 5 November 2001.

22. *Newsweek* (October 2001).

23. *New York Times,* 13 November 2001.

24. *The Multiracial Activist* (June/July 2002).

25. *New York Times,* 13 November 2001.

26. *International Herald Tribune,* 16 November 2001.

27. *New York Times,* 1 December 2001.

28. Electronic Privacy Information Center, October 2001.

29. Ibid.

30. *The Hill,* 18 November 2002.

31. Homeland Security, vii.

32. Ibid., viii, ix.

33. Ibid., 22.

34. *New York Times,* 19 November 2002.

35. Homeland Security, 23.

Chapter 10: Fortress North America

1. Homeland Security, 21.
2. Ibid.
3. *Toronto Star*, 12 September 2001, and Canadian Press, 13 September 2001.
4. *Toronto Sun*, 14 September 2001.
5. *Christian Science Monitor*, cited in *Globe and Mail*, 27 September 2001.
6. *Seattle Times*, cited in ibid.
7. *Globe and Mail*, 27 September 2001.
8. House of Commons, *Debates*, 20 September 2001 and 27 September 2001.
9. Ibid., 1 October and 22 October 2001.
10. *Toronto Sun*, 19 September 2001.
11. House of Commons, *Debates*, 26 September 2001.
12. cbc.ca, 2 November 2001.
13. *Globe and Mail*, 27 September 2001.
14. Department of Justice, Canada, 20 November 2001.
15. *Washington Post*, 3 December 2001.

Chapter 11: Deep Integration

1. House of Commons, *Debates*, 28 May 2002.
2. Robert A. Pastor, *Toward a North American Community: Lessons from the Old World for the New* (Washington: Institute for International Economics, 2001).
3. *Toronto Star*, 9 December 2002.
4. *Washington Post*, 10 December 2002.
5. *Globe and Mail*, 12 September 2002.
6. *Globe and Mail*, 14 September 2002.
7. *Report of the Royal Commission on the Economic Union and Development Prospects for Canada*, vol. 1 (Ottawa: Supply and Services Canada, 1985), 375.
8. *Statistical Abstract of the United States*, 1994, 2001.
9. George Grant, *Lament for a Nation: The Defeat of Canadian Nationalism* (Toronto: McClelland and Stewart, 1965), 69–70.
10. *Globe and Mail*, 19 December 2001.
11. *Globe and Mail*, 5 November 2002.
12. BBC News, 31 March 2001.

Appendix Source Notes

I have depended substantially in the appendix on a remarkable work published on the eve of World War I. *Canada and Its Provinces* was the first major multi-volume Canadian history published in English. In some ways, it remains the most ambitious. One volume of the twenty-three volume work, volume 8, is devoted to the matter of Canada's borders. The correct citation for that volume is as follows: Adam Shortt and Arthur G. Doughty (eds.), *Canada and Its Provinces*, (The Publishers' Association of Canada Ltd., Toronto, 1913), Volume 8. In addition, I have used Rob Huebert, "Climate Change and Canadian Sovereignty in the Northwest Passage", *Isuma* 2, no. 4 (Winter 2001); John Honderich, *Arctic Imperative: Is Canada Losing the North?* (University of Toronto Press, Toronto, Buffalo, London, 1987); Edgar McInnis, *Canada: A Political and Social History* (Holt, Rinehart and Winston, New York, 1962); and in one instance, Canada, House of Commons, *Debates*.

Acknowledgments

I am indebted to many people who aided me in writing *The Border*, some who advised me on my travels, some who suggested useful source material and others who offered feedback and advice on the manuscript or parts of it.

Maya Mavjee at Doubleday Canada came up with the concept of a book about the border. I was captivated at once by the idea, which opened doors to travel, adventure and exploration of much of the continent, as well as of the long and complex Canada–American relationship. Meg Taylor, my initial editor, was a faithful collaborator who pored over maps and mouldering texts with me, and the fact that this book has seen the light of day is due in no small part to her. When Martha Kanya-Forstner took over as in-house editor, she brought boundless energy to the project and great ideas on many subjects—all important in honing the manuscript. Meg Masters jumped into the process at a propitious moment and did a wonderful job editing and helping shape the book. I am grateful as well to John Sweet for his thoughtful copy-edit, to Alison Reid for her close and careful read, and to Brad Martin and Scott Sellers for their generous support and input.

On the road, among those who helped were Mo Simpson in Vancouver, Suzanne Poppema and John Cramer in Everett, Washington. Several intrepid Canada Customs officials, based in British Columbia, pointed me in useful directions. Other westerners who came to my aid were Gord Laxer and Judith Beirs. I am indebted as well to East Coast friends Elaine Landry and Francis Coutellier.

To those who assisted and inspired me—Ethan Poskanzer, Judy Niesenholt, Stan Kjellberg, Joni Boyer, Norm and Mary Jane Simon, Gerald Kaplan, Carol Phillips, Patsy Aldana, Linda and John Hutcheson, Liz Pinto, Daphne Intrator, Catherine Yolles, Souad Sharabani, Lina Nadar, Suzanne Dubeau and my offspring Michael, Kate, Emily and Jonathan (who also did research)—I offer my gratitude. Thanks to Albert, Natalie and Geoffrey.

Jackie Kaiser, my literary agent, was there with support to get me past the swamps along the way.

Finally, my heart goes out to my partner, Sandy Price, who travelled with me along the border from Skagway, Alaska, to Campobello, New Brunswick. I am thankful to her for invaluable research, for taking photos, for thinking about the themes of the book and for offering comfort and support along the way.

Index